On Wordsworth's *Prelude*

... and a thing unprecedented
in literary history that a man should talk so
much about himself.

> Wordsworth, in a letter to Sir
> George Beaumont, while completing the first
> full draft of *The Prelude*.

... that Lay
More than historic, that prophetic Lay
Wherein (high theme by thee first sung aright)
Of the foundations and the building up
Of a Human Spirit thou hast dared to tell
What may be told, to the understanding mind
Revealable. . . .

> Coleridge, "To William Wordsworth:
> Composed on the Night after his Recitation of
> a Poem on the Growth of an Individual Mind"

ON WORDSWORTH'S

Prelude

BY HERBERT LINDENBERGER

PRINCETON · NEW JERSEY

PRINCETON UNIVERSITY PRESS

Printed in the United States
of America

To Claire

FOREWORD: "WAYS OF LOOKING"

THIS study does not seek to propound a thesis, nor does it work toward any one conclusion. It is, rather, an attempt to illuminate a single major literary work from a number of points of view. I might well have called it "Thirteen Ways of Looking at *The Prelude*," for it is essentially a series of related essays, each designed to approach the poem from a single direction, and each, in turn, complementary to and sometimes even corrective of the others.

Dr. Johnson's remark about his contemporaries' attitude toward *Paradise Lost*—that it is "one of the books which the reader admires and lays down, and forgets to take up again"—could as well be made about the place *The Prelude* today holds in the minds of most serious readers. The poem is looked upon with greater respect than at any time since its publication little more than a century ago; indeed, it holds a more elevated place than any long poem in English since *Paradise Lost*. Its text, in its different versions, has been edited with the best of modern care; its literary sources have been scrupulously hunted down; and its philosophical affinities have been variously labelled, if not altogether agreed upon. When T. S. Eliot, in a discussion of the fate of long poems, noted of *The Prelude* that, "however tedious in many places, [it] has to be read entire,"[1] he was voicing what seems to me the most typical modern attitude—admiring and dutiful at once—toward the poem. *The Prelude*, in short, has been relegated (or elevated) to the role of Sunday reading in the modern secular world.

The fundamental aim which guides this study is to pre-

[1] *On Poetry and Poets* (London, 1957), p. 174.

sent the poem in all its freshness as a work of living literature; to accomplish this, I employ whatever resources I
can find among those available to the modern literary
historian to demonstrate the variety and complexity of the
poem and to "place" it within an appropriate context of
literary traditions. The first three chapters are concerned
centrally with the poem's language, and, above all, with
the barriers which stand between Wordsworth's blank-
verse style and the stylistic biases of many modern readers.
Chapter One examines certain elements of style, including the conceptions of genre and decorum, which Wordsworth inherited from the eighteenth century. The following two chapters define in detail the type of discourse
which Wordsworth developed to render his spiritual experiences and his processes of introspection. I refer to this
language as Wordsworth's characteristic "rhetoric of interaction," for it is a language at once different from the
more traditional rhetoric which I discuss in Chapter One
and from the language which poets since the Symbolist
Movement have employed to portray meditative experience.

The three middle chapters of this study originated in
my attempt to come to terms, though in sharply varying
ways, with the organization of the poem. Chapter Four
considers the problems which Wordsworth, writing at a
time when the definition of poetry was increasingly being
narrowed down to include only the more lyrical varieties,
faced in sustaining a long poem. Chapters Five and Six
explore the implications, for both the meaning and structure of *The Prelude*, of Wordsworth's intense concern
with time—time in two separate meanings, in its role,
first, as memory and introspection, then in its more traditionally metaphysical sense as the antithesis of eternity.

Although the major portion of this study concentrates
on *The Prelude* as a record of the poet's inward experi-

ence, the two chapters entitled "The Social Dimension" interpret those parts of the poem depicting Wordsworth's relations to other men and to society as a whole. The final chapter examines the fortunes of the poem within the history of English criticism and, despite Wordsworth's failure to find a significant public outside the English-speaking countries, attempts to define the affinities between Wordsworth's manner in *The Prelude* and certain strains within European Romanticism.

Although this is preeminently a study of a single poem, I have not limited my remarks to *The Prelude* among Wordsworth's works. For instance, the study of "Home at Grasmere" and *The Excursion* often helps shed light on *The Prelude*, especially since all these poems were designed to form part of Wordsworth's large, uncompleted life-work, *The Recluse*. Moreover, since nearly all of Wordsworth's major poetry was written during the years that covered the composition of *The Prelude*, much of his other work is directly relevant to the interests of this study. For instance, the role of the various solitaries in *The Prelude* can only be understood through reference to the solitaries who people *Lyrical Ballads* and such a poem as "Resolution and Independence." Indirectly, then, this study attempts to illuminate much of Wordsworth's major poetry from the focal point of *The Prelude*.

The fact that so many of the longer studies of Wordsworth's work have been organized in terms of the poet's development has created what I take to be an unnecessarily narrow limitation of the context in which his poems may be viewed. A single and quite compelling question governs the argument behind much that is most admirable in modern Wordsworthian study: how are we to account for the brief flowering and rapid decline of the genius of one of our greatest poets? Thus, the perspective through which any single work is viewed is determined by the relationship of the work to the particular answer the critic has given to this question. The Lucy poems, for example, are read primarily as moments in the history of the poet's ideological waverings, or of his guilt feelings regarding his relations with Annette or Dorothy. One cannot, of course, ignore the personal frame of reference which so explicitly encloses Wordsworth's work (and to a far greater degree than it does any major poet before his time). But this is by no means the only frame of reference which yields insights into his poems, or for that matter into the man himself.

The organization of this study, then, stands at an opposite extreme from such distinguished earlier books on Wordsworth as those of Sir Herbert Read and F. W. Bateson.[2] Instead of choosing a single frame of reference within which to view the history of his career, I have chosen to concentrate on his major poem, and to set it in successively different lights. Each chapter—and sometimes individual sections of chapters—suggests a way of looking at the poem and then pursues its theme as far as it may profitably go. In certain instances the emphases of different chapters may seem distinctly opposed to one another. The first chapter, for example, stresses the traditional rhetorical elements present in the poem, while the chapters on Wordsworth's "time-consciousness" attempt to isolate certain elements which seem akin to the characteristic preoccupations of much modern literature. I must answer that both of these frames of reference seem to me applicable to *The Prelude* and that any study which would stress one at the expense of the other would work to distort the meaning of the poem. I venture to think that this method, which involves a constant readjustment of the reader's perspective on the poem, will help lead the reader into a

2 Read, *Wordsworth* (London, 1930); Bateson, *Wordsworth: A Reinterpretation* (London, 1956).

gradually more complex and deepened understanding of *The Prelude* than would a single, over-arching argument.

It may also be objected that the various frames of reference I have brought together are arbitrarily chosen and incomplete. I might, for instance, have shed some light on *The Prelude* by comparing its moments of spiritual illumination with poems within the Christian mystical tradition such as those of St. John of the Cross or with such more prosaic accounts of mystical experience as Jakob Boehme's. Or, as Roy Harvey Pearce suggests in his recent study of the assumptions underlying American poetry,[3] *The Prelude* could be read as an analogue of such peculiarly "American" epics as *Song of Myself* and *The Cantos*. I can only answer that the areas of the poem's relevance are doubtless far greater than I may have suggested in this study. The topics I have chosen to pursue were determined by my particular interests and fields of competence, and what seemed to me most important to say at the present time. I did not, for instance, feel prepared to seek out archetypal patterns of meaning in the poem. Nor did it seem necessary to expound the poem's essential thought structure or trace its literary sources, as the two earlier full-length studies of *The Prelude*—those, respectively, of Raymond Dexter Havens and Abbie Findlay Potts—have done once and for all.[4] On the other hand, I found that such an apparently unimportant question as the circumstances surrounding the poem's poor reception in 1850—a subject which had not been investigated before—could help provide a fresh perspective on the meaning of the poem.

My use of the word *meaning* here may need some clari-

[3] *The Continuity of American Poetry* (Princeton, 1961), p. 7.
[4] Havens, *The Mind of a Poet: A Study of Wordsworth's Thought with Particular Reference to "The Prelude"* (Baltimore, 1941); Potts, *Wordsworth's Prelude: A Study of Its Literary Form* (Ithaca, N.Y., 1953).

fication. Throughout this study I am perhaps somewhat more concerned with the larger relevancies of *The Prelude* within the literary tradition than I am with the explication of its paraphrasable meaning. In a stimulating recent essay on the nature of literary interpretation E. D. Hirsch, Jr., distinguishes between the "objective" meaning which the interpreter defines in a given work (by which he means more or less the author's intended meaning) and those "outer horizons" of meaning which the critic discerns when he relates works to one another or to other environments of thought.[5] I am not so sure that these two areas of critical endeavor can be separated as neatly as Hirsch suggests, yet the distinction he makes has helped me define the nature of my inquiry. Thus, Havens' study of *The Prelude* seems to me an attempt to explicate what Hirsch calls the "objective" and "textual" meaning of the poem, for his frame of reference, for the most part, remains securely within the area of Wordsworth's own pronouncements of biases and intentions. Yet, though the present study often wanders into seemingly remoter areas, it is written with the full conviction that an inquiry into the poem's place within a larger literary framework would serve the contemporary reader as a guide on how to read the poem itself. For instance, a reader generally unsympathetic to expressions of "Romantic pantheism" is likely to read a passage such as "There was a Boy" in the spirit which Wordsworth intended if he can note the difference between Wordsworth's way of celebrating the interaction of man and nature and Byron's halting attempts to achieve similar effects in *Childe Harold*.

The fact that *The Prelude* generally reveals its "objective" meaning on the level of direct statement—in con-

5 "Objective Interpretation," PMLA, LXXV (1960), pp. 463-479.

trast to poems such as *The Faerie Queene* or Blake's prophetic books—makes an explicatory reading, in the usual
sense of the term, seem unnecessary. Certainly the poem
does not reveal a hidden allegory, nor does it convey its
central meanings with any of the ambiguities which make
works so diverse as *Gulliver's Travels* and *Endymion* difficult to read correctly. Yet the very directness with which
it seems to speak has created its own set of difficulties for
the interpreter. For instance, it is difficult to demonstrate
the nature of Wordsworth's "rhetoric of interaction" with
the usual tools of modern criticism (tools which, for that
matter, were developed for the analysis of Metaphysical
and modern poetry). Moreover, the poem wavers quite
explicitly between two areas of reference (suggested by
the two epigraphs I have taken for this study): the poem
as personal history and as prophetic utterance. But the
presence of these two apparently incompatible areas does
not leave the poem unresolved; much of the success of
the poem is, in fact, due to the manner in which Wordsworth was able to find a mode of language and organization to encompass both areas at once.

It is perhaps as a consequence of the peculiar difficulties
with which *The Prelude* teases the modern critic that, in
the course of my study, I gradually found myself approaching the poem from a multiplicity of directions. The directions which my lines of inquiry have taken were suggested
less often, I think, by the characteristic paths of earlier
Wordsworth scholarship (to which, however, I owe the
factual grounding in which my notions must inevitably
be rooted) than by ways of thinking which I have encountered in critics not primarily concerned with Wordsworth or the Romantics. William Empson's remarks on
Wordsworth's manipulation of the word *sense*, plus an
analysis of a passage from *The Prelude* in Donald Davie's

study of the syntax of English verse,[6] proved crucial in teaching me how to read the language in which Wordsworth expressed his spiritual experiences. Georges Poulet's studies of the significance of time in French writers guided me toward an understanding of Wordsworth's "time-consciousness."[7] If the reader recognizes a diversity of critical voices behind these essays—voices as diverse as those of Poulet, F. R. Leavis, Ernst Robert Curtius, and Northrop Frye—this is surely no accident, for this book is above all a record of my questionings and my enthusiasms during the years in which I have tried to come to terms with the great poem to which these essays are designed to do service.

ACKNOWLEDGMENTS

AMONG the many who have helped this study along in various ways, I wish to express my gratitude to the following: to Donald J. Greene, friend and former colleague, for the initial encouragement to undertake the project; to my colleagues Thomas R. Edwards, Frederick J. Hoffman, and Douglass S. Parker, for a critical reading of the manuscript; to the Humanities Faculty Seminar, University of California, Riverside, for the opportunity to present portions of the chapters on Wordsworth's "time-consciousness" during the period in which I was re-working these chapters; to D. J. Gordon, of the University of Reading, England, for the opportunity to present an earlier version of parts of Chapter IX before the staff and students in English at his university; to David V. Erdman, for permission to reprint portions of my article, "The Reception of Wordsworth's *Prelude*," *Bulletin of the New York Public Library*,

---

6 Empson, *The Structure of Complex Words* (London, 1951), pp. 289-305; Davie, *Articulate Energy: An Enquiry into the Syntax of English Verse* (London, 1955), pp. 106-116.

7 *Studies in Human Time* (Baltimore, 1956), and the article "Timelessness and Romanticism," JHI, XV (1954), pp. 3-22.

LXIV (1960), 196-208; to Miss Helen Darbishire and Miss Phoebe Johnson, for the opportunity to use the Wordsworth Archive, Dove Cottage, Grasmere; to the administration of the University of California, Riverside, for a sabbatical leave during the fall semester of 1958 to begin work on this book, and to the Research Committee of this university for funds for clerical assistance; to Mrs. Douglass S. Parker, for the kind of typing that should more properly be termed a form of editorial assistance; to Mrs. Laverne F. Lippert, to my students Robert A. Lee and Mrs. Charles R. Livingston, and to my wife, Claire F. Lindenberger, for additional typing and bibliographical help.

Riverside, California   H.L.
April 28, 1962

CONTENTS

CONTENTS

CONTENTS

On Wordsworth's *Prelude*

KEY TO ABBREVIATIONS

co: *Critical Opinions of William Wordsworth*, ed. M. L. Peacock, Jr., Baltimore, 1950.

EL: *Early Letters of William and Dorothy Wordsworth (1787-1805)*, ed. E. de Selincourt, Oxford, 1935.

PW: *Poetical Works of William Wordsworth*, ed. E. de Selincourt and H. Darbishire, Oxford, 1940-49, 5 vols.

PREL.: *The Prelude or Growth of a Poet's Mind*, ed. E. de Selincourt, rev. H. Darbishire, 2nd ed., Oxford, 1959. This abbreviation will be used to refer only to the notes and critical apparatus of this edition. Quotations from the poem itself will be identified by book and line numbers alone. Unless otherwise indicated, they are drawn from the 1805 version as printed in this edition. Quotations from *The Excursion* will also be identified by book and line numbers.

PROSE WORKS: *Prose Works of William Wordsworth*, ed. A. B. Grosart, London, 1876, 3 vols.

CHAPTER ONE

THE PRELUDE AND THE OLDER RHETORIC

And I would give,
While yet we may, as far as words can give,
A substance and a life to what I feel.

(XI, 339-341)

---

1 . THE PUBLIC TONE

IN recent years we have come increasingly to view *The Prelude* as a kind of modern poem. To the degree to which it is a poem of personal experience, attempting to render what a critic of Wordsworth has called the "unmediated vision,"[1] it is an expression of what we like to think of as the modern sensibility—at once spontaneous and self-conscious in its zeal to explore experience in all its immediacy. What most appeals to the modern reader in *The Prelude* is what most appeals to him in the poetry since Romanticism—the intimate tone, the evocation of the processes of introspection. In short, he reads *The Prelude* as a record of personal, private vision, much as he reads such later, more specialized explorations of the realm of consciousness as *Illuminations* and *Four Quartets.*

In a later section of this book, in my study of Wordsworth's "time-consciousness," I shall stress certain peculiarly "modern" aspects of *The Prelude.* But Wordsworth

---

[1] I refer to the title and theme of Geoffrey Hartman's study of four poets, *The Unmediated Vision* (New Haven, 1954); the affinities of *The Prelude* with various modern poems have been demonstrated at length in such works as Robert Langbaum's *The Poetry of Experience* (Ithaca, N.Y., 1957) and Elizabeth Sewell's *The Orphic Voice* (New Haven, 1960).

in *The Prelude* speaks with a public voice as well, although the modern reader is not likely to seek out such passages as George Eliot (who was not insensitive to Wordsworth's more introspective moments) recommended to a friend as memorable texts:[2]

> The human nature unto which I felt
> That I belonged, and reverenced with love,
> Was not a punctual presence, but a spirit
> Diffused through time and space, with aid derived
> Of evidence from monuments . . .
>
> (VIII, 608-612 [1850])

or

> There is
> One great society alone on earth:
> The noble Living and the noble Dead.
>
> (XI, 393-395 [1850])

These lines, both in what they say and in the explicit, assertive way in which they say it, remind us of that Augustan side of Wordsworth which could define a poet as "a man speaking to men," who could speak of the object of poetry as "truth, not individual and local, but general, and operative," and boast that he had endeavored "to dwell with truth upon these points of human nature in which all men resemble each other, rather than on those accidents of manners and character produced by times and circumstances" (PW, II, 393, 394; CO, 119).

As M. H. Abrams has reminded us, behind the obviously unique contributions which Wordsworth made to poetic theory, there stands an "assumption that human nature, in its passions and sensibilities no less than its reason, is everywhere fundamentally the same."[3] Though

---

[2] *Letters*, ed. Gordon Haight (New Haven, 1955), VII, 261.

[3] *The Mirror and the Lamp* (New York, 1958), p. 104.

much of his theory, as indeed much of his poetry, worked to undermine this very assumption, the fact that it could still be meaningful to Wordsworth—as it was not to writers after him—served to give his work a motivation and a coloring distinctly foreign to those of the modern poet.

In one of his latter-day discussions of his own verse, T. S. Eliot depicted his development from a lyric to a dramatic poet by speaking of "three voices" through which his work has successively passed. What is perhaps most significant about Eliot's theory is that he distinguishes the voices according to the poet's relation to an audience. Thus, the first voice is that of "the poet talking to himself—or to nobody," the second that of "the poet addressing an audience," the third, "the poet when he attempts to create a dramatic character."[4] If one might borrow Eliot's distinctions for a moment, one could speak of *The Prelude* as a poem in which the second voice is constantly trying to emerge out of the first. To put it another way, what goes on in the poem is a constant flight from the subjectivity of private experience to the assertion of publicly communicable and valid truths. The pattern from private to public is evident in the closing phase of most of the visionary moments within the poem. In the episode about the stolen boat, for instance, after the subjectivity implicit in his "dim and undetermin'd sense / Of unknown modes of being," we observe an attempt to communicate an essentially private experience in publicly apprehensible terms:

> In my thoughts
> There was a darkness, call it solitude,
> Or blank desertion, no familiar shapes
> Of hourly objects, images of trees,

[4] *On Poetry and Poets*, p. 89.

> Of sea or sky, no colours of green fields;
> But huge and mighty Forms that do not live
> Like living men . . .   (I, 420-426)

If we remember the famous statement about Words-worth's solipsism—"He used to be frequently so rapt into an unreal transcendental world of ideas that the external world seemed no longer to exist in relation to him, and he had to reconvince himself of its existence *by clasping a tree*, or something that happened to be near him" (PW, IV, 467)—we might think of the composition of *The Prelude* as Wordsworth's way of giving objective form to highly subjective states, or, to put it another way, of his effort to create an external reality for his private, transcendental world.

The fact that the poem is addressed throughout to Coleridge is, as it were, a guarantee of its movement from the first to the second voice, from revery and personal vision to public statement. Thus, in that visionary moment in Book IV where he depicts his walk home after the dance he addresses Coleridge just at the point when he is about to interpret the meaning of his experience:

>   Magnificent
> The morning was, a memorable pomp,
> More glorious than I ever had beheld.
> The Sea was laughing at a distance; all
> The solid Mountains were as bright as clouds,
> Grain-tinctured, drench'd in empyrean light;
> And, in the meadows and the lower grounds,
> Was all the sweetness of a common dawn,
> Dews, vapours, and the melody of birds,
> And Labourers going forth into the fields.
> —*Ah! need I say, dear Friend, that to the brim
> My heart was full*; I made no vows, but vows
> Were then made for me; bond unknown to me

Was given, that I should be, else sinning greatly,
A dedicated Spirit.   (IV, 330-344; italics mine)

The epistolary convention becomes a means of achieving
the sense of an audience—if only an audience of one—and
thus of giving a public definition to a state of mind which
might otherwise have remained meaningful to the poet
alone. In an analogous way the invocations to nature and
its various aspects throughout the poem serve to broaden
Wordsworth's area of reference from the private to the
public realm. For instance, at the end of the ice-skating
passage:

> Yet still the solitary Cliffs
> Wheeled by me, even as if the earth had roll'd
> With visible motion her diurnal round;
> Behind me did they stretch in solemn train
> Feebler and feebler, and I stood and watch'd
> Till all was tranquil as a dreamless sleep,
>
> (I, 484-489)

concluding as it does in revery and relaxation of the will,
he shifts directly to a tone of invocation, which, in the
succeeding lines, serves as a way of setting the earlier experience within a larger, more public perspective:

> Ye Presences of Nature, in the sky
> Or on the earth! Ye Visions of the hills!
> And Souls of lonely places! can I think
> A vulgar hope was yours when Ye employ'd
> Such ministry, when Ye through many a year
> Haunting me thus among my boyish sports,
> On caves and trees, upon the woods and hills,
> Impress'd upon all forms the characters
> Of danger or desire. . . .   (I, 490-498)

One cannot help noting that these objects of Wordsworth's
address—Coleridge, Nature, as well as Dorothy, whom

he eulogizes in the last book of the poem—were *in fact* Wordsworth's real audience. "One of the most important differences between Wordsworth and the other major poets of the eighteenth and nineteenth centuries," F. W. Bateson writes, "is that whereas they wrote for the silent reader, *i.e.* for the eye, he wrote most of his poems to be declaimed, *i.e.* for the ear," and he goes on to remind us of the long recitations to which Wordsworth subjected friends and family, and also of the solitary walks witnessed by astonished neighbors as he composed his poems aloud.[5] Lacking that sense of a larger literary public to whom he could adjust the tone of his verse, Wordsworth was forced to accept a makeshift audience, which, as it turned out, consisted of the handful of devotees who happened to be in his physical proximity. Unlike Horace and Pope, he could not, in the privacy of his country retirement, assume himself in communication with an urban society with whom he shared a common order of values: in fact, his very flight to the country was a sign of his search for a different, more peculiarly personal set of values. In the light of his isolation it seems a wonder that Wordsworth was able to speak with a public voice at all and that he was not, like poets of a later time, confined to the poetry of the first voice, to that private mode of contemplation which we have come to associate with the ivory tower and the castle of Axël.

Within the total line of Wordsworth's development the years that mark the composition of *The Prelude* (1798-1805) are also those in which Wordsworth spoke in his most private voice. For his early loco-descriptive poems, and even for *Guilt and Sorrow*, he had at hand a conventional, non-personal (or pseudo-personal) rhetoric out of which, had he so wanted, he might have gone on issuing poems indefinitely. We might view such a ready-made rhetoric as a sign of a poet's commitment to the public realm, or

[5] *Wordsworth: A Re-interpretation*, pp. 187-197.

at least of his desire to maintain the illusion that such a commitment and such a realm still have a meaningful existence for him. The poems of the Great Decade (whatever the exact dates with which we choose to circumscribe it) represent an attempt both to find a set of personal values and to develop a language with which to define these values. Once the search was completed, and the values fully defined, Wordsworth was once again able to speak with a public voice. The public tone toward which we feel him moving in *The Prelude*—and the process with which he seeks to achieve it is one of the enduring pleasures of the poem—eventually became the basis for a new rhetoric, one that left no room for introspection and that could quite comfortably take up the public role which his later duties of poet laureate demanded.

2 . THE EPIC TASK

It was not the mere presence of someone to declaim to that gave *The Prelude* a public voice. For Wordsworth still retained a sense of the objective reality of the traditional literary genres and could seriously hold the notion that there existed a style appropriate to each. When, in his Preface of 1815, he speaks of "the laws and appropriate graces of every species of composition" (PW, II, 432), he is expressing a principle of decorum which would have been taken for granted by any earlier writer but which, by the time of his death, could not have been voiced by any serious critic. If readers have been reluctant to link Wordsworth with the classical past, it is only because the more revolutionary aspects of his contribution, above all his expressive theory of poetry as "spontaneous overflow," has remained predominant in their minds. But it would be far more accurate to see Wordsworth, and above all the Wordsworth of *The Prelude*, as standing at a sort of meeting-point between two views of literary form: the modern view that the form of a work results from the demands and rhythms of personal vision, and the traditional view of objectively existing styles and structures to which the writer accommodates his personal interests. The Wordsworth who created the "spot of time"—centered as it is on the exploration of personal experience—as a significant literary form is a distinctly modern type of poet. But the Wordsworth who, when nearing the completion of *The Prelude*, could vow henceforth "to write a narrative Poem of the Epic kind," adding that he should then "consider the *task* of my life as over" (CO, 441), spoke words which might have been voiced by Milton and Dryden but which would have had little meaning after his time. We can understand *The Prelude*—its frequently Miltonic rhetoric, its largeness of scope—only if we remain aware of the epic conception behind the poem (and to the extent that Wordsworth held a classical view of literary form his generic intentions, whether or not they were realized, are very relevant to the meaning of the poem). We know, of course, that *The Prelude* was merely the introduction—the "portico" or "ante-chapel," as he variously described it—to the great poem, *The Recluse*, which was to be his lifework. And though he never brought this work to completion, and even described *The Prelude* as its "least important" part, it is still true that *The Prelude* derives its energy and momentum, its dignity and its religious aura, from the larger epic mission toward which it was to lead.[6]

The very conception of a single major work toward which he was to prepare himself ("To this work [*The Recluse*] I mean to devote the prime of my life, and the chief force of my mind," he wrote to De Quincey in 1804—

[6] Miss Sewell's fine appreciation of the epic qualities of *The Prelude* (in *The Orphic Voice*, pp. 302-309) appeared after I had completed this chapter.

co, 439) with the consequent reduction of his remaining work to the role of "minor pieces," "adjuncts," "little cells," "oratories," is sufficient indication of his traditional sense of the pattern of an epic poet's career. That Wordsworth should take his epic task so seriously seems only natural when we remember the nature of his early training, the solemnity with which he declared himself a "dedicated Spirit, else sinning greatly," and, finally, the encouragement and goading he received for years from Coleridge. It is of course ironic that by the later nineteenth century so fervent an admirer as George Eliot could refer to *The Prelude* and *The Excursion* as "the 'dull' poems."[7]

Throughout Wordsworth's correspondence during the writing of *The Prelude*, as well as in critical remarks to be found in the poem itself (remarks which, considering Milton's precedent, were fully appropriate to a poem in the high style), one feels that Wordsworth was somewhat uneasy about the nature of the poem he was writing. His statement, "It will be not much less than 9000 lines,—not hundred but thousand lines long,—an alarming length! and a thing unprecedented in literary history that a man should talk so much about himself" (co, 441), directly voices the astonishment of a poet who by training conceived of a long poem as dealing with a public order of experience, but who found himself drifting, as it were, into a genre inappropriate to his particular subject. We know from his own testimony that he undertook *The Prelude* because he did not yet feel ready for the epic task: "I was unprepared to treat any more arduous subject, and diffident of my own powers" (*ibid.*), or as he expressed it within the poem itself,

> 'Tis a theme
> Single and of determined bounds; and hence

---

[7] *Letters*, p. 261. Her quotes around *dull* indicate that this judgment was less hers than that of her contemporaries.

> I chuse it rather at this time, than work
> Of ampler or more varied argument.
>
> (I, 668-671)

Yet the modesty he shows here only partly describes his real conception of the work, for at several points he expresses a far more ambitious one:

> Of Genius, Power,
> Creation and Divinity itself
> I have been speaking, for my theme has been
> What pass'd within me. Not of outward things
> Done visibly for other minds, words, signs,
> Symbols or actions; but of my own heart
> Have I been speaking, and my youthful mind.
> O Heavens! how awful is the might of Souls,
> And what they do within themselves, while yet
> The yoke of earth is new to them, the world
> Nothing but a wild field where they were sown.
> This is, in truth, heroic argument,
> And genuine prowess.   (III, 171-183)

By echoing Milton ("Sad task, yet argument/Not less but more Heroic than the wrath/Of stern Achilles . . .") he not only points up the epic impulse behind the poem, but calls on Milton's precedent in justifying new areas worthy of epic: for if Milton must defend himself for writing an epic about man's moral rather than his military history, Wordsworth in turn claims to find heroic argument in man's (and, indeed, in *one* man's) personal history. If modern readers are reluctant to award the laurels of epic poet to Wordsworth, it is not only that they are indifferent to the high claims of the genre, but perhaps also that *The Prelude* is deficient in that aspect of the "epic spirit" which E. M. W. Tillyard, in his admirable book on *The English Epic*, calls the "choric element" that we associate with epic:

the feeling that "behind the epic author is a big multitude of men of whose most serious convictions and dear habits he is the mouthpiece."[8] If we are ready to grant *The Prelude* the other three epic qualities which Tillyard distinguishes—high seriousness, sustained exercise of the will, and even amplitude and breadth—we are hard put to think of *The Prelude*, for all its declamatory moments, as a spokesman for its age: the egotistical sublime must by its very nature reject such demands.

Had Wordsworth been pressed to describe the species to which *The Prelude*, as distinct from the rest of the projected *Recluse*, belonged, he might well have called it a composite of several genres. The word *composite*, at any rate, was what Wordsworth used to describe Young's *Night Thoughts* and Cowper's *Task*, neither of which directly fit any one of the six genres of poetry which he distinguished in the Preface of 1815. (It is characteristic of the mixture of Augustan and Romantic in Wordsworth that this same preface, which begins with a description of the literary genres, closes with his definitive statement on the difference between fancy and imagination.) His very method of dividing the genres, though not very logically argued, reflects the traditionalism inherent in his critical thought. The first two, epic and drama, are distinguished, as they were by Plato, according to the voice through which the poet speaks—in the former the poet being "the source from which everything primarily flows," in the latter, "the whole action [being] carried on by speech and dialogue of the agents" (PW, II, 432-433). The third genre, the "lyrical," he characterizes, if not in a manner parallel to that of the first two, at least in an equally traditional way, for he here distinguishes those forms—hymn, ode, elegy, song, ballad—for which, "for the production of their *full* effect, an accompaniment of music is indispensable."

[8] *The English Epic* (London, 1954), p. 12.

The remaining three genres are classified by subject matter. The idyllium becomes a catch-all for much eighteenth-century poetry (Thomson, Burns, Goldsmith, Shenstone), and is defined by its largely descriptive quality: "descriptive chiefly either of the processes and appearances of external nature . . . or of characters, manners, and sentiments." It is noteworthy that *The Prelude* not only is concerned with both these areas of subject matter—nature and the human realm—but specifically focuses upon their interaction. The last two genres mentioned in the Preface are the "didactic" ("the principal object of which is direct instruction") and "philosophical Satire, like that of Horace and Juvenal." The didactic impulse of *The Prelude*, though not as direct as in *De Rerum Natura* and the *Georgics*—two of Wordsworth's examples of the genre— is still one of the most pervasive elements in the poem, while the satirical mode, though not prevalent in the poem as a whole, dominates the books on Cambridge and London (one remembers Coleridge on the plan of *The Recluse*: "Then he was to describe the pastoral and other states of society, assuming something of the Juvenalian spirit as he approached the high civilization of cities and towns"[9]).

The Prelude thus remains epic by Wordsworth's broad definition, while, like *Night Thoughts* and *The Task*, sharing in the idyllic, didactic, and satirical modes. (But the very self-consciousness which it so often reveals about its own nature makes it seem, rather, a poem in search of a genre.) By the time it was published, the older generic distinctions—and particularly those relevant to the eighteenth-century genres which Wordsworth brought together in the poem—were sufficiently forgotten that its early readers were baffled at what Wordsworth was really trying

[9] *Table-Talk*, July 21, 1832.

to do. "Wordsworth's 'Prelude' is not quite solid enough in its texture; is rather a poetical pamphlet, though proceeding from a new and genuine experience," Emerson wrote in his journal; "it is like Milton's Areopagitica, an immortal pamphlet."[10] *The Prelude*, for most of its early readers, belonged to no recognizable type: if it was meant to be an autobiography, asked one of its early reviewers, why was it not in prose, with all the richness of detail of Goethe's *Dichtung und Wahrheit?*[11] If it was meant to be a poem, why, to use the words of Lord Macaulay, "the endless wildernesses of dull, flat, prosaic twaddle"?[12] Above all, its early readers—and, in fact, many of its later ones—remained oblivious to the epic impulse which informs the whole and helps fuse its elements into a composite whole.

3. THINKING IN CATEGORIES

a. *The Idealized Character*

But this is passion over-near ourselves,
Reality too close and too intense,
And mingled up with something, in my mind,
Of scorn and condemnation personal,
That would profane the sanctity of Verse.

(x, 641-645)

At the opening of Book IV, after the affecting details of Wordsworth's first homecoming from Cambridge—"I bounded down the hill, shouting amain / A lusty summons to the farther shore / For the old Ferryman"—the modern reader is likely to respond less readily when he comes upon these lines, addressed to the poet's old landlady, Anne Tyson:

[10] *Journals*, ed. E. W. Emerson and W. E. Forbes (Boston, 1913), IX, 51-152.
[11] *British Quarterly Review*, XII (1850), 554.
[12] G. O. Trevelyan, *Life and Letters of Lord Macaulay* (Leipzig, 1876), V, 45.

The thoughts of gratitude shall fall like dew
Upon thy grave, good Creature! While my heart
Can beat I never will forget thy name.
Heaven's blessing be upon thee where thou liest,
After thy innocent and busy stir
In narrow cares, thy little daily growth
Of calm enjoyments, after eighty years,
And more than eighty, of untroubled life,
Childless, yet by the strangers to thy blood
Honour'd with little less than filial love.
Great joy was mine to see thee once again,
Thee and thy dwelling; and a throng of things
About its narrow precincts all belov'd,
And many of them seeming yet my own.
Why should I speak of what a thousand hearts
Have felt, and every man alive can guess?

(IV, 19-34)

For this is a highly formal passage, totally lacking in the
specific and, in fact, homey, detail of its surrounding passages. What little we learn about Anne Tyson remains on
a general level—that she lived a long, busy, domestic life
and that she was beloved by many. The language, though
free of the eighteenth-century circumlocutions which
Wordsworth so disliked, recalls Thomson and Cowper. It
is above all a "public" passage, not emanating, as does most
of *The Prelude*, from Wordsworth-in-the-process-of-pri-
vately-experiencing, but from Wordsworth the Public
Spokesman. The last two lines are indeed an acknowledg
ment of its public status, in which Wordsworth takes full
advantage of his opportunity to declare the universality
of the feelings he shares with the rest of humanity.

But several pages later we come across another portrai
of Anne Tyson, this one of an entirely different character

>   With new delight,
> This chiefly, did I view my grey-hair'd Dame,
> Saw her go forth to Church, or other work
> Of state, equipp'd in monumental trim,
> Short Velvet Cloak (her Bonnet of the like)
> A Mantle such as Spanish Cavaliers
> Wore in old time. Her smooth domestic life,
> Affectionate without uneasiness,
> Her talk, her business pleas'd me, and no less
> Her clear though shallow stream of piety,
> That ran on Sabbath days a fresher course.
> With thoughts unfelt till now, I saw her read
> Her Bible on the Sunday afternoons;
> And lov'd the book, when she had dropp'd asleep,
> And made of it a pillow for her head.
>   (IV, 207-221)

Both passages are related to the ancient genre known as the "character," a term which long ago passed out of the active vocabulary of criticism. What distinguishes the two is Wordsworth's sense of decorum. The earlier passage is a eulogy and as such followed the rule prescribed by Wordsworth in his essay on epitaphs: "The character of a deceased friend or beloved kinsman is not seen, no—nor ought to be seen, otherwise than as a tree through a tender haze or a luminous mist, that spiritualises and beautifies it; that takes away, indeed, but only to the end that the parts which are not abstracted may appear more dignified and lovely; may impress and affect the more" (PW, v, 452).

And then, sensing a possible conflict between this "spiritualising" process and his customary demands for sincerity, he adds the following note: "Shall we say, then, that this is not truth, not a faithful image; and that, accordingly, the purposes of commemoration cannot be answered?—

It *is* truth, and of the highest order; for, though doubtless things are not apparent which did exist; yet, the object being looked at through this medium, parts and proportions are brought into distinct view which before had been only imperfectly or unconsciously seen: it is truth hallowed by love—the joint offspring of the worth of the dead and the affections of the living!" But in the second portrait of Anne Tyson there is no attempt to "spiritualise" or "beautify." Though affectionate, Wordsworth is clearly intent on capturing the essence of her character: the concrete image of her reclining on the Bible, to take up Wordsworth's metaphor, portrays both the "clear" and "shallow" aspects of her piety.

The sense of decorum which distinguishes these two portraits of Anne Tyson is still essentially the same that distinguishes the types of portraits which we find in Pope —on the one hand, the pious eulogy to his father in the *Epistle to Arbuthnot*:

> Born to no Pride, inheriting no Strife
> Nor marrying Discord in a Noble Wife,
> Stranger to Civil and Religious Rage,
> The good Man walk'd innoxious thro' his Age . . .

on the other hand, the merciless *character* of Sporus, from the same poem:

> Whether in florid Impotence he speaks,
> And, as the Prompter breathes, the Puppet squeaks;
> Or at the Ear of *Eve*, familiar Toad,
> Half Froth, half Venom, spits himself abroad. . . .

I have chosen these examples from Pope because we know how little Wordsworth would have appreciated them; even in the passage on Pope's father he would doubtless have complained of a lack of "spiritual" quality, or, to draw from his discussion of Pope's epitaphs in the "Essay

upon Epitaphs," he would have demanded more "stillness,"
"sweetness," "stable grandeur," "repose" (PW, II, 55-68,
passim). Yet the mode of thinking which characterizes
Wordsworth's choice of diction and tone in each passage,
which in fact determines that there be one set of words
for piety, another for less elevated purposes, has far more
in common with the past than with the poetry since his
time.

Or, consider these lines:

> Thine be those motions strong and sanative,
> A ladder for thy Spirit to reascend
> To health and joy and pure contentedness;
> To me the grief confined that Thou art gone
> From this last spot of earth where Freedom now
> Stands single in her only sanctuary,
> A lonely wanderer, art gone, by pain
> Compell'd and sickness, at this latter day,
> This heavy time of change for all mankind. . . .
> Thou tak'st thy way, carrying a heart more ripe
> For all divine enjoyment, with the soul
> Which Nature gives to Poets, now by thought
> Matur'd, and in the summer of its strength.
> Oh! wrap him in your Shades, ye Giant Woods,
> On Etna's side, and thou, O flowery Vale
> Of Enna! is there not some nook of thine,
> From the first playtime of the infant earth
> Kept sacred to restorative delight?   (x, 978-1006)

Although this is Wordsworth speaking to Coleridge, we are
about as far from a personal, intimate tone as we can get.
For one thing, we learn nothing about their relationship,
and all we learn of Coleridge himself is the fact that he is
ill and has gone to Sicily for reasons of health. The attitude expressed is what might be called a stock attitude:
"Since we value you and since you are ill, we hope you may

recover soon." The pious tone is as though determined in advance—by the formal occasion, rather than by any spontaneous sentiment—and, unlike such exploratory passages as the spots of time, allows no free play for the imagination. One even suspects that if Coleridge had gone to Spain or Southern France there would have been no reason for the passage. As it is, the Miltonic echo ("O flowery Vale of Enna") and the specific references to Sicily evoke the whole pastoral tradition and serve mainly to lend a classical weight to the poem. Essentially the passage follows the form of an epistle to a distant friend; it is formal and impersonal in much the same way as the following lines in Thomson's "Spring," addressed to the poet's friend and patron Lyttelton:

> These are the sacred feelings of thy heart,
> Thy heart informed by reason's purer ray,
> O Lyttelton, the friend! Thy passions thus
> And meditations vary, as at large,
> Courting the muse, through Hagley Park you stray—
> Thy British Tempè! There along the dale
> With woods o'erhung, and shagged with mossy rocks
> Whence on each hand the gushing waters play,
> And down the rough cascade white-dashing fall
> Or gleam in lengthened vista through the trees,
> You silent steal. . . .   (ll. 904-914)

Again we note the unbendingly formal attitude and the refusal to indulge in personal detail; the scenic background, in fact, literally encloses the individual, as though to divert attention from any demand for the purely personal. If the "characters" who people Thomson's poem are chiefly men of public eminence, Wordsworth's are figures within his own private realm—Beaupuy, Dorothy, Coleridge, Raisley Calvert—who, by virtue of the formal machinery of eighteenth-century literary portraiture, are raised to public status.

The idealized passages in *The Prelude* are doubtless those that the modern reader, conditioned as he is by a century and a half of increasingly realistic techniques in the novel, finds most difficult to accept. Thus, in that most characteristic of modern epics, *The Cantos*, the method of treating character has come full swing from that of *The Prelude*. One might note, for instance, the portrait of Yeats (who, as past friend and collaborator, plays a role in the later *Cantos* somewhat analogous to that of Coleridge in *The Prelude*) in Canto LXXXIII:

> so that I recalled the noise in the chimney
> as it were the wind in the chimney
>   but was in reality Uncle William
> downstairs composing
> that had made a great Peeeacock
>   in the proide ov his oiye
>   had made a great peeeeeeecock in the . . .
> made a great peacock
>   in the proide of his oyyee
>
> proide ov his oy-ee
> as indeed he had, and perdurable
>
> a great peacock aere perennius
>   or as in the advice to the young man to
> breed and get married (or not)
>   as you choose to regard it
>
> at Stone Cottage in Sussex by the waste moor
>   (or whatever) and the holly bush
>   who would not eat ham for dinner
> because peasants eat ham for dinner
>   despite the excellent quality
> and the pleasure of having it hot

> well those days are gone forever
> and the traveling rug with the coon-skin tabs
> and his hearing nearly all Wordsworth
> for the sake of his conscience but
> preferring Ennemosor on Witches . . .

Pound's memory of his stay with Yeats in Sussex could be said to correspond to Wordsworth's memory of the summer of 1798:

> But, beloved Friend,
> When, looking back, thou seest in clearer view
> Than any sweetest sight of yesterday
> That summer when on Quantock's grassy Hills
> Far ranging, and among the sylvan Coombs,
> Thou in delicious words, with happy heart,
> Didst speak the Vision of that Ancient Man,
> The bright-eyed Mariner, and rueful woes
> Didst utter of the Lady Christabel.
>
> (XIII, 390-398)

The decorum that controls such lines as these is no doubt responsible for Pound's noting that Wordsworth could be read only "for the sake of conscience." For Pound's lines are in every way antithetical to Wordsworth's. Instead of being idealized, Yeats is caught in the most informal of poses: he is reduced, though with affection, to "Uncle William," his accent and process of composition are poked fun at, and he is surrounded by commonplace domestic detail (though Yeats, if not Pound, had decorum enough to resist eating the same fare as the peasants). For Pound, unlike Wordsworth, there is no longer any conflict possible between the demands of decorum and those of sincerity; the indecorous, the intimate detail, the observed eccentricity—these are the very substance of his portraits of the great public men who parade through his poem. But

Pound is perhaps not quite so free of poetic conventions as he might think: his. portraits, one could argue, derive much of their energy and charm from their conscious violation of all epic decorum.

b. *Pathos* and *Ethos*

When we come across these lines:

> And I grew up
> Foster'd alike by beauty and by fear,
>
> (I, 305-306)

we are likely to read them primarily as personal confession, as a summary of what Wordsworth took to be the two chief formative influences of his childhood. We all too easily imagine him thinking back on his early experiences—the theft of the little boat, the trips to the islands in Lake Windermere—and then deciding what qualities could best summarize the effects they had on him. But I should suggest that the thought process may have worked the other way around—that Wordsworth quite naturally assumed a dichotomy between conceptions of "beauty" and "fear," and that behind his use of these words there stands a whole century of discussion on the nature of the beautiful and the sublime.[13] To Wordsworth, reared as he was in the culture of the eighteenth century, these terms and all their areas of reference were second nature. As it had been for every writer from Addison onward, the sublime was as-

---

[13] Throughout this section I am concerned not so much with Wordsworth's exact intellectual relationship to earlier writers on aesthetics as with the way he used their concepts and terminology, sometimes rather imprecisely, for his artistic purposes. For the most illuminating studies of these terms throughout eighteenth-century thought, see Samuel H. Monk, *The Sublime* (New York, 1935); R. S. Crane's review of Monk's book in *Philological Quarterly*, xv (1936), 165-167; Marjorie H. Nicolson, *Mountain Gloom and Mountain Glory: The Development of the Aesthetics of the Infinite* (Ithaca, N.Y., 1959); and Ernest L. Tuveson, *The Imagination as a Means of Grace: Locke and the Aesthetics of Romanticism* (Berkeley and Los Angeles, 1960).

sociated in his mind with such attitudes and concepts as fear, admiration, passion, grandeur, and power; the beautiful, with loveliness, love, tenderness, calmness, gentleness. One need only note the combinations in these lines (the italics are mine):

> To early intercourse,
> In presence of *sublime* and *lovely* Forms
> With the adverse principles of *pain* and *joy* . . .
>
> (XIII, 145-147)

> From nature doth *emotion* come, and *moods*
> Of *calmness* equally are nature's gift,
> This is her glory.
>
> (XII, 1-3)

> Two feelings have we also from the first,
> [?] of *grandeur* and of *tenderness*;
> We live by *admiration* and by *love*
> And ev'n as these are well and wisely fixed
> In dignity of being we ascend.
>
> (From an early draft, in *Prel.*, p. 571)

The dichotomy between the beautiful and the sublime is evident in the scribblings found in the so-called Manuscript JJ, the earliest known draft (1798-99) of any longer passage in *The Prelude*:

> A storm not terrible but strong
> With lights and shades and with a rushing (power?)
> With *loveliness* and *power*.   (*Prel.*, p. 642)

It is noteworthy that for Wordsworth, as for many eighteenth-century theoreticians, these dual qualities were used not only to characterize the opposing poles within the outer world, but also to indicate the range of human emotions. One is often not quite sure whether he is speaking primarily of the physical or the mental landscape. And if

Wordsworth easily applied the categories of "beautiful" and "sublime" to either realm, to nature or the mind, it was also natural for him to transfer these concepts to the discussion of literary styles and genres. In this respect, as Klaus Dockhorn demonstrated in two important papers published in Germany more than a decade ago, Wordsworth betrays his training in that ancient rhetorical tradition which distinguishes between *pathos* and *ethos* as the opposing types of emotion which poetry seeks to depict, or which possess the orator at alternate moments.[14] "Emotions," wrote Quintilian, "as we learn from ancient authorities, fall into two classes; the one is called *pathos* . . . the other *ethos*. . . . The more cautious writers . . . explain *pathos* as describing the more violent emotions and *ethos* as designating those which are calm and gentle: in the one case the passions are violent, in the other subdued, the former command and disturb, the latter persuade and induce a feeling of goodwill."[15] As Dockhorn has, I think, shown conclusively, Wordsworth's critical writings take for granted the traditional distinctions between *pathos* and *ethos*. Thus, when Wordsworth speaks of "a natural delineation of human passions, human characters, and human incidents" (PW, II, 383), he refers to *pathos* and its various attributes under the term "passions," to *ethos* under "characters" and "incidents." In other spots Wordsworth employs such terms as "lofty," "profound," "general," "sublime" to indicate *pathos*, and "manners," "circumstances," "habitual," "common," and "pathetic" (the last-named having lost its associations with its origin by Words-

[14] "Wordsworth und die rhetorische Tradition in England," *Nachrichten der Akademie der Wissenschaften in Göttingen*, Phil.-Hist. Kl. (1944), 255-292, and "Die Rhetorik als Quelle des vorromantischen Irrationalismus in der Literatur- und Geistesgeschichte," in the same publication and series in 1949, pp. 109-150.

[15] *Institutio*, VI, ii.

worth's time) for *ethos*. The two conceptions are brought together, for instance, in the "Essay upon Epitaphs":

"The first requisite, then, in an Epitaph is, that it should speak, in a tone which shall sink into the heart, the *general language of humanity* as connected with the subject of death. . . . This general language may be uttered so strikingly as to entitle an epitaph to high praise; yet it cannot lay claim to the highest unless *other* excellencies be superadded. Passing through all intermediate steps, we will attempt to determine at once what these excellencies are, and wherein consists the perfection of this species of composition.—It will be found to lie in a due proportion of the common or universal feeling of humanity to sensations excited by a distinct and clear conception, conveyed to the reader's mind, of the individual, whose death is deplored and whose memory is to be preserved. . . . The general sympathy ought to be quickened, provoked, and diversified, by particular thoughts, *actions*, images,—*circumstances* of age, occupation, *manner of life*, prosperity which the deceased had known, or adversity to which he had been subject; and these ought to be bound together and solemnised into one harmony by the general sympathy. The *two powers* should temper, restrain, and exalt each other" (PW, V, 451-452; italics mine).

Note the contrast between the "general language of humanity" and the "distinct and clear conception of the individual": *pathos* and *ethos*, the lofty and common, the general and particular—all interacting with one another to "temper" (presumably the influence of *ethos* upon *pathos*), "exalt" (the influence of *pathos* upon *ethos*), and "restrain" (perhaps the mutual effect of each upon the other). Note also that Wordsworth, through the use of these key terms, can speak at once of the feelings and attitudes which are the *source* of poetry, of the *language* of poetry, and of the *effect* of poetry upon the reader; one is none too sure, in fact, whether "the common or universal feeling of humanity" is something that exists in the human mind from the start, or whether it inheres primarily in the epitaph itself, or whether it is aroused in the reader as a result of his reading the epitaph.

But above all, Wordsworth could still take for granted the doctrine that there existed a correspondence between the language a poet chose and the subject matter he was depicting, and that certain forms of language were more appropriate to certain areas of subject matter than others (one could in fact interpret his attack on eighteenth-century diction as a reassertion of this very doctrine: the forced loftiness of eighteenth-century personification and circumlocution was inappropriate to, and out of proportion with, the objects discussed). The Preface of 1800, moreover, is quite clear about the fact that lofty subjects demand a lofty style: "If the Poet's subject be judiciously chosen, it will naturally, and upon fit occasion, lead him to passions the language of which, if selected truly and judiciously, must necessarily be dignified and variegated, and alive with metaphors and figures" (PW, II, 392). As Dockhorn reminds us, the words "dignified" and "variegated" are traditional attributes of the high style.[16] And in the Introduction to *The Prelude*, when sorting out possible epic themes, he employs the terms "lofty" and "variegated" to give epic justification to a "Tale told from my own heart," in contrast to the more obviously epic subjects—Odin, Gustavus, Wallace—which he had noted earlier:

> Sometimes it suits me better to shape out
> Some Tale from my own heart, more near akin
> To my own passions and habitual thoughts,
> Some variegated story, in the main

[16] "Wordsworth und die rhetorische Tradition in England," p. 258.

Lofty, with interchange of gentler things.

(I, 220-224)

Here again he introduces the *pathos-ethos* dichotomy—
"passions" and "lofty" representing one pole, habitual
thoughts and gentler things, the other. Though his tale
be "in the main lofty"—that is, in the high style—it is
to be "variegated"—with those aspects of life which were
associated with the concept of *ethos* (eighteenth-century
commentaries on epic often called for variation of language within a poem to suit changes in subject matter).[17]
Since it is a "tale" which he is here considering, one suspects he refers not so much to the personal subject matter
of *The Prelude* as to some projected later portion of *The
Recluse*. But in the "Prospectus" to *The Excursion*, in a
version that probably goes back as early as 1798, we are
aware of a certain uneasiness on his part in reconciling
the purely personal elements of his theme—those which
we categorize as *ethos*—with the loftiness of his epic mission:

> Come thou prophetic Spirit, Soul of Man
> Thou human Soul of the wide earth that hast
> Thy metropolitan Temple in the hearts
> Of mighty Poets, unto me vouchsafe
> Thy guidance, teach me to discern and part
> Inherent things from casual, what is fixed
> From fleeting, that my verse may live and be
> Even as a light hung up in heaven to chear
> Mankind in times to come.

Thus far, his conception of the epic task.

And if with this

I blend more *lowly matter* with the thing

---

[17] See H. T. Swedenberg, Jr., *The Theory of the Epic in England: 1650-
1800* (Berkeley and Los Angeles, 1944), pp. 336, 369, 371-372.

Contemplated describe the mind and man
Contemplating and who and what he was
The *transitory Being* that beheld
This vision when and where and how he lived
With all his *little realties of life*
Be not the labour useless: if such theme
With *highest things* may mingle then great God
Thou who art breath and being, way and guide
And power and understanding, may my life
Express the image of a better time
More wise desires and simple manners, nurse
My heart in genuine freedom, all pure thoughts
Be with me and uphold me to the end.

(PW, V, 339; italics mine)

If at first he asked to be purged of all transitory things, he now asks for the "lowly matter," the "little realties of life" that constitute *ethos*, to be worthy of their more lofty accompaniment. If Wordsworth wishes to liberalize the laws of decorum, he is no less aware of the traditional meaning of decorum.

One could, in fact, speculate that it was Wordsworth's traditional sense of decorum which led him to cut two extended passages of the 1805 *Prelude* from the later version. The first of these, the so-called "Matron's Tale," about the boy and the lone sheep lost in the fog, is written in the same restrained tone as "Michael," of which it was presumably first intended to form a part:

Down to the Brook he went, and track'd its course
Upwards among the o'erhanging rocks; nor thus
Had he gone far, ere he espied the Boy
Where on that little plot of ground he stood
Right in the middle of the roaring Stream,
Now stronger every moment and more fierce.
The sight was such as no one could have seen

Without distress and fear. The Shepherd heard
The outcry of his Son, he stretch'd his Staff
Towards him, bade him leap, which word scarce said
The Boy was safe within his Father's arms.

                                            (VIII, 301-311)

The style could be described as a "middle style," mediating
between the sublime of the rest of *The Prelude* and the
lower order of most of *Lyrical Ballads*. As in "Michael,"
much of the charm resides in the discrepancy between the
formal blank verse and the simple diction and syntax,
which, every now and then, threaten to return to the sublime mode ("Now stronger every moment and more
fierce"). In its original place in Book VIII the tale has
something of a doctrinal purpose, for it demonstrates the
nature of "true" pastoral in contrast to the artifice of
literary pastoral. Yet in the lines directly following those
above we are aware of a sharp break in style, as Wordsworth, recounting the shepherds of the classical past, takes
up the Miltonic sublime:

Smooth life had Flock and Shepherd in old time,
Long Springs and tepid Winters on the Banks
Of delicate Galesus; and no less
Those scatter'd along Adria's myrtle Shores:
Smooth life the Herdsman and his snow-white Herd
To Triumphs and to sacrificial Rites
Devoted. . . .   (VIII, 312-318)

But we feel an even sharper breakdown in decorum
in "Vaudracour and Julia," that other long passage which
Wordsworth removed from *The Prelude*. The breakdown,
I think, is something intrinsic to the text itself and has
nothing to do with our modern reaction to the way he
covered up the Annette episode in this passage. What we
most object to is the inevitable transition from the lofty

tone established at the start—full worthy of the highest
strains in *The Prelude*:

> Earth liv'd in one great presence of the spring,
> Life turn'd the meanest of her implements
> Before his eyes to price above all gold,
> The house she dwelt in was a sainted shrine,
> Her chamber-window did surpass in glory
> The portals of the East, all paradise
> Could by the simple opening of a door
> Let itself in upon him . . .   (IX, 585-592)

to the more modest style demanded by the "little realties
of life":

>   It consoled him here
> To attend upon the Orphan and perform
> The office of a Nurse to his young Child
> Which after a short time by some mistake
> Or indiscretion of the Father, died.
>
>   (IX, 903-907)

In fact, it is to Wordsworth's uneasiness about the propriety of his subject matter that we can ascribe some of the
most unfortunate lapses in *The Prelude*, especially in the
early version:

>   Alas! I feel
>   That I am trifling,
>
>   (VIII, 706-707)

or, directly after the powerful line "I would enshrine the
spirit of the past / For future restoration":

>   Yet another
>   Of these, *to me*, affecting incidents
>   With which we will conclude.
>
>   (XI, 343-345; italics mine)

[31]

In historical terms we might think of Wordsworth as veering between two irreconcilable literary systems: between the demands of decorum and the demands of sincerity, or, to put it another way, between the responsibilities imposed by the recognition of a hierarchy of styles and the responsibilities he felt to the truth of his personal experience.

The dichotomies that guided Wordsworth's thought have still other implications for a study of his poetry. If we look at the three major philosophical poems of the Great Decade—"Tintern Abbey," the "Immortality Ode," and *The Prelude*—we can distinguish in each a transition from the realm of *pathos* to that of *ethos*. Consider, for instance, the terms in which he expresses the history of his growth in "Tintern Abbey." In early childhood, characterized as it is by "coarser pleasures" and "glad animal movements," and even later, when he was "more like a man / Flying from something that he dreads" rather "than one / Who sought the thing he loved," there still prevailed in him those attitudes which we associate with *pathos*:

> The sounding cataract
> Haunted me like a passion: the tall rock,
> The mountain, and the deep and gloomy wood,
> Their colours and their forms, were then to me
> An appetite; a feeling and a love,
> That had no need of a remoter charm,
> By thought supplied, nor any interest
> Unborrowed from the eye.—That time is past,
> And all its aching joys are now no more,
> And all its dizzy raptures.

In their place have come the attitudes of *ethos*:

> Not for this
> Faint I, nor mourn nor murmur; other gifts

Have followed; for such loss, I would believe,
Abundant recompense. For I have learned
To look on nature, not as in the hour
Of thoughtless youth; but hearing oftentimes
The still, sad music of humanity,
Nor harsh nor grating, though of ample power
To chasten and subdue.

These new attitudes are characterized by the calmer, gentler aspects of life ("still, sad music," "nor harsh, nor grating"), and they are distinctly concerned with the human, as against the merely natural, scene. (The word *humanity*, which retained considerably more of its Latin meaning in the eighteenth century than it does today, was traditionally associated with *ethos*.) In the culminating statement,

> And I have felt
> A presence that disturbs me with the joy
> Of elevated thoughts,

as Dockhorn reminds us, Wordsworth interweaves the attributes of the two realms: "disturbs" and "elevated thoughts" referring to *pathos*; "joy" and perhaps even "presence" to *ethos*. What Wordsworth says, in effect, is not only that the loss of *pathos* in favor of *ethos* has had "abundant recompense," but that his moment of vision is made possible only through the fusion—of the "mind of man" with the more sublime aspects of nature—he has been able to perceive within the two realms:

> A sense sublime
> Of something far more deeply interfused,
> Whose dwelling is the light of setting suns,
> And the round ocean and the living air,
> And the blue sky, and in the mind of man.

The quietude which makes possible the visionary state must come from *ethos,* but the intensity and range of his vision derive from *pathos.*

In something of the same way we can read the concluding stanza of the "Immortality Ode" as a celebration of the new, mature "philosophic mind" which synthesizes the lost visionary gleam of *pathos* with the sympathies and affections of *ethos*:

> I only have relinquished one delight
> To live beneath your more *habitual* sway.
> I love the Brooks which down their channels fret,
> Even more than when I tripped lightly as they;
> The innocent brightness of a new-born Day
> Is *lovely* yet;
> The Clouds that gather round the setting sun
> Do take a *sober* colouring from an eye
> That hath kept watch o'er *man's mortality*;
> Another race hath been, and other palms are won.
>
> (italics mine)

And when describing the character of the "Happy Warrior" the attainment of the qualities of *ethos* are not only an occasion for celebration, but also a matter of doctrine:

> He who, though thus endued as with a sense
> And faculty for *storm* and *turbulence,*
> Is yet a Soul whose master-bias leans
> To *homefelt pleasures* and to *gentle scenes.*
>
> (italics mine)

It is strangely characteristic of Wordsworth's transitional place in literary history that he can assert the value of smaller, gentler things while employing the verse forms and diction of the Great Ode and the Epic. *The Prelude* contains numerous passages in which he rejects the sublime in favor of the human realm. Take, for instance, the lines on Mont Blanc:

> That day we first
> Beheld the summit of Mont Blanc, and griev'd
> To have a soulless image on the eye
> Which had usurp'd upon a living thought
> That never more could be: the wondrous Vale
> Of Chamouny did, on the following dawn,
> With its dumb cataracts and streams of ice,
> A motionless array of mighty waves,
> Five rivers broad and vast, make rich amends,
> And reconcil'd us to realities.
> There small birds warble from the leafy trees,
> The Eagle soareth in the element;
> There doth the Reaper bind the yellow sheaf,
> The Maiden spread the haycock in the sun,
> While Winter like a tamed Lion walks
> Descending from the mountain to make sport
> Among the cottages by beds of flowers.
>
> (VI, 452-468)

The two modes, *pathos* and *ethos*, are clothed in opposing styles: the mountain is depicted in Wordsworth's characteristic language of personal vision, what, in the next two chapters, I describe as his "rhetoric of interaction" (note the deliberate blurring of tenor and vehicle; or his use of the word *usurp'd*, as in the lines on the Simplon Pass: "in such strength / Of usurpation, in such visitings / Of awful promise . . ."); in sharp contrast, the "realities" of the human realm below are poetically conventional (as in the generalized images of the reaper and maiden, the neat parallelisms, the absence of run-ons). It is as though, having arrived among known, apprehensible entities, he must turn to a more universal, time-honored mode of language. The final image of winter recapitulates the whole process from *pathos* to *ethos* (an alternate version is more explicit:

> While Winter like a Lion that had issued
> In threats and anger from his darksome cave
> Among the mountains, to a gentler mood. . . .
>
> [*Prel.*, p. 205])

On a less specifically personal level he complains that English historians too often excluded the qualities of *ethos* from their works:

> 'Tis true the History of my native Land,
> With those of Greece compar'd and popular Rome,
> Events not *lovely* nor *magnanimous*,
> But *harsh* and *unaffecting* in themselves
> And in our *high-wrought* modern narratives
> Stript of their *harmonising* soul, the life
> Of *manners* and *familiar* incidents,
> Had never much delighted me.
>
> (VIII, 770-777; italics mine)

Had Wordsworth chosen an historical theme for his long poem he would surely have sought to vary his story, though "in the main / Lofty, with interchange of gentler things."

The progress from *pathos* to *ethos* is Wordsworth's image of the history of his own life, and as such it provides a pattern of organization for *The Prelude*. Thus, whenever he attempts to summarize the course of his personal history (especially in the two "summarizing" books, VIII and XIII), he resorts to the vocabulary customarily associated with these terms. In the concluding book, for instance, he defines Dorothy's influence as a force which helped draw him from *pathos* to *ethos*:

> Even to the very going out of youth,
> The period which our Story now hath reach'd,

I too exclusively esteem'd that love,
And sought that beauty, which, as Milton sings,
Hath terror in it. Thou [Dorothy] didst soften down
This over-sternness; but for thee, sweet Friend,
My soul, too reckless of mild grace, had been
Far longer what by Nature it was framed,
Longer retained its countenance severe,
A rock with torrents roaring, with the clouds
Familiar, and a favorite of the Stars. . . .
When every day brought with it some new sense
Of exquisite regard for common things,
And all the earth was budding with these gifts
Of more refined humanity, thy breath,
Dear Sister, was a kind of gentler spring
That went before my steps. (XIII, 222-246)

We note once more the familiar terminology: the earlier Wordsworth is associated with "terror," "over-sternness," "recklessness," "a rock with torrents roaring"; Dorothy, with "gentleness," "more refined humanity," and "common things." The mature Wordsworth is, as it were, a synthesis of the two principles, with an emphasis on *ethos*. In something of the same way the creative imagination which reveals itself to him on Mt. Snowdon ultimately has its effects in the human realm. "The universal spectacle throughout / Was shaped for *admiration* and *delight*" (italics mine), he tells us, echoing the traditional attributes of *pathos* and *ethos*, and the power which it can generate among men is conducted through all human activities, even the mildest:

Such minds are truly from the Deity,
For they are Powers; and hence the highest bliss
That can be known is theirs, the consciousness
Of whom they are habitually infused
Through every image, and through every thought,

And all impressions; hence religion, faith
And endless occupation for the soul
Whether discursive or intuitive;
Hence sovereignty within and peace at will
Emotion which best foresight need not fear
Most worthy then of trust when most intense.
Hence chearfulness in every act of life
Hence truth in moral judgements and delight
That fails not in the external universe.

(XIII, 106-119)

The whole sequence here is from great to small, from the "highest bliss" to "chearfulness" and "delight." The ability of great things to influence and exalt smaller ones is stated even more forcefully in an earlier passage, when he speaks of Nature's power "to breathe / Grandeur upon the very humblest face / Of human life" (XII, 284-286).

The title of Book VIII, "Retrospect.—Love of Nature Leading to Love of Mankind," not only sums up the argument of the first half of the poem, but also indicates the movement of the second half. If the first half moves from the awesome visionary experiences of early childhood to the "tamer argument," as he puts it, of the human world of London, the second half progresses from his experience of the terrors of the Revolution—with the corresponding turmoil that ensued within his mind—to his attainment of inner peace in rural retirement. Like *Paradise Lost, The Prelude* moves from the cosmic to the human realm, from heroic to domestic sentiments.

But the *pathos-ethos* dichotomy was obviously not a rigid formula which Wordsworth used to determine the form and meaning of his work in advance. Rather, we might view it as a somewhat loose set of associations—its very looseness is evident in the way he and his predecessors could retain the same general category for such varied notions as Longinus' association of the "sublime" with greatness, and Burke's with terror—which Wordsworth could take for granted as a normative, universal way of viewing reality. In the unselfconscious ease with which he could voice these concepts, both in his criticism and his poetry, he reveals himself as more closely akin to the writers of the eighteenth century than to any poet since his time. We might, moreover, look at these concepts as a kind of lens through which he could look back on, evaluate, and give form and meaning to his past experience. Their formative influence upon the raw material of Wordsworth's personal history is perhaps analogous to that of the machinery of classical epic upon the Biblical themes out of which *Paradise Lost* was built; in both poems, though less readily in *The Prelude*, one discerns a traditional literary culture working to shape and interpret materials which might otherwise have assumed more modest poetic forms. We might, finally, think of *pathos* and *ethos* as a kind of language in and through which Wordsworth thought—a language which came to him so naturally that he could not have separated these concepts from the experiences and memories which they attempt to describe. It must, for example, have seemed natural to him to think of Dorothy as an incarnation of the qualities of *ethos*, or of his childhood experience plundering bird-nests as an instance of the workings of *pathos*. To the degree that he sensed a ready correspondence between his experience and such traditional concepts—and *The Prelude* reveals a high degree of correspondence— the demands of literary convention were able to consort well with the demands of sincerity.

CHAPTER TWO

THE RHETORIC OF INTERACTION (1): LANGUAGE AS REENACTMENT

He was to treat man as man,—a subject of eye, ear, touch, and taste, in contact with external nature. . . .

> (COLERIDGE, on Wordsworth's plan for a long poem)

For his understanding of the relationship of inner and outer is Wordsworth's principal claim to greatness. He had something new to say about mental and physical.

> (JOHN JONES, *The Egotistical Sublime*)

1 . PROCESS AND EXPLORATION

IN one of the few nineteenth-century discussions of *The Prelude* that show any real insight into the poem, De Quincey, writing more than a decade before the poem was published, singled out part of the passage which was already known to the public under the title "There Was a Boy":

> And they [the owls] would shout
> Across the watry Vale, and shout again,
> Responsive to his call, with quivering peals,
> And long halloos, and screams, and echoes loud
> Redoubled and redoubled; concourse wild
> Of mirth and jocund din! And when it chanced
> That pauses of deep silence mock'd his skill,
> Then sometimes, in that silence, while he hung

Listening, a gentle shock of mild surprize
Has carried far into his heart the voice
Of mountain torrents; or the visible scene
Would enter unawares into his mind
With all its solemn imagery, its rocks,
Its woods, and that uncertain Heaven, receiv'd
Into the bosom of the steady Lake.

(v, 399-413)

"This very expression, 'far,'" wrote De Quincey, "by which space and its infinities are attributed to the human heart, and to its capacities of re-echoing the sublimities of nature, has always struck me as with a flash of sublime revelation."[1] What De Quincey observed here was something little noted by Wordsworth's early critics: his unique method of portraying the interworking of physical with mental phenomena, of the external, observable world with the hidden inner world which is revealed to us at crucial moments in the poem. But the word "far" is only part of a much more elaborate strategy which Wordsworth employs to shift from the purely physical plane of hootings and screams along the lakeside to the landscape of the mind. The casual tone of "And when it chanced . . ." is the first sign of a slowing-up process, a shift away from the wild physical activity of the preceding lines, and the syntactical interruptions of the phrases "in that silence" and "while he hung / Listening," in suspending the rest of the sentence, prepare us for the mysterious processes about to take place. The "deep silence" (with the word "silence" carefully repeated in the following line) stands in striking contrast to the sense of confusion and noise he had conveyed immediately before. The process of interaction begins with "shock" and "surprize," though the suddenness is offset by the adjectives "gentle" and

---

[1] *Literary Reminiscences* (Boston, 1852), I, 310.

"mild." The interworking of the natural and human spheres that De Quincey noted in the word "far" is sustained in the following lines, when the outer scene assumes the active role which had earlier belonged to the boy; indeed, the word "unawares," with its double sense of "unexpectedly" (referring back to "shock" and "surprize") and "unconsciously" (the latter applicable both to the boy and the landscape) serves as a kind of pivot on which the changing relationship of landscape and mind turns.

We note here a type of poetry centrally concerned with process and movement, not only in its explicitly stated theme, but above all in the way it attempts to enact its theme for the reader. The sentence we have discussed is itself like a developing organism the course of whose growth we are unable to foresee as we begin to read it. In its attempt to reenact the processes of private experience it is wholly different in character from those set pieces of "public" rhetoric which we took up in the preceding chapter. Through the phrases interrupting its movement and such words as "far" and "unawares" we feel ourselves hovering at the edge of something new and unpredictable; and although the culminating image of the lake seems to deflect from the main business of interaction, in its actual effect—through the stabilizing qualities suggested by the words "bosom" and "steady"—it serves to bring the process to a temporary rest.

Though Wordsworth left us few really penetrating discussions about his own style, there is a passage in his Preface of 1815 concerning the interaction of objects within his poems. While illustrating his distinction between the fancy and the imagination, he quotes from "Resolution and Independence" to demonstrate the workings of the imagination when it is "employed upon images in a conjunction by which they modify each other":

As a huge stone is sometimes seen to lie
Couched on the bald top of an eminence,
Wonder to all who do the same espy
By what means it could thither come, and whence,
So that it seems a thing endued with sense,
Like a sea-beast crawled forth, which on a shelf
Of rock or sand reposeth, there to sun himself.

Such seemed this Man; not all alive or dead
Nor all asleep, in his extreme old age.

. . . .

Motionless as a cloud the old Man stood,
That heareth not the loud winds when they call,
And moveth altogether if it move at all.

"The stone," writes Wordsworth, "is endowed with some-thing of the power of life to approximate it to the sea-beast; and the sea-beast stripped of some of its vital qual-ities to assimilate it to the stone; which intermediate image is thus treated for the purpose of bringing the original image, that of the stone, to a nearer resemblance to the figure and condition of the aged Man; who is divested of so much of the indications of life and motion as to bring him to the point where the two objects unite and coalesce in just comparison" (PW, II, 438).

Although Wordsworth never discussed anything from *The Prelude* in comparable detail, this habit of inter-changing qualities of the animate and inanimate, of the mind and external nature, is central to *The Prelude* (and its satellite poems such as "Tintern Abbey" and those parts of *The Excursion* written contemporaneously with it) as it is to no other part of his work. It is the natural method with which he communicates his early spiritual experiences and accounts in poetic terms for his mental and emo-tional development; above all, it is his way of recapturing

poetically that sense of the unity of all existence which he
had felt on so intuitive a level in early childhood. In
The Prelude, unlike the passage from "Resolution and
Independence," he does not merely portray the interwork-
ings of discernible objects, but creates a lively interplay of
what we would normally call abstract concepts. Thus, in
the phrase "The Power which . . . Nature thus / Thrusts
forth upon the senses" (XIII, 84-86) the abstractions are
brought to life through the highly charged physical activity
suggested by the verb. In this passage:

> Thus the pride of strength,
> And the vain-glory of superior skill
> Were interfus'd with objects which subdu'd
> And temper'd them, and gradually produc'd
> A quiet independence of the heart,
>
> (II, 69-73)

the word "heart" is the closest we get to any tangible object. Yet he creates a brief but intense drama centered
about the assertiveness of the human ego, which, in the
process of "interfusion," loses the upper hand to the unnamed objects of external nature, which in turn—after
the suggestions of bold but controlled activity in the verbs
"subdu'd" and "temper'd"—succeed in bringing the conflict to a peaceful conclusion. Sometimes the processes that
Wordsworth depicts are wholly internal, with external nature playing only an indirect role, as in these lines,

> Thus sometimes were the shapes
> Of wilful fancy grafted upon feelings
> Of the imagination, and they rose
> In worth accordingly,   (VIII, 583-586)

where the process achieves a certain concreteness through
the organic metaphor underlying "grafted." Wordsworth's
reenactment of the processes of interaction thus often de-

pends on the metaphoric power of a single word within a longer passage.

This power, moreover, does not issue only from the verbs, as in the above examples, but sometimes from seemingly abstract nouns. In the following lines,

> [I] felt
> Incumbences more awful, visitings
> Of the Upholder of the tranquil Soul . . . ,
> (III, 114-116)

the chief burden of reenactment is carried neither by the verb, which is weak, nor by the two capitalized quasi-deities, "Upholder" and "Soul," but by the portentous nouns and adjective of the middle line, which seems to uncover new perspectives with each succeeding word. "Incumbences," for instance, encompasses both the physical and spiritual realms. The word is defined in the NED—which quotes Wordsworth's line, albeit in the 1850 version, where it reads "incumbencies"—as "condition of lying or pressing upon something; brooding; a spiritual brooding or over-shadowing." It could thus be said to combine the two seventeenth-century usages also listed in the NED—the first of these of distinctly spiritual reference, "the peculiar incumbency and direction of the holy Ghost," the other physical, "the chill incumbency of other wildfoul." William Empson, in one of the most penetrating essays ever written on Wordsworth, calls attention to a favorite Wordsworthian noun, "the apparently flat little word *sense*," which, especially when it appears at the end of a line, functions as a kind of mediator between ordinary and new, still uncharted ways of perception:

> [The soul] retains an obscure sense
> Of possible sublimity. . . .
> (II, 336-337)

                                          My brain
Work'd with a dim and undetermin'd sense
Of unknown modes of being.

                              (I, 418-420)

"There is a suggestion here from the pause at the end of
the line," writes Empson, "that he had not merely 'a feeling of' these unknown modes but something like a new
'sense' which was partly able to apprehend them—a new
kind of sensing had appeared in his mind."[2]

The uniqueness of Wordsworth's way of coming to
terms with interacting forces can best be seen by setting
any of the above passages next to something like the following, part of a speech from Coleridge's *Osorio*:

> With other ministrations thou, O Nature!
> Healest thy wandering and distemper'd child:
> Thou pourest on him thy soft influences,
> Thy sunny hues, fair forms, and breathing sweets,
> Thy melodies of woods, and winds, and waters,
> Till he relent, and can no more endure
> To be a jarring and a dissonant thing,
> Amid this general dance and minstrelsy;
> But, bursting into tears, wins back his way,
> His angry spirit heal'd and harmoniz'd
> By the benignant touch of Love and Beauty.

Like Wordsworth later, Coleridge is here concerned with
the effect of nature on the individual mind, yet the result strikes one as flat and wooden. Despite the attempt
at rhetorical heightening in the opening apostrophe, the
lifeless effect of the verbs, the conventionality of the epi-
thets ("sunny hues," "fair forms"), and the inhibited flow
of the syntax throughout the course of the sentence all
contribute to a static quality which informs the whole.
What F. R. Leavis once wrote of Wordsworth's blank verse

[2] *The Structure of Complex Words*, pp. 289-290.

at its best—that he "produces the mood, feeling or experience and at the same time appears to be giving an explanation of it"[3]—can scarcely be said of this Coleridgean passage, which (under the title "The Dungeon") appeared but a few pages apart from "Tintern Abbey" in the first edition of *Lyrical Ballads*; Coleridge, one might say, has merely explained the process of interaction without successfully reenacting it. But the above example, despite its inclusion in *Lyrical Ballads*, is not entirely fair to Coleridge, for my comparison ignores the contribution he made through his so-called "conversation poems"—beginning with "The Eolian Harp" in 1795—to the type of poetic structure which Wordsworth later developed in "Tintern Abbey" and *The Prelude*.[4] Yet if Coleridge, somewhat crudely at first, pointed the way toward a poetry which would run the gamut from physical sense experience to larger spiritual insight, it remained for Wordsworth to perfect a rhetoric which would adequately encompass the physical and mental realms; indeed, Coleridge's greatest triumphs in the genre which he created, the "Dejection Ode" of 1802 and the poem "To William Wordsworth," composed in 1807 in response to a reading of *The Prelude*, reflect the characteristic Wordsworthian language of interaction:

> To her may all things live, from pole to pole,
> Their life the eddying of her living soul!

>   Of moments awful,
> Now in thy inner life, and now abroad,
> When power streamed from thee, and thy soul received
> The light reflected, as a light bestowed.

[3] *Revaluation* (New York, 1947), p. 159.

[4] See, for instance, G. M. Harper's ground-breaking essay, "Coleridge's Conversation Poems," *Quarterly Review*, CCXLIV (1925), 284-298, and a searching recent study by A. Gérard, "The Systolic Rhythm: The Structure of Coleridge's Conversation Poems," *Essays in Criticism*, X (1960), 307-319.

Byron, too, above all in *Childe Harold*, tried to cope with the phenomenon of interaction:

> I live not in myself, but I become
> Portion of that around me; and to me
> High mountains are a feeling, but the hum
> Of human cities torture: I can see
> Nothing to loathe in nature, save to be
> A link reluctant in a fleshly chain,
> Class'd among creatures, when the soul can flee,
> And with the sky, the peak, the heaving plain
> Of ocean, or the stars, mingle, and not in vain.
>
> (III, lxxii)

Though at moments we recognize the customary precision of Byron's conversational tone ("I can see / Nothing to loathe in nature"), he is working toward the expression of a type of experience completely foreign to his real talent. The omission of the indefinite article before "portion" and the deliberate vagueness of "high mountains are a feeling" are unsuccessful attempts to create an aura of mystery (Wordsworth once described the tone of Byron's nature enthusiasm as *assumed* rather than natural"—co, 205), while the off-handed cataloguing of sky, peaks, ocean, and stars in the final lines need only be compared with Wordsworth's

> The visible scene
> Would enter unawares into his mind
> With all its solemn imagery, its rocks,
> Its woods, and that uncertain Heaven, receiv'd
> Into the bosom of the steady Lake,

to make us aware of the incompatibility of the swift, casual Byronic tone with the transcendental longings he is trying to express. Byron tried his hand, as well, at manipulating the "flat little word *sense*" (which he would not

have known from *The Prelude*, but from "Tintern Abbey"—"a sense sublime / Of something far more deeply
interfused"):

> All is concenter'd in a life intense,
> Where not a beam, nor air, nor leaf is lost,
> But hath a part of being, and a sense
> Of that which is of all Creator and defence.
>
> (III, lxxxix)

The mystery which he sought to achieve in the transition
to the "Creator" fails to come through; the reader is left
with an example of Byronic flatness without his saving
grace of irony.

But Wordsworth, too, had lost touch with this mode of
experience soon after completing *The Prelude*, to a certain
degree even before the poem was complete. Consider the
following passage from *The Excursion*:

> The sun is fixed,
> And the infinite magnificence of heaven
> Fixed, within reach of every human eye;
> The sleepless ocean murmurs for all ears;
> The vernal field infuses fresh delight
> Into all hearts. Throughout the world of sense,
> Even as an object is sublime or fair,
> That object is laid open to the view
> Without reserve or veil; and as a power
> Is salutary, or an influence sweet,
> Are each and all enabled to perceive
> That power, that influence, by impartial law.
>
> (IX, 209-220)

The characteristic vocabulary—"power," "influence,"
"murmurs," even so effective a verb of process as "in-
fuses"—is still present, but the life and movement are
gone. The tone is no longer personal, but official; the syn-

tax is no longer a vehicle for exploration, but for what seems little more than direct statement; the reader no longer feels new perspectives opening, but must content himself with commonplace two-dimensional reality.

2. THE STRUGGLE TOWARD DEFINITION

Among the rhetorical strategies which Wordsworth developed to mediate between the physical and mental realms was one which sought to embody the full process of visionary experience, from perception of the world of the senses to spiritual illumination. The visionary experiences recorded in the poem generally begin with a down-to-earth, often prosaic statement closely rooted in the world of ordinary perception. "There was a Boy," he starts the famous passage discussed at the opening of this chapter. The culminating vision of the poem, the ascent of Mt. Snowdon, begins with a matter-of-fact account punctiliously recording all the circumstances that mark the occasion:

> In one of these excursions, travelling then
> Through Wales on foot, and with a youthful Friend,
> I left Bethkelet's huts at couching-time,
> And westward took my way to see the sun
> Rise from the top of Snowdon. Having reach'd
> The Cottage at the Mountain's foot, we there
> Rouz'd up the Shepherd, who by ancient right
> Of office is the Stranger's usual Guide;
> And after short refreshment sallied forth.
>   It was a Summer's night . . .   (XIII, 1-10)

From here on there is a steady probing inward (and upward, in a sense, for the passage literally follows the ascent up the mountain), until the mountain loses its physical reality in the climactic lines:

> And it appear'd to me
> The perfect image of a mighty Mind,
> Of one that feeds upon infinity,
> That is exalted by an under-presence,
> The sense of God, or whatsoe'er is dim
> Or vast in its own being . . .   (68-73)

The inner world, the moment of vision is never, of course, defined exactly: when Wordsworth approaches this realm of experience he cannot proceed with the straightforwardness with which he depicted the beginning of his journey. We are, after all, prepared to accept the reality of Bethkelet and the shepherd's cottage, but the vision toward which he builds can be presented verbally only by the most indirect means. In the lines above he approaches it in a number of ways, none of which is really parallel to any other. First he translates it into a possible metaphorical equivalent ("image of a mighty Mind"); next, he explains it by its peculiar form of activity ("feeds upon infinity"); finally, he retreats from the problem of what it *is* or *does* and he tells us instead what it is "exalted by," what lurks behind it, what it is related to. It seems that each time he has found a way to define his object, he must move back and seek out a new approach. The grammatically parallel phrases and clauses—"under-presence," "sense of God," "whatsoe'er is dim"—do not function primarily to add descriptive detail about the object but, rather, to suggest new perspectives (the traditionally religious dimension in "sense of God," the hidden, mysterious depths in "under-presence," a word which Wordsworth coined himself) through which the object may be viewed. But even to speak of an "object" or "inner world" as such seems to imply something static or substantial toward which Wordsworth moves. Indeed, the reader is not shown any images so concrete as the flame at the end of Dante's journey or Keats's fairy realm of the imagination. Rather, what he experiences in such passages in *The Prelude* is the poet's verbal struggle to define his moment of spiritual illumination.

This struggle toward definition which characterizes Wordsworth's visionary passages makes for a peculiarly rhetorical type of art—one much more foreign to the contemporary reader than the symbol-centered method used by writers like Keats and Eliot to record spiritual experiences.[5] Wordsworth's method can be seen at its most typical in "Tintern Abbey," which served him as a kind of trial-run for the visionary experiences recorded in *The Prelude*:

> These beauteous forms,
> Through a long absence, have not been to me
> As is a landscape to a blind man's eye:
> But oft, in lonely rooms, and 'mid the din
> Of towns and cities, I have owed to them
> In hours of weariness, sensations sweet,
> Felt in the blood, and felt along the heart;
> And passing even into my purer mind,
> With tranquil restoration:—feelings too
> Of unremembered pleasure: such, perhaps,
> As have no slight or trivial influence
> On that best portion of a good man's life,
> His little, nameless, unremembered, acts
> Of kindness and of love. Nor less, I trust,

[5] Through Wordsworth's insistence on discussing literally the process by which he achieved his visionary experiences, his accounts of these experiences stand in obvious contrast to the imaginary symbolic journeys of Dante, St. John of the Cross, and Keats. Lowry Nelson, Jr., in an essay on these three poets, makes a distinction between "poetry *about* the idea of having a mystical experience and . . . poetry that tries to communicate the experience itself" ("The Rhetoric of Ineffability: Toward a Definition of Mystical Poetry," *Comparative Literature*, VIII [1956], 324). The poetry that Nelson commends is of course the latter. I suggest, with Dr. Leavis (in the passage quoted in the preceding section), that Wordsworth, whom Nelson does not take up in his essay, manages to do both at once.

To them I may have owed another gift,
Of aspect more sublime; that blessed mood,
In which the burthen of the mystery,
In which the heavy and the weary weight
Of all this unintelligible world,
Is lightened:—that serene and blessed mood,
In which the affections gently lead us on,—
Until, the breath of this corporeal frame
And even the motion of our human blood
Almost suspended, we are laid asleep
In body, and become a living soul:
While with an eye made quiet by the power
Of harmony, and the deep power of joy,
We see into the life of things.

                    If this
Be but a vain belief, yet, oh! how oft—
In darkness and amid the many shapes
Of joyless daylight; when the fretful stir
Unprofitable, and the fever of the world,
Have hung upon the beatings of my heart—
How oft, in spirit, have I turned to thee
O sylvan Wye! thou wanderer thro' the woods,
How often has my spirit turned to thee!

  And now, with gleams of half-extinguished
        thought,
With many recognitions dim and faint,
And somewhat of a sad perplexity,
The picture of the mind revives again:
While here I stand, not only with the sense
Of present pleasure, but with pleasing thoughts
That in this moment there is life and food
For future years. And so I dare to hope,
Though changed, no doubt, from what I was
        when first

I came among these hills; when like a roe
I bounded o'er the mountains, by the sides
Of the deep rivers, and the lonely streams,
Wherever nature led: more like a man
Flying from something that he dreads than one
Who sought the thing he loved. For nature then
(The coarser pleasures of my boyish days,
And their glad animal movements all gone by)
To me was all in all.—I cannot paint
What then I was. The sounding cataract
Haunted me like a passion: the tall rock,
The mountain, and the deep and gloomy wood,
Their colors and their forms, were then to me
An appetite; a feeling and a love,
That had no need of a remoter charm,
By thought supplied, nor any interest
Unborrowed from the eye.—That time is past,
And all its aching joys are now no more,
And all its dizzy raptures. Not for this
Faint I, nor mourn nor murmur; other gifts
Have followed; for such loss, I would believe,
Abundant recompense. For I have learned
To look on nature, not as in the hour
Of thoughtless youth; but hearing oftentimes
The still, sad music of humanity,
Nor harsh nor grating, though of ample power
To chasten and subdue. And I have felt
A presence that disturbs me with the joy
Of elevated thoughts; a sense sublime
Of something far more deeply interfused,
Whose dwelling is the light of setting suns,
And the round ocean and the living air,
And the blue sky, and in the mind of man:
A motion and a spirit, that impels

All thinking things, all objects of all thought,
And rolls through all things.

I have quoted at length because one becomes aware
of the full movement of thought only through extended
passages; and this forward movement toward the vision of
the concluding lines is all-important here, despite the variety of things that are discussed along the way (there is
good reason, after all, that this passage has been more useful than any other to those who wish to extricate Wordsworth's philosophy from his work). In the lines preceding
the passage he had established a solid external world, with
its mountain-springs, its "steep and lofty cliffs," its "plots
of cottage-ground," yet a world which, like the pastoral
world sketched in before the ascent of Snowdon, serves
essentially as a base for a journey into something more
inward. The spiritual journey in "Tintern Abbey" is not,
as in the vision from Snowdon, correlated with an actual
physical journey; it remains, rather, a discursive journey
within the mind. Throughout we are aware of a probing
toward something, a forward movement broken at frequent intervals by shifts into new directions of thought.

This forward movement is signalled, for instance, by
intensifying words: "even into my *purer* mind," "of aspect
more sublime," "of something far *more* deeply interfused";
by repetition of such words as "deep": "deep power,"
"deep rivers," "deep woods," "deeply interfused"—with its
suggestions of the hidden and the inward; or "all": "all
this unintelligible world," "nature to me was all in all,"
"all objects of all thought"—which not only asserts wholeness and unity, but acts at the end of the passage as a kind
of tonic chord resolving the whole.

The probing, moreover, is constantly interrupted by
qualifications and rhetorical back-tracking. Strong assertions are tempered by phrases such as "no doubt," "I

trust," "if this be but a vain belief," "somewhat of."
Through frequent use of negatives (fully seven of the
twelve lines beginning with "That had no need of a remoter charm" contain forms of negation) he defines by a
process of elimination. At one point he even speaks of the
impossibility of verbal communication: "I cannot paint /
What then I was." We move back and forth between abstract thought ("that serene and blessed mood, / In which
the affections gently lead us on") and description of the
natural setting ("the sounding cataract / Haunted me
like a passion") from which he began and to which he
can always return before starting out on further explorations. There are also frequent, if also gradual shifts in the
tone, which ranges from the intimate ("On that best portion of a good man's life") to the formally poetic ("How
oft, in spirit, have I turned to thee, / O sylvan Wye"). But
despite the shifts and interruptions we never lose sight of
the goal ahead. Whatever the divagations along the way,
there is still a continuity and progression from one sentence
to the next ("And now. . . ," "And so I dare to hope. . . ,"
"And I have felt. . . .")—until the culminating lines, where,
through the rows of parallel phrases, and the heavy, regular repetitions, the long, elaborate process of definition
gradually comes to an end. Yet the spiritual essence toward
which the poet has moved is rendered for us no more
clearly than is the vision on Snowdon: we know it only by
its dwelling-place ("the light of setting suns," etc.) and by
the objects of its motivating power ("all thinking things,"
etc.). If we succeed in "experiencing" what it is, that is
because we have been made to share the full course of the
poet's movement of thought.

Something of the same backward-and-forward movement
is present throughout those portions of *The Prelude* devoted to the poet's visionary experiences. The following
passage presents this movement, from vision to rational

deliberation and back to vision, within the course of a few
lines:

> And I would stand,
> Beneath some rock, listening to sounds that are
> The ghostly language of the ancient earth,
> Or make their dim abode in distant winds.
> Thence did I drink the visionary power.
> I deem not profitless those fleeting moods
> Of shadowy exultation: not for this,
> That they are kindred to our purer mind
> And intellectual life; but that the soul,
> Remembering how she felt, but what she felt
> Remembering not, retains an obscure sense
> Of possible sublimity, to which
> With growing faculties she doth aspire,
> With faculties still growing . . .
>
> (ii, 326-339)

While we are busy following the turnings of the deliber-
ating mind ("I deem not profitless," "not for this . . .
but") the poet has once again moved us toward the realm
of spiritual essence, but only *toward*, for like the soul's
"growing faculties," we "aspire" toward a goal which we
never fully reach.

In thus recapturing the mind's struggle for expression of
the inexpressible, Wordsworth stands apart from such
visionaries as Boehme, or the Blake of the prophetic books,
who set down their visions directly, without creating the
rhetorical bridge from the observable world of the reader
to the new world to be uncovered. "And thus we give you
to understand what this world's existence is," writes
Boehme with all the self-assurance of the doctrinalist,
"nothing else than a coagulated smoke from the eternal
aether, which thus had a fulfilment like the Eternal."[6]

[6] I quote from one of the Boehme passages listed by Newton P. Stallknecht as possible Wordsworthian sources: see *Strange Seas of Thought*,
2nd ed. (Bloomington, Ind., 1958), p. 118.

It is the inevitable difference between the philosopher and the poet. Indeed, one is tempted at this point to correct Coleridge's notion of Wordsworth as a philosophical poet: in describing the plan for *The Recluse* as a whole he wrote that "Wordsworth should assume the station of a man in mental repose, one whose principles were made up, and so prepared to deliver upon authority a system of philosophy" (CO, 438). But in his great introductory poem to *The Recluse*, Wordsworth can hardly be said to assume a "station of mental repose." One is impressed, for one thing, by the immense intellectual energy concentrated in the language; and however well Wordsworth's "system of philosophy" was already "made up," the poem reveals, above all, the process by which it came into being.

As a literary method the struggle toward definition was useful to Wordsworth only so long as there was something to define or discover. Once the discovery was complete, or the pressure to recapture the feeling of discovery was gone, the intensity of his vision was lost, as we are all too well aware when we try to read *The Excursion*. It was a method, then, peculiar to the Wordsworth of "Tintern Abbey" and *The Prelude*, and it seems to have left no substantial imprint either on his later work or on the future course of English poetry. In inept hands it resulted in something like this, from Samuel Rogers' *Italy* (itself an imitation of Byron, who derived the method from "Tintern Abbey"):

> Who first beholds those everlasting clouds . . .
> But instantly receives into his soul
> A sense, a feeling that he loses not,
> A something that informs him 'tis an hour,
> Whence he may date henceforward and for ever?[7]

[7] *Poetical Works* (London, 1856), p. 262.

3 . MEDITATIVE ENERGY AND FULLNESS

Distinctions between the concrete and the abstract in the discussion of poetic language are relevant only to an age, such as ours, which has been dedicated to the clear, precisely framed image as the most appropriate vehicle for the enforcement of poetic meaning. "The great aim is accurate, precise and definite description"—so runs T. E. Hulme's famous dictum, which, for better and worse, has stood behind most of the significant poetry and criticism of the first half of the twentieth century. Inevitably, concreteness of diction has become a term of honor in our criticism, and we have come to associate it, in one way or another, with such sought-after qualities as dramatic objectivity, functional metaphor, and general cleanness of style. At the opposite extreme, associated with the abstract, we generally find such critical terms as "hazy," "subjective," and "rhetorical." But a critical system useful in defining the qualities of one set of poets is meaningless when applied literally to poetry characterized by an entirely foreign set of qualities. Certainly the language of *The Prelude* will strike us as "abstract" if we approach it directly from a reading of, say, Donne, Rimbaud, Eliot, or even *Lyrical Ballads*. But the whole modern dichotomy between concrete and abstract is applicable to *The Prelude* only if we are willing to observe not the individual words—any word-count, I am sure, would reveal an overwhelming number of abstractions—but the way they work in context. In his searching analysis of some of our most cherished critical assumptions Donald Davie singled out *The Prelude* as a type of poetry that differs sharply from our contemporary norm: "The diction of *The Prelude* is neither abstract nor concrete, but something between the two. . . . The nouns are not concrete; but the verbs are, and may be lingered over. In short, this is poetry where the syntax counts enormously, counts for nearly everything."[8] What he is saying is much the same, I think, as what I meant when I spoke of Wordsworth's as a poetry of process and movement, a poetry less interested in illuminating individual objects than in enacting the process of perception and the movement of the contemplating mind. Davie's remarks were made with specific reference to the lines beginning "Blest the infant Babe," a passage which, one suspects, is about as far removed from modern taste as anything to be found in a major English poet:

> Thus, day by day,
> Subjected to the discipline of love,
> His organs and recipient faculties
> Are quicken'd, are more vigorous, his mind spreads,
> Tenacious of the forms which it receives.
> In one beloved Presence, nay and more,
> In that most apprehensive habitude
> And those sensations which have been deriv'd
> From this beloved Presence, there exists
> A virtue which irradiates and exalts
> All objects through all intercourse of sense.
> No outcast he, bewilder'd and depress'd;
> Along his infant veins are interfus'd
> The gravitation and the filial bond
> Of nature, that connect him with the world.
>
> (II, 250-264)

The example seems useful since the proportion of Latinate abstractions is probably higher here than in *The Prelude* as a whole. Yet the concreteness that Davie notes in the verbs (for instance, "spreads," "irradiates," "interfus'd") extends as well to some of the adjectives: "tenacious," which gathers energy, as it were, from "spreads," or "apprehensive," which gains almost an active verbal sense through the context of motion within which it appears;

[8] *Articulate Energy*, pp. 107, 110-111.

even such substantives as "gravitation" and "intercourse of
sense" gather a certain vitality from their surroundings.
Indeed, in the discussion of such a passage the real dichotomy is not between abstract and concrete, but between activity and inertia.

One might contrast the above passage, with all its life
and activity, with the following passage from Akenside,
who is attempting here to depict the creative process:

> By degrees, the mind
> Feels her young nerves dilate: the plastic powers
> Labour for action: blind emotions heave
> His bosom. . . .
>
> Then with Promethean art,
> Into its proper vehicle he breathes
> The fair conception; which, embodied thus,
> And permanent, becomes to eyes or ears
> An object ascertain'd: while thus inform'd,
> The various organs of his mimic skill,
> The consonance of sounds, the featur'd rock,
> The shadowy picture and impassion'd verse,
> Beyond their proper powers attract the soul
> By that expressive semblance. . . .[9]

Although we are told much *about* the transfer of energy—
both within the artist and from the artist into his work—
the language fails to demonstrate the act itself. In the
opening lines, for instance, the phrase "labour for action"
literally labors to imitate an action which never takes place,
while the idea of young nerves dilating or of emotions
heaving seems too obviously self-conscious an attempt to
root the action in concrete psychological processes. In the
later lines the verbs "attract" and "ascertain'd" do not,
like "spreads" and "irradiates" in the Wordsworth passage,

[9] *Pleasures of Imagination*, in Alexander Chalmers, *Works of the English Poets* (London, 1810), XIV, 73-74.

work to magnetize the surrounding context with their concretizing influence; above all, we miss that delicate counterbalancing movement so conspicuous in Wordsworth, whereby the accumulated weight of adjectives and nouns is continually offset by the action of the verbs. Yet there are moments when Akenside anticipates the type of movement which Wordsworth was later to bring to perfection; I cite these lines, which are as close to the characteristic Wordsworthian mode as anything in eighteenth-century poetry:

> Then Nature speaks
> Her genuine language, and the words of men,
> Big with the very motions of their souls,
> Declare with what accumulated force
> The impetuous nerve of passion urges on
> The native weight and energy of things.[10]

But the inherited conventions of eighteenth-century Miltonic blank verse, of which Akenside's is doubtless one of the finer examples (we might remember Dr. Johnson's remark about Akenside, that "in the general fabrication of his lines he is perhaps superior to any other writer of blank verse"[11]), were not easily adapted to the dynamic mode of language which its subjects often demanded. For energy and movement in the eighteenth century we must look primarily to the language of the Augustan tradition, with its swiftly changing currents of thought. Yet the blank verse conventions which Wordsworth inherited and refined were able to lend themselves—as those of the couplet emphatically did not—to a peculiarly meditative type of poetry, one which often had to give up in energy and activity what it gained in fullness. Much of the fascination of *The Prelude*, in fact, lies in the fullness and sub-

[10] *Ibid.*, xiv, 66.
[11] *Ibid.*, xiv, 55.

tlety with which Wordsworth succeeded in characterizing the meditative process.

Josephine Miles, who has gone to greater lengths than any other critic to define the qualities peculiar to Wordsworth's meditative verse, notes this fullness in her comments on the following passage:

> Humility and modest awe themselves
> Betray me, serving often for a cloak
> To a more subtle selfishness, that now
> Doth lock my functions up in blank reserve,
> Now dupes me by an over-anxious eye
> That with a false activity beats off
> Simplicity and self-presented truth.
>
> (I, 245-251)

"In this more abstract phase of the descriptive-essay style," Miss Miles writes, "one sees the constant functioning of modification, the step-by-step refining of terms. Awe is modest, selfishness is subtle . . . ; no one of these terms startles by radical alteration of the nature of its noun, yet none merely repeats, either, the sense of its noun; each makes the phase of the noun special enough to be [a] specific part of the specific complex of mood which here is being defined."[12]

Although the chief activity emanates from the verbs in this passage, the adjectives create a movement—slow and even somewhat weighty—of their own. Like the adjectives used to modify the personifications of eighteenth-century poetry, they call attention to themselves through their specificity, yet in the frequency and regularity with which they appear (one in almost every line of the above passage) they set up and sustain that "step-by-step refining" process to which Miss Miles refers. One might think of this

---

[12] *Major Adjectives in English Poetry*, "University of California Publications in English," Vol. XII, No. 3 (Berkeley and Los Angeles, 1946), p. 350.

process as a somewhat less spectacular version of that "struggle toward definition" which goes on, in a more dramatic manner, in Wordsworth's more distinctly visionary passages, those that we commonly refer to as "spots of time." But this refining process goes on throughout *The Prelude*, lending a sense of movement to the whole so as to justify, within the very texture of the work, Wordsworth's repeated likening of the poem's organization to a journey.

If Wordsworth, as I have suggested, relies largely on his verbs to pinpoint the main movements of his thought, he relies on adjectives and qualifying phrases to re-create the full ebb and flow of the meditative process. His poetry is not argumentative, at least not in the Augustan manner; rather, it is ruminative and discursive, concerned with the wide expanses of thought existing between the extreme positions which argumentative verse normally assumes. As Dr. Leavis, approaching Wordsworth with a distinctly Augustan bias, once put it, "[He] will appear to be preoccupied with a scrupulous nicety of statement, with a judicial weighing of alternative possibilities, while actually making it more difficult to check the argument from which he will emerge, as it were inevitably, with a far from inevitable conclusion."[13] (The closest prose equivalent to Wordsworth's meditative verse, one ventures to say, is perhaps the later style of Henry James.) One might look at one of the more "meditative" passages in *Descriptive Sketches* to note how foreign the meditative style of *The Prelude* is to the Augustan couplet:

> But, ah! th' unwilling mind may more than trace
> The general sorrows of the human race:
> The churlish gales, that unremitting blow
> Cold from necessity's continual snow,

13 *Revaluation*, p. 162.

To us the gentle groups of bliss deny
That on the noon-day bank of leisure lie.

Yet more; the tyrant Genius, still at strife
With all the tender Charities of life,
When close and closer they begin to strain,
No fond hand left to staunch th' unclosing vein,
Tearing their bleeding ties leaves Age to groan
On his wet bed, abandon'd and alone.

(1793 version, ll. 602-613)

The movement is one of sharp flashes rather than the endless slow process of modification that characterizes *The Prelude*. The couplet, with its affinity for violent contrasts, can give us the mind at its most highly charged, but only in the type of blank verse that Wordsworth developed in "Tintern Abbey" and *The Prelude* can we find the meditating mind in all its fullness.

And it is this fullness which seems most conspicuously lacking in the major poetry of our own century. One turns to one of the more discursive passages in *Ash-Wednesday*:

Because I know that time is always time
And place is always and only place
And what is actual is actual only for one time
And only for one place
I rejoice that things are as they are and
I renounce the blessèd face
And renounce the voice
Because I cannot hope to turn again
Consequently I rejoice, having to construct
    something
Upon which to rejoice
And pray to God to have mercy upon us
And I pray that I may forget
These matters that with myself I too much
    discuss . . .

Here we have all the twists and turns of the meditating process, but the fullness of the experience is gone. The stress is all on the connectives, like "because" and "consequently," which act essentially as signals of a larger process which we must accept on faith. Eliot has here come about as close to discursive poetry as is possible within the confines of the Symbolist method he was pursuing so rigorously in his early work (though he later approached the fullness, if not the energy, of Wordsworthian meditation in *Four Quartets*). Yet it is a type of poetry which, like the couplets quoted above from *Descriptive Sketches*, must inevitably restrict itself to a high level of intensity; and it is something perhaps more closely related to argument than to the free, full range of the meditating mind that is Wordsworth's characteristic achievement in *The Prelude*.

CHAPTER THREE

THE RHETORIC OF INTERACTION (2): IMAGES OF INTERACTION

1 . WIND AND WATER

THE distinctive thing about the images of *The Prelude* is that they provide the basic setting for the poem: water, islands, mountains, breezes, and growing things. When Wordsworth describes a stream he knew in childhood he can start out wholly on the level of literal description— the poem is, after all, an autobiography—and before the reader has gone much further the stream has become a metaphor for the workings of the imagination. It is difficult to distinguish between the literal and metaphorical level in Wordsworth, for the literal becomes figurative and then literal again. Distinctions between tenor and vehicle, crucial as they are to the understanding of Renaissance and metaphysical verse, are of little avail in this type of poetry. Wordsworth's use of imagery stands at an opposite extreme, one might say, from that of a Shakespearean play. When we speak of the imagery of sickness in *Hamlet* we think of a body of images which, however closely they seem to grow out of the play's action, can still, for purposes of discussion at least, be viewed as distinct from the plot. The characters are not physically sick in the literal sense: the images are essentially an imaginative extension of the dramatic situation that Shakespeare is probing. We could conceivably cut the metaphorical element out of *Hamlet* and still have a substantial, though certainly impoverished drama. But to rob *The Prelude* of its images is to rob it of its whole plot and continuity.

One might think of the imagery of *The Prelude* as a kind of *donnée*, something concretely observed by the poet, and something he must constantly return to as he narrates the events of his life; yet it is also something he thinks *through*, a mode of language which continually leads him away from itself to encompass larger areas of human experience. In the opening lines of the poem he starts with the simple fact of the breeze that blows upon him as he leaves London:

> Oh there is blessing in this gentle breeze
> That blows from the green fields and from the
>   clouds
> And from the sky: it beats against my cheek,
> And seems half-conscious of the joy it gives.

From the beginning the breeze seems both rooted in the sensory, observable world and at the same time ("half-conscious of the joy it gives") connected to higher powers. A few lines later the poet speaks of his own breathings:

> I breathe again;
> Trances of thought and mountings of the mind
> Come fast upon me,   (I, 19-21)

and soon thereafter the two processes, the breathings within nature and within the poet, are brought together, and then connected with the creative process:

> For I, methought, while the sweet breath of
>   Heaven
> Was blowing on my body, felt within
> A corresponding mild creative breeze,
> A vital breeze which travell'd gently on
> O'er things which it had made, and is become
> A tempest, a redundant energy
> Vexing its own creation. 'Tis a power
> That does not come unrecogniz'd, a storm,
> Which, breaking up a long-continued frost

Brings with it vernal promises, the hope
Of active days, of dignity and thought. . . .

(41-51)

Although the field of reference has moved from the physical
world to the mental world of the poet, we are still reminded—in the metaphor of the storm breaking up the
frost—of the physical origins of the figure. What started
out as literal observation has become metaphor, and in the
course of this shift the image has unobtrusively changed
character from a "gentle breeze" to a storm: the flexibility
we noted in the rhetorical roles which the image plays is
accompanied by a corresponding flexibility of meaning.

The dominating images of *The Prelude* are wind and
water, images which by their very nature—their flowing,
transforming quality, their ability to interact with other
natural elements, and also their traditional associations—
allow the poet free range between the observable world
and the higher transcendental reality which he wishes to
make visible to us. Their chief function, one might say, is
to act as intermediaries between the two worlds. In the
incident about the stolen boat in Book I the water remains
throughout a part of the observed scene:

The moon was up, the Lake was shining clear
Among the hoary mountains.

. . . Not without the voice
Of mountain-echoes did my Boat move on,
Leaving behind her still on either side
Small circles glittering idly in the moon,
Until they melted all into one track
Of sparkling light. (383-384; 389-394)

Yet as we follow the play of moonlight upon the water we
feel ourselves gradually being led into a deeper reality,
something which, at the end of the passage, will culminate

in the vision of the "huge and mighty Forms that do not live / Like living men . . ." (425-426). Soon after this passage, directly after the apostrophe "Wisdom and Spirit of the universe," we return to the literal image of water, not only in its usual state, but in the form of mist:

> In November days,
> When vapours, rolling down the valleys, made
> A lonely scene more lonesome; among woods
> At noon, and 'mid the calm of summer nights,
> When, by the margin of the trembling Lake,
> Beneath the gloomy hills I homeward went
> In solitude, such intercourse was mine;
> 'Twas mine among the fields both day and night
> And by the waters all the summer long.
>
> (443-451)

We have returned to the observable world, yet in the rolling of vapors and the trembling of waters the reader still feels himself in an atmosphere of vision. Only somewhat later does Wordsworth make explicit the water's role as intermediary:

> Even then,
> A Child, I held unconscious intercourse
> With the eternal Beauty, drinking in
> A pure organic pleasure from the lines
> Of curling mist, or from the level plain
> Of waters colour'd by the steady clouds.
>
> (588-593)

But in the course of the poem we come to take the transcendental meanings of the wind and the water so for granted that we are immediately aware of their relevance even in a naturalistic description such as the following:

> And in the shelter'd coppice where I sate,
> Around me, from among the hazel leaves,

Now here, now there, stirr'd by the straggling
  wind,
Came intermittingly a breath-like sound,
A respiration short and quick, which oft,
Yea, might I say, again and yet again,
Mistaking for the panting of my Dog,
The off-and-on Companion of my walk,
I turn'd my head, to look if he were there.

                                          (IV, 172-180)

The dog is something of a deflecting agent: it is as though
Wordsworth is too reticent to remind us once more of the
transcendental associations of the breeze, yet these associations have been so thoroughly established in the poem
thus far that the reader is less easily fooled by the nature
of the breeze than was the young Wordsworth.

One could speak of the wind and water as functioning
on two separate levels: on the one hand, as we have seen,
they are *literally* intermediaries between the visible and
the invisible worlds, but they also have a rhetorical function, for they serve to prepare the reader for the great
moments of vision. They are, one might say, a mode of
transition both between the parts of the poet's universe
and between the reader and the visionary experience which
the poet is preparing him for. Thus, at the beginning of
the ascent of Snowdon the stress is all on the low, thick
mist:

      It was a Summer's night, a close warm night,
      Wan, dull and glaring, with a dripping mist
      Low-hung and thick that cover'd all the sky,
      Half threatening storm and rain.

                                          (XIII, 10-13)

Momentarily we feel our senses dulled, as though we must
be cut off from familiar ways of thinking and feeling before we are ready for new ones. Above all, there is a qual-

ity of imminence (as well as immanence) about the scene, of something larger about to happen than merely the "half threatening storm and rain."

In their gentler aspects, as we have seen, the wind and water help bring together the divergent orders of Wordsworth's world, but in their harsher moments they serve yet another function—as manifestations of power and vitality in the universe. Thus, on the Simplon Pass we are shown

> The stationary blasts of water-falls,
> And every where along the hollow rent
> Winds thwarting winds, bewilder'd and forlorn,
> The torrents shooting from the clear blue sky,

culminating in the vision of

> Characters of the great Apocalypse,
> The types and symbols of Eternity,
> Of first and last, and midst, and without end.
>> (VI, 558-561; 570-572)

Again, in the vision on Snowdon, as the mist begins to lift we see

> A fracture in the vapour,
> A deep and gloomy breathing-place through which
> Mounted the roar of waters, torrents, streams
> Innumerable, roaring with one voice.

As in the passage on the Simplon, we are first shown the elements in all their immediacy; only then are we prepared for the explanation of their meaning:

> The universal spectacle throughout
> Was shaped for admiration and delight,
> Grand in itself alone, but in that breach
> Through which the homeless voice of waters rose,
> That dark deep thoroughfare had Nature lodg'd

The Soul, the Imagination of the whole.

(XIII, 56-65)

Often, when the context does not permit Wordsworth to represent wind and water as part of the surrounding scene, he makes use of their symbolic value by introducing them on the figurative level. Thus, on seeing a blind beggar on the London streets, he reflects, "My mind did at this spectacle turn round / As with the might of waters . . ." (VII, 615-616). Here the whole previously established context exerts its pressure in the simile, while at the same time the Biblical phrase confirms our sense of the transcendental powers inherent in the water image.[1] In the following discursive passage, which attempts to generalize upon his experience in London, all the nature images which had hitherto appeared on the literal level become part of an extended simile:

> And not seldom
> Even individual remembrances,
> By working on the Shapes before my eyes,
> Became like vital functions of the soul;
> And out of what had been, what was, the place
> Was throng'd with impregnations, like those wilds
> In which my early feelings had been nurs'd,
> And naked valleys, full of caverns, rocks,
> And audible seclusions, dashing lakes,
> Echoes and Waterfalls, and pointed crags

[1] In these lines from Exodus the Lord's power is seen manifesting itself both in wind and water:

> Thou didst blow with Thy wind, the sea covered them;
> They sank as lead in the mighty waters. (15:10)

Biblical phrases, whether used on the literal level or as expressed metaphors are a central part of the Romantic world of images from Blake through Melville. Through his sense of the particular Biblical context—whether a prophetic outcry or a celebration of divine immanence in nature—the reader of Romantic literature is expected to transfer the Biblical meaning to the modern passage.

That into music touch the passing wind.

(VIII, 786-796)

The simile is meant to do considerably more than illustrate the effect that the memory of London had on him. Not only has the memory process taken on visible and audible shape, but the powers that are unleased in the natural setting return us to a more directly observable form of reality than the mental processes which he had been trying to depict. Indeed, the simile acts less to illustrate these processes than to turn us away from them and celebrate once more his native domain. Again, similarly to the Biblical overtones that emanated from the phrase "might of waters," the final line of this passage takes us out of the immediate context by a play on our associations: we think of the "Aeolian visitations" at the poem's opening, perhaps even more specifically of Coleridge's famous lines,

> And what if all of animated nature
> Be but organic Harps diversely fram'd,
> That tremble into thought, as o'er them sweeps
> Plastic and vast, one intellectual breeze,
> At once the Soul of each, and God of all?
>
> ("The Eolian Harp")

Wordsworth's simile has not only drawn us back to physical nature, but through the implicit image of the harp, has extended the poem's range of reference once more to the mental realm.

The all-pervasiveness of the wind and the water in *The Prelude* is apparent throughout the very fabric of the language, as when we read of nature's power

> To breathe
> Grandeur upon the very humblest face
> Of human life.   (XII, 284-286)

In the lines:

> By simple strains
> Of feeling, the pure breath of real life,
> We were not left untouch'd,
>
> (VI, 471-473)

the equating of "strains of feeling" with breath immediately links them to the vital impulse of the universe.
The verb *spread*, with its implicit plastic qualities, often
acts as a kind of conducting agent in the interaction
process:

> Such a holy calm
> Did over*spread* my soul . . .
>
> (II, 367-368)

> Man . . . daily *spreads* abroad
> His being with a strength that cannot fail.
>
> (IV, 159-161)

In its most memorable instance it serves as a medium for
a larger imaginative apprehension of the life that flows
through all things: thus, after starting with the proposition

> I, at this time
> Saw blessings *spread* around me like a sea,
>
> (II, 413-414)

he lets the word, with its implicit metaphor, set into motion a childlike jubilation in the oneness of life:

> I was only then
> Contented when with bliss ineffable
> I felt the sentiment of Being spread
> O'er all that moves, and all that seemeth still,
> O'er all, that, lost beyond the reach of thought
> And human knowledge, to the human eye
> Invisible, yet liveth to the heart,

> O'er all that leaps, and runs, and shouts, and
>   sings,
> Or beats the gladsome air, o'er all that glides
> Beneath the wave, yea, in the wave itself
> And mighty depth of waters.   (II, 418-428)

By the end of the passage we have come full swing from
the water as metaphor to the water itself, though the Biblical echo in the final line suggests a new and higher order
of symbolic meaning.

Of the four formal epic similes in *The Prelude*, two take
us back to the water: one to a still lake (IV, 247-261), the
second to a river (IX, 1-7). Even the "characters" of the
poem are related in one way or another to the wind and
water. Michel Beaupuy's peripatetic discussions with the
poet take place along the Loire (the water can set the scene
for political as well as visionary meditation), and Beaupuy's
death is reported—mistakenly—having occurred while he
was "fighting in supreme command / Upon the Borders
of the unhappy Loire" (IX, 430-431). The poet pays tribute
to Raisley Calvert for having "clear'd a passage for me,
and the stream / Flowed in the bent of Nature" (XIII,
366-367). Dorothy assumes the role of nature goddess—
somewhat like the unhappy Lucy for whom she may well
have served as model—and gives the breath of life back to
Nature:

>   Methought such charm
> Of sweetness did her presence breathe around
> That all the trees, and all the silent hills
> And every thing she look'd on, should have had
> An intimation how she bore herself
> Towards them and to all creatures.
>
>   (XI, 216-221)

Even when the wind and water do not function as a
means toward transcendental vision—and this is often so

in later parts of the poem—they remain part of the poet's habit of mind, a way through which he can approach other, less boldly exploratory modes of experience.

2. ISLANDS

If the wind and the water serve to portray relationship—to link the observable with the inner world, the powers of the human mind with those within the physical universe—there is also a type of image within *The Prelude* that portrays separation, the isolation of one element from another. Its most obvious manifestation is in the recurrence of islands within the poem. Like the wind and the water, the island is part of the natural setting of Wordsworth's background, and, in consequence, of the poem itself. When we read a passage like the following, we hardly think of the island as a conscious symbol:

> When summer came
> It was the pastime of our afternoons
> To beat along the plain of Windermere
> With rival oars, and the selected bourne
> Was now an Island musical with birds
> That sang for ever; now a Sister Isle
> Beneath the oaks' umbrageous covert, sown
> With lillies of the valley, like a field;
> And now a third small Island where remain'd
> An old stone Table, and a moulder'd Cave,
> A Hermit's history. (II, 56-65)

Wordsworth here is far more the objective observer than the conscious symbolist.[2] Yet note the order in which the

[2] As an observer, however, his childhood memories of these islands on Windermere are considerably more romantic than the description he prepared for prospective tourists in his *Guide to the Lakes*: "The islands, dispersed among these lakes, are neither so numerous nor so beautiful as might be expected from the account that has been given of the manner in which the level areas of the vales are so frequently diversified by rocks, hills, and hillocks, scattered over them; nor are they orna-

islands are introduced: the first, joyous and paradise-like; the next shaded and subdued, as though suited to the contemplative mood, yet through its flowers still sharing somewhat in the joyous atmosphere of the first; the last wholly and uncompromisingly dedicated to contemplation and solitude.

The island (with its companion trope, the lone boat) is one of the great Romantic images, and to record its history from Saint-Pierre to Innisfree is to encompass much of the essential history of Romanticism. Here I merely wish to suggest that Wordsworth's conception of islands is something more than the result of personal observation, that it is, in fact, rooted in a far larger context of thought. One remembers, for instance, the twin islands in the Lac de Bienne which Rousseau describes at the end of his *Confessions*; the first of these, the isle of Saint-Pierre, "has fields, meadows, orchards, woods, vineyards; and all this, thanks to the diversified and hilly nature of the ground, provides a most pleasing variety of landscape. . . . The western part . . . has been planted with a long avenue, broken in the middle by a large hall in which all the inhabitants of the neighbouring shores gather on Sundays during the grape harvest to dance and enjoy themselves. There is only one house on the island, where the receiver lives. But it is large and comfortable, and situated in a hollow which protects it from the wind."

With its joyous peasants, its benign vegetation, and its house protected from the elements, Rousseau's island is the perfect embodiment of the idyllic mode of life. But "five or six hundred yards to the south of the island is

---

mented (as are several of the lakes in Scotland and Ireland) by the remains of castles or other places of defence; nor with the still more interesting ruins of religious edifices. Every one must regret that scarcely a vestige is left of the Oratory, consecrated to the Virgin, which stood upon Chapel-Holm in Windermere. . . ." (*Prose Works*, II, 247)

another, much smaller, which is uncultivated and uninhab-
ited, and appears to have been broken away at some time
from the larger one by storms. Its gravelly soil produces
nothing but willows and persicaria; it has, however, one
considerable eminence, which is grassy and very pleasant."[3]

The notion of contrasting islands—the one idyllic, the
other harsh and unfriendly—goes back to Rousseau's
favorite book, *Robinson Crusoe*, in which the two landscapes can be found on the same island. One need not
seek romantic meanings in the setting of Defoe's classic;
but from Rousseau onward the island—in both its *allegro*
and *penseroso* aspects—serves as the ideal scenic background for contemplation. "It seemed to me," Rousseau
writes, "that on that island I should be further removed
from men, safer from their insults, and more forgotten by
them; freer, in a word, to surrender to the pleasures of
idleness and the contemplative life."[4] And directly following these passages Rousseau launches into his famous ex-
position of the art of revery, which he practiced along the
lake shore or while drifting in his boat, itself an even
more appropriate setting for revery than the more solid,
substantial island.

Wordsworthian revery generally takes a more austerely
visionary form than the gentler delights celebrated by
Rousseau. But Wordsworth sometimes approaches Rousseau's idyllic domain when he speaks of shores, boats, and
islands, as in the following passage:

> But ere the fall
> Of night, when in our pinnace we return'd
> Over the dusky Lake, and to the beach
> Of some small Island steer'd our course with one,
> The Minstrel of our troop, and left him there,
> And row'd off gently, while he blew his flute

[3] *Confessions*, tr. J. M. Cohen (London, 1955), p. 588.
[4] *Ibid.*, p. 589.

Alone upon the rock; Oh! then the calm
And dead still water lay upon my mind
Even with a weight of pleasure, and the sky
Never before so beautiful, sank down
Into my heart, and held me like a dream.[5]

(II, 170-180)

It is worth noting that Wordsworth here projects himself
in the form of two solitaries: in his own person in the
boat, and as the other boy playing music on the rock. In
something of the same way he often refers to hermits—as
at the opening of "Tintern Abbey" or in the passage on
the three islands quoted at the start of this section—while
preparing to relate his own solitary musings. Just as Wordsworth's images move at will between the literal and figurative levels, so it is little more than an academic question
whether his solitaries appear in the first or third person.[6]
Indeed, one of his most memorable uses of the island
image occurs on the figurative level, when he encounters
one of his solitaries in the fog and depicts him as though
on a floating island:

Along a narrow Valley and profound
I journey'd, when, aloft above my head,

[5] The mode of interaction which Wordsworth experiences in this revery
is paralleled in his discussion of islands in the *Guide to the Lakes*: "The
water is also of crystalline purity; so that, if it were not for the reflections
of the incumbent mountains by which it is darkened, a delusion might be
felt, by a person resting quietly in a boat on the bosom of Winandermere or
Derwent-water, similar to that which Carver so beautifully describes when
he was floating alone in the middle of lake Erie or Ontario, and could
almost have imagined that his boat was suspended in an element as pure
as air, or rather that the air and water were one." (*Prose Works*, II, 248)
Characteristically, Wordsworth's direct source is not a literary one, but a
travel book, Jonathan Carver's *Travels through the Interior Parts of North
America* (London, 1778). For the Carver passage, see C. N. Coe, *Wordsworth and the Literature of Travel* (New York, 1953), pp. 34-35.

[6] One might note that Wordsworth presents himself in the third person
in the passage "There was a Boy" (v, 389-422), while the dream of the Arab,
shell and stone (v, 49-139), related in the third person in the 1805 *Prelude*
is in the first person in the revised version.

Emerging from the silvery vapours, lo!
A Shepherd and his Dog! in open day:
Girt round with mists they stood and look'd about
From that enclosure small, inhabitants
Of an aerial Island floating on,
As seem'd with that Abode in which they were,
A little pendant area of grey rocks,
By the soft wind breath'd forward.

(VIII, 92-101)

Separated as they are from the solid world, shepherd and
dog gather a visionary aura about themselves. Somewhat
later, the lone shepherd appears in a more explicitly visionary setting:

Mine eyes have glanced upon him, few steps off,
In size a giant, stalking through the fog,
His Sheep like Greenland Bears; at other times
When round some shady promontory turning,
His Form hath flash'd upon me, glorified
By the deep radiance of the setting sun:
Or him have I descried in distant sky,
A solitary object and sublime,
Above all height! like an aerial Cross,
As it is stationed on some spiry Rock
Of the Chartreuse, for worship.

(VIII, 400-410)

One could speak of a tendency throughout *The Prelude*
to isolate objects in order to connect them later at a deeper
level: islands, whether real or figurative, are places which
cut you off so that these connections may be made. In
the last passage there is no specific mention of an island,
yet the same principle is at work here as in the earlier example: when Wordsworth suddenly spies the shepherd and
his flock in their isolation, not only does he view them in

a unique visual perspective ("his Sheep like Greenland Bears"), but this very perspective creates the transition by which we are enabled to view the shepherd as a spiritual manifestation. In the same way, as we saw earlier, the fog that enclosed the poet in his ascent up Mt. Snowdon was essentially a way of cutting him off from the earthly sphere before he could attain his higher vision. Isolation becomes the means toward interaction. We can, in fact, speak of an image of vacancy, whereby the objects of the visible world are systematically eliminated before our eyes to prepare for the revelation of a new way of seeing things. We feel something of this, for instance, in the passage concluding the incident of the stolen boat:

> In my thoughts
> There was a darkness, call it solitude,
> Or blank desertion, no familiar shapes
> Of hourly objects, images of trees,
> Of sea or sky, no colours of green fields;
> But huge and mighty Forms that do not live
> Like living men mov'd slowly through my mind
> By day and were the trouble of my dreams.
>
> (I, 420-427)

The island is less a physical entity than a way of thinking and feeling; "huge and mighty Forms" cannot emerge until the conventional world—whose fading presence we still experience despite the negatives—is reduced to a chaos of emptiness. In far lengthier fashion than above, he creates an elaborate image of emptiness in order to prepare for the meeting with the discharged soldier at the end of Book IV:

> On I went
> Tranquil, receiving in my own despite
> Amusement, as I slowly pass'd along,
> From such near objects as from time to time,

Perforce intruded on the listless sense
Quiescent, and dispos'd to sympathy,
With an exhausted mind, worn out by toil. ...
                    Above, before, behind,
Around me, all was peace and solitude,
I look'd not round, nor did the solitude
Speak to my eye; but it was heard and felt.
                    (IV, 375-381; 388-391)

Quietness, fatigue, a sense of total calmness about himself, when solitude becomes a tangible thing, "heard and
felt"—these are the necessary conditions for the visionary
mood. When the soldier later appears, the reader per-
ceives him in all his ghostly grandeur, but only because
he has gradually felt himself removed from the earthly
sphere (one need only compare the difference in effect of
the 1850 version, from which Wordsworth omitted the
crucial preparatory passage). In a work like *The Prelude*,
which constantly mediates between inner and outer worlds,
emptiness becomes an image of transition, the vision itself
a type of island. Wordsworth's designation of his visionary
moments as "spots of time" (XI, 258) is, in fact, a geograph-
ical metaphor which suggests the island-like qualities of
these moments. Indeed, in some early (though later rejected) jottings toward *The Prelude* he equates his childhood memories directly with islands:

Those recollect(ed) hours that have the charm
Of visionary things—
                    islands in the unnavigable depth
Of our departed time.   (*Prel.*, p. 641)

3 · CAVERNS AND MOUNTAINS

There is still another image, even less articulated,
through which Wordsworth records intimations of the
inner world. We become aware of it, for instance, each

THE RHETORIC OF INTERACTION (2)

time we encounter such words as *under-thirst, under-presence, under-soul,* all of them, De Selincourt tells us in his edition (p. 622), apparent coinages of Wordsworth's. Its most memorable use occurs in the vision on Snowdon,

> The perfect image of a mighty Mind,
> Of one that feeds upon infinity,
> That is exalted by an under-presence,
> The sense of God, or whatsoe'er is dim
> Or vast in its own being,
>
> (XIII, 69-73)

where it is one of several alternatives that take part in the poet's struggle toward definition. It is no more than an intimation, but as such it hints at a hidden, subterranean reality which itself is never further defined. Yet one senses a relationship between these *under*-elements and those much-mentioned hiding-places and inner recesses within the human soul:

> Oh! mystery of Man, from what a depth
> Proceed thy honours!
> . . . The hiding-places of my power
> Seem open; I approach, and then they close.
>
> (XI, 329-330; 336-337)

> 'Tis thine,
> The prime and vital principle is thine
> In the recesses of thy nature. . . .
>
> (XIII, 193-195)

Behind these terms there stands what David Perkins, in his recent study of Romantic symbolism, calls "the image of the cavern or abyss." Perkins discerns a double function for this image in Wordsworth: first, as symbolic of "an inevitable, and fearful, isolation from any external medium through which the mind can be healthfully governed," and second, as suggestive of "fertility and creation."[7] Like all of Wordsworth's central images, the cavern can stand potentially for several things, even apparent opposites. But the cavern differs from the other images in one important respect: it occurs but inconspicuously in the literal narrative. Wordsworth lists it, for instance, among the spots where nature's "presences" dwell: "On caves and trees, upon the woods and hills" (I, 496). It plays a role in the episode of the stolen boat, where the "rocky cave" from which the poet steals the boat later becomes deified, in the course of the passage, into the "Cavern of the Willow tree" (I, 395, 414). And, in turn, it comes to suggest the dark recesses of the poet's mind from which issues that "dim and undetermin'd sense / Of unknown modes of being" (419-420). The image is also used occasionally in a totally figurative sense, as in the somewhat tedious epic simile which compares the opposing ways in which Wordsworth had come to evaluate his London experience with a traveller's ways of looking at a cave (VIII, 711-751); then, too, he speaks of those "caverns . . . within my mind" (III, 246) which were left inviolate amid the social temptations of Cambridge. Indeed, a reading of *The Prelude* leaves one with far less memory of actual caverns than of such caverns of the mind—both the individual human mind and the universal mind. Unlike the wind, water, and mountains, which dominate the poem's scenic background, the cavern functions chiefly as a metaphor, in fact, a literally submerged metaphor, one which we sense but dimly through the unnamed (and unnamable) depths and under-agents which Wordsworth has such frequent occasion to invoke.

Yet there is one extension of the cavern image which, though it occurs only twice in *The Prelude*, leaves one of

[7] *The Quest for Permanence* (Cambridge, Mass., 1959), p. 24.

the most powerful impressions among any of the natural scenes of the poem. I refer here to the mountain chasm which plays such a central role in his experiences at the Simplon Pass and on Mt. Snowdon. One might note first that mountains *in themselves*—when they seem remote and solid entities, without direct contact with man or the natural elements—are of little interest to Wordsworth. His imagination is stimulated only if the human mind, in some way, is able to interact with them. Mont Blanc, for instance, turned out to be a disappointment, not only since the reality failed to live up to Wordsworth's anticipations, but because, in its imperious self-sufficiency, the mountain had something final and dead about it:

> That day we first
> Beheld the summit of Mont Blanc, and griev'd
> To have a soulless image on the eye
> Which had usurp'd upon a living thought
> That never more could be.   (VI, 452-456)

Only after he turned away from the summit and looked downward at the "dumb cataracts and streams of ice" (458) were his imagination's cravings satisfied. The "perilous ridge" (I, 347) on which he hung alone while plundering birds' nests was meaningful not only in itself, but through its "half-inch fissures," its blasts of wind, and the perilousness of his own position. The "huge cliff" in the episode of the stolen boat achieves its memorable power through the darkness and the surrounding scenery of water and cave. The Simplon Pass made no impression in itself; in fact, he and his companion went by it thinking there were still higher reaches to attain. Only after they entered the gorge on the other side did they encounter an appropriately visionary setting: indeed, the winds, torrents, crags, and mists with which they are surrounded bring together—though in their most violent form—most of *The Prelude*'s

prevailing images. The top of Snowdon, as I have suggested, is essentially an island in the mist; but even after
the transition has been made and the everyday world cut
off, Wordsworth cannot apprehend its inner meaning until he encounters "a fracture in the vapour" (it hardly
matters whether it is a real mountain gorge or not):

> A deep and gloomy breathing-place through which
> Mounted the roar of waters, torrents, streams
> Innumerable, roaring with one voice.
>   . . . But in that breach
> Through which the homeless voice of waters rose,
> That dark deep thoroughfare had Nature lodg'd
> The Soul, the Imagination of the whole.
>
>   (XIII, 57-59; 62-65)

Thus, despite the obvious symbolic value that Wordsworth felt in elevation, and specifically in the physical
act of ascent, one notes that his visionary experience on
mountains was more centrally concerned with depths
rather than heights, with the continually intensifying in-
wardness suggested by the interaction of water, air, and
rock in the deeper regions of the earth.

4 . SOME REFLECTIONS ON WORDSWORTH'S
NATURE IMAGERY

Wordsworth's deliberate blurring of tenor and vehicle,
his insistence on fusing the literal level of things with their
larger symbolic meanings—these are more than rhetorical
strategies, for they are, in fact, central to the meaning and
intent of his major poetry. The following statement by
Coleridge, made in a letter to William Sotheby in 1802,
suggests a program which brings together the realm of
rhetoric with that of metaphysics: "Nature has her proper
interest; & he will know what it is, who believes & feels,
that every Thing has a Life of it's own, & that we are all

one Life. A Poet's *Heart* & *Intellect* should be *combined, intimately* combined & *unified*, with the great appearances in Nature—& not merely held in solution & loose mixture with them, in the shape of formal Similies. I do not mean to exclude these formal Similies—there are moods of mind, in which they are natural—pleasing moods of mind, & such as a Poet will often have, & sometimes express; but they are not his highest, & most appropriate moods."[8]

"*Combined, intimately* combined & *unified*" (the italics are of course Coleridge's)—the interaction of man and nature as a demonstration of the "one life" becomes the central motive of the poet. The older rhetorical system with its "formal Similies" and its separation of tenor and vehicle would obviously not suffice for the lofty task which Coleridge contemplated for the poet. As works written not in a "pleasing mood of mind," but in the poet's "highest, & most appropriate mood," Wordsworth's major poems, like the "Dejection Ode" which Coleridge had written a few months before the letter to Sotheby, had by necessity to speak a language which would demonstrate the unity of the poet's inner world and the external world of nature. The rhetorical method which Wordsworth developed to fulfill this task became, one might say, a re-enactment of the process of interaction. In reading poetry which makes such a radical attempt to fuse inner and outer, the reader trained to approach poetic imagery according to the methods of Renaissance or even of twentieth-century poetry is likely to keep asking which particular realm—nature or the mind—Wordsworth is actually talking about. But the question is scarcely necessary or germane to his poetry, for Wordsworth usually speaks of both realms at once. The "huge and mighty Forms" which pursue the poet for days after the stolen-boat incident exist at once in his own mind, in the external landscape, and,

[8] *Letters*, ed. E. L. Griggs (Oxford, 1956), II, 864.

for that matter, in the universal mind as well. In something of the same way the imagination which is revealed
to him atop Mt. Snowdon is a faculty within the mind of
an individual poet, a manifestation of the universal mind,
and even a part of the mountain ("in that breach . . .
had Nature lodg'd / The Soul, the Imagination of the
whole"). A recently published early draft, in fact, has
shown that certain of the lines used to characterize Mt.
Snowdon—"The perfect image of a mighty Mind, / Of
one that feeds upon infinity, / . . . or whatso'er is dim /
Or vast in its own being" (XIII, 69-70, 72-73)—were originally intended to characterize the mind of the poet:

> But also such an one must have been used
> To feed his soul upon infinity
> To deal with whatsoe'er be dim or vast
> In his own nature. . . .   (*Prel.*, p. 620)

I can think of no interpretative task so difficult as trying
to define Wordsworth's concept of the imagination on
the basis of the utterances found in his poetry; indeed,
the essentially analytical process of definition is quite antithetical to Wordsworth's constant endeavors to synthesize
his concepts and percepts into dazzlingly new rhetorical
formations.

Yet, despite his efforts to wipe out distinctions between
outer scene and inner thought, one discerns a special significance in the literal level of discourse in *The Prelude*.
This literal level—the level of real lakes and real mountains, of the real boy Wordsworth—throughout the poem
provides a transition to guide the reader from his accustomed way of looking at things to the transcendental
reality which Wordsworth repeatedly celebrates. The real
world functions rhetorically both as something to start
from and something to fall back on between the often
bewildering visionary assertions of his intenser moments.

Dr. Leavis, in pitting Shelley against Wordsworth, has remarked, for instance, on the younger poet's "weak grasp on the actual"; he compares the opening of Shelley's "Mont Blanc":

> The everlasting universe of things
> Flows through the mind, and rolls its rapid waves,
> Now dark—now glittering—now reflecting gloom—
> Now lending splendour, where from secret springs
> The source of human thought its tribute brings
> Of waters . . .

with Wordsworth's lines on the Simplon:

> Black drizzling crags that spake by the way-side
> As if a voice were in them, the sick sight
> And giddy prospect of the raving stream,
> The unfetter'd clouds and region of the Heavens,
> Tumult and peace, the darkness and the light
> Were all like workings of one mind, the features
> Of the same face. . . .   (VI, 563-569)

Leavis notes "the unobtrusiveness with which [in the Wordsworth passage] 'outer' turns into 'inner'. . . . What is characteristic of Wordsworth is to grasp surely (which, in the nature of the case, must be delicately and subtly) what he offers, whether this appears as belonging to the outer world—the world as perceived, or to inner experience." In Shelley, so Leavis goes on with his comparison, "the metaphorical and the actual, the real and imagined, the inner and the outer, could hardly be more unsortably and indistinguishably confused."[9] Despite E. R. Wasserman's recent efforts to show what Shelley was really doing in "Mont Blanc"—and Wasserman demonstrates exhaustively that there was real method in Shelley's frenzy[10]—

[9] *Revaluation*, pp. 206, 212-214.
[10] *The Subtler Language* (Baltimore, 1959), pp. 195-240.

next to Wordsworth's lines, "Mont Blanc" remains a more distinctly private type of poetry, a significant enough visionary meditation, but of a less persuasively universal order of experience.

It has not perhaps been sufficiently remarked how Wordsworth's major images seem even on the literal level to suggest the directions for their symbolic expansion. Kenneth MacLean, writing of the water image in *The Prelude*, has noted the following properties of water which Wordsworth chose to build from: "[Water] has the power to move and sound; to freshen and make float; to wash and to cleanse; the power to reflect; to distort, to sparkle magically; the power to be free; and finally, the power to create that rhythm, which, however it comes to life, can moderate, soothe, and give pleasure."[11] One hardly need list the various potentialities that Wordsworth found in breezes, mountains, islands, caverns, and, above all, in the combination of these images. It is significant, in fact, that in those parts of the poem where he did not have the natural landscape to work from, his imagery assumes far more conventional forms than those I have described in this chapter. The passages on the French Revolution, for instance, are dominated by storm imagery:

> In both her clamorous Halls,
> The National Synod and the Jacobins
> I saw the revolutionary Power
> Toss like a Ship at anchor, rock'd by storms . . .
>
> (IX, 46-49)

But these storms function essentially as background imagery: like the dominant strain of imagery within a Shakespearean play, they help define and give dramatic coloring to the central situation, but they are always rhetori-

[11] "The Water Symbol in *The Prelude*," *University of Toronto Quarterly*, XVII (1948), 387.

cally, at least, distinguishable from the narrative which they are intended to embellish. Yet Wordsworth was also aware that beyond their natural proclivities, his major images also contained innumerable literary and cultural associations to which his readers would automatically respond. "A stranger to mountain imagery naturally on his first arrival looks out for sublimity in every object that admits of it; and is almost always disappointed," he wrote in his *Guide to the Lakes* (*Prose Works*, II, 291-92). Obviously he did not need to go to much trouble convincing his readers of the grandeur and fascination of natural scenery. Moreover, as Marjorie Nicolson and Ernest Tuveson have painstakingly shown in their recent books on the development of the "aesthetics of the infinite," poetry and aesthetic theory had been preparing readers to find religious meaning in sublime scenery—above all, in mountains and caverns—for a whole century before Wordsworth.[12] In the light of their researches, in fact, Wordsworth's attempt to locate visionary power in natural scenery seems less the beginning of a tradition—as conventional literary history would have it—than the culmination of a way of thinking for which the groundwork had been laid long before. Wordsworth's distinctive achievement, one ventures to say, was not so much in the attitudes he expressed toward scenery as in the language he succeeded in devising for the interaction of the mind with external nature. After the suppleness of "Tintern Abbey" and *The Prelude*, the language of the eighteenth-century "sublime" poems—I refer to the term which Josephine Miles has employed to describe a genre that extends across the century from Blackmore through Akenside to Blake[13]—

12 Nicolson, *Mountain Gloom and Mountain Glory*, esp. pp. 271-369; Tuveson, *The Imagination as a Means of Grace*.

13 *Eras and Modes in English Poetry* (Berkeley and Los Angeles, 1957), pp. 48-77.

could no longer seem appropriate to a living body of literature.

The eighteenth century anticipated Wordsworth not only in the grander types of scenery, but also in those that made less urgent claims on the infinite. If islands were associated with romantic reveries from Rousseau onward, throughout the century—chiefly through the impact of *Robinson Crusoe*—they had provided scenic background for the study of solitude. W. K. Wimsatt, in his incisive account of the nature of Romantic nature imagery, has suggested the stylistic evolution of this imagery by examining three sonnets—by Thomas Warton, William Lisle Bowles, and the early Coleridge, respectively—addressed to local streams.[14] A long genealogy extending back to the beginning of our civilization stands behind the "Aeolian visitations" with which *The Prelude* so ecstatically opens; but if archetypal critics like Maud Bodkin have stressed the traditionality of the divinely inspired breeze, M. H. Abrams has lately insisted on the distinctly Romantic manner in which Wordsworth and his contemporaries treated the wind motif.[15]

Wordsworth's attempt to build his major poems out of images he had himself observed was rooted not only in his love of nature, but even more specifically in the epistemology which had come down to him. Tuveson has reminded us, for instance, how the unity of image and idea, of outer and inner, follows naturally from Locke's epistemology: "From the nature of the mind as described by Locke, we could expect a new poetry to be highly visual in nature, for the faculty of sight came to monopolize the analysis of intellectual activity. Since ideas are images,

---

[14] "The Structure of Romantic Nature Imagery," *The Verbal Icon* (Lexington, Ky., 1954), pp. 103-116.

[15] "The Correspondent Breeze: A Romantic Metaphor," in *English Romantic Poets: Modern Essays in Criticism*, ed. Abrams (New York, 1960), esp. pp. 44-52.

since even complex ideas are multiple pictures, and since understanding itself is a form of perception, the visual and the intellectual would tend to become amalgamated."[16]

Tuveson is speaking here of post-Lockian poetry in general—not only the eighteenth-century "sublime" poem and nature lyric, but the image-centered poetry of Romanticism and of our own century. Again, what makes Wordsworth's poetry unique is not the fact that he combined the sense-impressions of nature with more complex ideas, but the peculiar method which he developed to draw the intellectual from the visual. His need to combine both these realms in his poetry—and Locke's epistemology, as Tuveson shows, provides the rationale for such amalgamation—is also what keeps Wordsworth from being what we commonly consider a "landscape" poet. The true landscape poet is one who, like John Clare or Edward Thomas, keeps primarily to visual impressions and only incidentally, if at all, to the more complex ideas toward which these might lead. Indeed, the attempt of modern poets in the Hulme-Pound tradition to build poems fully out of sense impressions and to keep the intellectualizing observer out of the poem seems in the present context an extreme and all too narrow application of Lockian epistemology to poetry. The modern poet pretends to represent the external world "as it is"—spontaneously perceived, unspoiled by the intrusion of abstract thought.

Wordsworth, on the other hand, represents the external world only in order to get beyond it; if he lets his intellectualizing self intrude, the intrusion seems to follow so naturally from the concretely perceived premise with which he started that the reader is scarcely aware he has crossed the border which commonly separates the simple idea from the complex, the empirical realm from the transcendental. In a terse statement that Wordsworth once

16 *The Imagination as a Means of Grace*, pp. 72-73.

made to his nephew, Christopher Wordsworth, he distinguished between the poetry that simply records sense-impressions and that which goes beyond them: "S——, in the work you mentioned to me, confounds *imagery* and *imagination*. Sensible objects really existing, and felt to exist, are *imagery*; and they may form the materials of a descriptive poem, where objects are delineated as they are. Imagination is a subjective term: it deals with objects not as they are, but as they appear to the mind of the poet" (*Prose Works*, III, 464). Unlike the modern imagist (and unlike many eighteenth-century descriptive poets), he did not attempt to give the impression that his "objects are delineated as they are": the center of his art was his explicit demonstration of what happened to objects as they interacted with the mind of the poet.

In the history of poetic imagery Wordsworth and his contemporaries occupy a position roughly half-way between the Renaissance mode, in which the image remains subservient to the demands of logic, and that peculiarly modern condition which—to employ a term used by Rainer Maria Rilke in hailing the achievement of one of his post-Symbolist contemporaries—is characterized by the "liberation of the poetic figure."[17] Wimsatt, in his paper on nature imagery cited earlier, pinpoints the Romantic position in this way:

"If we think of a scale of structures having at one end logic, the completely reasoned and abstracted, and at the other some form of madness or surrealism, matter or impression unformed and undisciplined (the imitation of disorder by the idiom of disorder), we may see metaphysical and neoclassical poetry as near the extreme of logic (though by no means reduced to that status) and

[17] *Briefe aus den Jahren 1914-1921*, ed. Ruth Sieber-Rilke and Carl Sieber (Leipzig, 1928), p. 126. The poet of whom he wrote was Georg Trakl.

romantic poetry as a step toward the directness of sensory presentation (though by no means sunk into subrationality)."[18]

If our age has proved slow to acknowledge the characteristic Romantic achievement, we must remember that the critical system in which we have been taught to think was dedicated primarily to defending the two extremes—the metaphysical and the modern—on Wimsatt's scale. And in our zeal to uphold these extremes we have often misunderstood—and hastily rejected—that "half-way position" which *The Prelude* so eminently represents.

[18] *The Verbal Icon*, p. 116.

CHAPTER FOUR

THE POSSIBILITY OF A LONG POEM

1. INSPIRATION AND THE CONSCIOUS WILL

"He not merely interposes level tracts between his heights, he is not only lavish of prose at a proper distance from his poetry, but he dashes his very poetry with prose; he thrusts into the very middle of a lofty burst or splendid description some feeble line, some slight remark; he throws our spirits into a glorious glow, and then suddenly makes us cool again, before we have had time to feel the divine heat."

SO spoke the *Prospective Review* in 1851,[1] in a review of *The Prelude*, which had appeared with little fanfare less than a year before. But the *Prospective*'s comment is quite representative of Victorian reaction to the poem, as witness the terse lines which Longfellow jotted down in his journal: "We have finished Wordsworth's Prelude. It has many lofty passages. It soars and sinks, and is by turns sublime and commonplace" or the comment of a popular American magazine, *Graham's*, which, picking up a line from the first page of the poem, wished that Wordsworth had supplied more "trances of thought and mountings of the mind."[2]

What stands behind these reactions is a major shift in attitude toward the structure and purpose of poetry that

[1] VII, 101.

[2] *Life of Henry Wadsworth Longfellow*, ed. S. Longfellow (Boston, 1886), II, 175, and *Graham's*, XXXVII (1850), 323.

took place in the half century between the composition and publication of *The Prelude*. It is a shift evident, for instance, in Tennyson's depiction of Pindar as "a kind of Australian poet; has long tracts of gravel, with immensely large nuggets imbedded";[3] in the vogue, during the early 1850's, of the so-called "spasmodic" poets—John Bailey, Sydney Dobell, and Alexander Smith—who sought to send their readers into fits and spasms through their intense lyric flights; but on its most explicit level it is evident in Poe's famous pronouncement "that the phrase, 'a long poem,' is simply a flat contradiction in terms." For Poe's essay, "The Poetic Principle," which, by one of those significant ironies of history, was published posthumously the same year as *The Prelude*, stands at the threshold of a new aesthetic, one so alien to the basic assumptions underlying *The Prelude* that it is no wonder the poem remained neglected for more than half a century after its publication. In Poe's aesthetic the prime criterion is that a poem maintain a high level of intensity throughout:

"I need scarcely observe that a poem deserves its title only inasmuch as it excites, by elevating the soul. The value of the poem is in the ratio of this elevating excitement. But all excitements are, through a psychal necessity, transient. That degree of excitement which would entitle a poem to be so called at all, cannot be sustained throughout a composition of any great length. After the lapse of half an hour, at the very utmost, it flags—fails—a revulsion ensues—and then the poem is, in effect, and in fact, no longer such."[4]

And Poe goes on to speak of *Paradise Lost* in much the same terms in which Croce was to speak of the *Divine*

[3] Quoted from Palgrave's "Personal Recollections" in Hallam Tennyson, *Alfred Lord Tennyson: A Memoir by His Son* (New York, 1897), II, 499.

[4] *Complete Poems and Stories*, ed. A. H. Quinn and E. H. O'Neill (New York, 1946), II, 1021.

Comedy a half century later: "There are, no doubt, many who have found difficulty in reconciling the critical dictum that the 'Paradise Lost' is to be devoutly admired throughout, with the absolute impossibility of maintaining for it, during perusal, the amount of enthusiasm which that critical dictum would demand. This great work, in fact, is to be regarded as poetical, only when, losing sight of that vital requisite in all works of Art, Unity, we view it merely as a series of minor poems. . . . After a passage of what we feel to be true poetry, there follows, inevitably, a passage of platitude which no critical prejudgment can force us to admire. . . . It follows from all this that the ultimate, aggregate, or absolute effect of even the best epic under the sun, is a nullity:—and this is precisely the fact."

In the course of the early nineteenth century the Longinian demand for intensity had gradually been narrowed down to the point where it was no longer satisfied by individual moments of elevation embedded within a larger structure, but, rather, insisted that the only proper business of poetry was the exclusive cultivation of these moments. And it is not surprising that in an age in which lyric intensity had replaced dignity as the measure of the high style in poetry and in which originality and sincerity were held antithetical to the artifice of convention, *The Prelude*, if it was read at all, was read only for its more elevated moments. Though the nineteenth-century reader was willing to spend long winter nights working his way through three-decker novels, he preferred his poetry in smaller pieces, or, if not always in the form of short lyrics, at least in individual idylls (which rarely passed the half-hour limit set by Poe) or in straight narratives which were essentially nothing more than novels in meter.

Even to this day, conditioned as we still are to certain conceptions of poetry that derive from Poe and the Symbolist aesthetic, we tend to look at *The Prelude* as a group of great lyrical passages—largely confined to the various spots of time, like the stolen boat episode, "There was a Boy," the vision on Mt. Snowdon—separated from one another by tedious stretches of prosaic matter. The tendency is evident, for instance, in such an admirable recent study as that of John Jones, who distinguishes sharply between *The Prelude* of 1798-99 and *The Prelude* of 1804-5. The former period, during which some of the best spots of time were composed, he sees as spontaneous and inspired, the latter as marked by a decline in imaginative power, with Wordsworth often forced to pad and fill in in order to carry out his chosen task.[5] Disregarding the fact that a number of passages generally acknowledged as "inspired," like Mt. Snowdon, were done in 1804, one must recognize at least two unfortunate consequences of this attitude. The first is that insofar as we value the major spots of time, we all too easily demand precisely the same set of values—lyric intensity, the sense of freshly uncovered insights, the aura of transcendental vision—from the rest of the poem. As a result we lump together all the long intervening stretches as essentially the same quality throughout—or, to be more accurate, we remain indifferent to their quality—and are unable to make the proper distinctions between them. We ignore the fact, for instance, that the books on the French Revolution represent a type of poetry unique in the history of English verse and a type as distinctly different from the spots of time as they are different from the Augustan satire in the passages on Cambridge and London. When we look at an extended period such as the following, on his retreat from Godwinism:

> Thus I fared,
> Dragging all passions, notions, shapes of faith,

5 Jones, *The Egotistical Sublime: A History of Wordsworth's Imagination* (London, 1954), pp. 125-127.

Like culprits to the bar, suspiciously
Calling the mind to establish in plain day
Her titles and her honours, now believing,
Now disbelieving, endlessly perplex'd
With impulse, motive, right and wrong, the ground
Of moral obligation, what the rule
And what the sanction, till, demanding *proof*,
And seeking it in everything, I lost
All feeling of conviction, and, in fine,
Sick, wearied out with contrarieties,
Yielded up moral questions in despair,
And for my future studies, as the sole
Employment of the inquiring faculty,
Turn'd towards mathematics, and their clear
And solid evidence—Ah! then it was
That Thou, most precious Friend! about this time
First known to me, didst lend a living help
To regulate my Soul, and then it was
That the belovèd Woman in whose sight
Those days were pass'd, now speaking in a voice
Of sudden admonition, like a brook
That does but cross a lonely road, and now
Seen, heard and felt, and caught at every turn . . .

(x, 889-913)

when we come upon such a passage we obviously cannot
read it the same way we read the celebrated visionary moments. It does not, for one thing, reveal its full power
out of context, as does the passage on the Simplon Pass,
but only when read as part of the larger inner drama
that makes up the books on the Revolution. The formal
diction, the formal parallelisms ("what the rule / And
what the sanction") are balanced by an intricate syntactical
maze that gives outward dramatic form to the fierce war
raging within the mind. Although we cannot deny these
lines the epithet *intensity*, this is emphatically not the in-

tensity of the "lofty burst" or the "divine heat" that meant so much to Poe and the *Prospective Review*; it is rather, intensity of a different kind, one more closely akin to the intensity of argumentation that marked the poetry of the seventeenth century. But more on the Revolution later.

A second consequence of our reading *The Prelude* for its visionary moments alone is that we miss an essential experience peculiar to the long poem. For the successful long poem—and their number among the modern European literatures is few—is something more than the sum of its parts. The very fact that it goes beyond Poe's half-hour limit enables a type of illusion which makes the reader feel he has explored a far more comprehensive area of life, and one less rooted in transient matters, than he does in a piece of shorter scope. Indeed, the cosmic and heroic themes and the elevation of style that have traditionally marked the long poem are essentially outward signs of the largeness of scope and weightiness toward which the epic poet strives. Although the novel of the last two centuries has often been able to emulate the epic in comprehensiveness, only rarely—in instances such as *Moby Dick* and *War and Peace*—has it approached both the seriousness and the monumentality which were once within the province of poetry alone.

It is significant that T. S. Eliot, whose early criticism was instrumental in renewing the life of Poe's doctrine for our own time, has in recent years declared that "the *art poétique* of which we find the germ in Poe, and which bore fruit in the work of Valéry, has gone as far as it can go."[6] In fact, the later Eliot, in a parenthetical remark which I cited at the beginning of this study, has said of *The Prelude* that, "however tedious in many places, [it] has to be read entire."[7] What he no doubt meant was that to read

6 "From Poe to Valéry," *Hudson Review*, II (1949), p. 342.
7 *On Poetry and Poets*, p. 174.

it entire was an experience wholly different from and ultimately more rewarding than knowing it by its touchstones
and moments of intensity.

But there is still another mode of discourse prevalent
throughout *The Prelude* that is far more inimical to the
modern sensibility than the introspective dialectic of the
passages on the French Revolution. I am thinking of those
many sections which we would dub "rhetorical," like the
following:

>   Beauteous the domain
> Where to the sense of beauty first my heart
> Was open'd, tract more exquisitely fair
> Than is that Paradise of ten thousand Trees,
> Or Gehol's famous Gardens, in a Clime
> Chosen from widest Empire, for delight
> Of the Tartarian Dynasty composed;
> (Beyond that mighty Wall, not fabulous,
> China's stupendous mound!) by patient skill
> Of myriads, and boon Nature's lavish help;
> Scene link'd to scene, an evergrowing change.
> Soft, grand, or gay! with Palaces and Domes
> Of Pleasure spangled over, shady Dells
> For Eastern Monasteries, sunny Mounds
> With Temples crested, Bridges, Gondolas,
> Rocks, Dens, and Groves of foliage taught to melt
> Into each other their obsequious hues
> Going and gone again, in subtile chace,
> Too fine to be pursued.   (VIII, 119-137)

Despite the image of the various elements "melting" into
one another, this is emphatically not an example of what,
in the last two chapters, I described as Wordsworth's rhetoric of interaction. We feel no sense of discovery, no
struggle to define new modes of feeling; rather, like the
eulogy to Anne Tyson and the epistle to Coleridge which

I discussed in my opening chapter, this is a set piece, an elaborate exercise in formal rhetoric. The fact that the method is obviously borrowed from Milton is irrelevant to our present discussion: without the example of Milton, Wordsworth—had he been inspired to write a long poem at all—would have found another model for his rhetoric. What was essential for him at this point was the formality itself, for it serves to assert the dignity and decorum of the poem, and, though he introduces the Gardens of Gehol only to reject them in favor of his native domain, their very presence also serves to widen the poem's scope and, in effect, to aid the illusion of comprehensiveness.

Rhetoric, moreover, provides the semblance of intensity when the more "genuine" intensity of the lofty burst can no longer be sustained. For the long poem demands at least the pretense of evenness (the very idea of pretense is of course repugnant to post-Romantic taste), which it achieves by maintaining a uniform meter and a uniform level of diction. A long poem of epic pretensions must ultimately depend on formal rhetoric for its sustenance. To read *The Prelude* correctly we must accept the presence of its rhetoric and willingly suspend our disbelief in the aesthetic validity of this art, which has suffered so great a decline in prestige during the last 150 years that by our own time it has been relegated to the realm of its probable origin, that of political oratory, and specifically the backwoods variety. For Wordsworth rhetoric could still serve as a sign of commitment to the public realm and of the poet's desire to maintain communications with the world of affairs. Indeed, the violent revolt of the French Symbolists and of the English poets of the 1890's against all traditional rhetoric can be taken as a sign of their commitment to a strictly private world.

The rhetoric of *The Prelude* serves still another, more central purpose, that of persuasion, for in its most elemental sense rhetoric attempts to be persuasive. On its most obvious level, the persuasive character of the poem is revealed in such a passage as the following, in Wordsworth's discussion of the deficiencies of his Cambridge education:

> Yet I,
> Methinks, could shape the image of a Place
> Which with its aspect should have bent me down
> To instantaneous service, should at once
> Have made me pay to science and to arts
> And written lore, acknowledg'd my liege Lord,
> A homage, frankly offer'd up, like that
> Which I had paid to Nature. Toil and pains
> In this recess which I have bodied forth
> Should spread from heart to heart; and stately
>   groves,
> Majestic edifices, should not want
> A corresponding dignity within. . . .
> Youth should be aw'd, possess'd, as with a sense
> Religious, of what holy joy there is
> In knowledge, if it be sincerely sought
> For its own sake, in glory, and in praise,
> If but by labour won, and to endure.
>
> (III, 380-400)

The passage is didactic in a double sense, for its persuasiveness is directed to the field of education itself. But if the didactic element is rarely so obvious as here, where the auxiliary *should*, in its imperative sense, governs virtually every sentence, it still remains a central motivating force behind the poem. When Wordsworth, in the midst of composing Book VII of *The Prelude*, wrote an acquaintance, "I pray God to give me life to finish these works [the total *Recluse*], which I trust, will live, and do good" (CO, 439), he was voicing an attitude directly antithetical

to the doctrine of enlightened purposelessness that underlies the theories of Poe and the Symbolists. However fal-
lacious they may seem to succeeding generations, Wordsworth's didactic intentions are an intrinsic part of the
meaning of his poem, if only to the extent that they supply
the motivating and staying power which makes a long
poem possible.

But the didacticism of *The Prelude* often retains a distinctly charming quality, even, I think, for those readers
most antipathetic to didactic verse. Throughout the poem
we are made aware that the poet's life (like *The Prelude*
itself) is essentially a preparation for another, still greater
didactic work, and as a result the poem retains an aura of
hopeful enthusiasm about future achievement:

> Prophets of Nature, we to them will speak
> A lasting inspiration, sanctified
> By reason and by truth; what we have loved,
> Others will love; and we may teach them how;
> Instruct them how the mind of man becomes
> A thousand times more beautiful than the earth
> On which he dwells, above this Frame of things
> (Which, 'mid all revolutions in the hopes
> And fears of men, doth still remain unchanged)
> In beauty exalted, as it is itself
> Of substance and of fabric more divine.
>
> (XIII, 442-452)

It is ultimately irrelevant that the great didactic purpose
was never fulfilled. What matters is the energy which
Wordsworth's optimism during composition lent to *The
Prelude* itself, which, even in its less overtly visionary passages, like the one above, often glows with the hope of
things to come.

Even if Wordsworth had been able to sustain his high
flights throughout, one wonders how readable the result-

ing poem might have been. Humankind, T. S. Eliot would say, cannot bear very much intensity. The comprehensiveness of scope which the successful long poem suggests inevitably demands the introduction of materials incompatible with the more lyrical qualities which, during the course of the nineteenth century, gradually claimed exclusive domain over the province of poetry. In reading *The Prelude* one is often impressed by the fact that Wordsworth was as successful as he was in withstanding the demands of the lyrical impulse to break down the larger structure and plan of the poem. In the lyrical mode, attempting, as it does, to give the effect of spontaneity and inspiration, the poet, in effect, denies the role of the conscious will in the making of poems. And without at least the stabilizing force of this will, the long poem—unless it rest content as a loosely organized collection of related lyrics, like *In Memoriam*—must remain an impossibility. In *The Prelude* we are aware of a conflict, on Wordsworth's part, between the traditional ambitions of the epic poet and the failure of the Romantic imagination to provide both the inspiration and staying power for his appointed task. The dilemma is obvious in such lines as the following, from the introduction:

> Then, last wish,
> My last and favourite aspiration! then
> I yearn towards some philosophic Song
> Of Truth that cherishes our daily life;
> With meditations passionate from deep
> Recesses in man's heart, immortal verse
> Thoughtfully fitted to the Orphean lyre;
> But from this awful burthen I full soon
> Take refuge, and beguile myself with trust
> That mellower years will bring a riper mind
> And clearer insight. Thus from day to day
> I live, a mockery of the brotherhood

> Of vice and virtue, with no skill to part
> Vague longing that is bred by want of power
> From paramount impulse not to be withstood,
> A timorous capacity from prudence;
> From circumspection, infinite delay.
>
> (I, 228-244)

The sensibility he betrays here is one far removed from that revealed by Milton in the various invocations of *Paradise Lost*; for it is essentially the sensibility of the modern poet—procrastinating, self-analytical, recoiling from the burden of his task, apprehensive of inadequacy and failure of the will. But the lines that directly follow these are an even more explicit demonstration of those peculiarly modern vices, rationalization, inhibition, anxiety, which follow one another in such ruthlessly logical order:

> Humility and modest awe themselves
> Betray me, serving often for a cloak
> To a more subtle selfishness, that now
> Doth lock my functions up in blank reserve,
> Now dupes me by an over-anxious eye
> That with a false activity beats off
> Simplicity and self-presented truth.
>
> (245-251)

"Simplicity and self-presented truth"—Wordsworth looks back longingly at what he conceives of, rightly or wrongly, as an earlier condition of poetry, much as Schiller in his essay "On Naïve and Sentimental Poetry," written only a few years before *The Prelude*, looked with envy upon the "naïve" older poets (Homer, Shakespeare, and, by a happy accident of history, his own contemporary Goethe) whom he viewed as creating directly out of nature, without the undue and inhibiting intrusion of the reflective faculty. After the lines quoted above we find the characteristic defense of the Romantic poet, a retreat into a state of indolence, which, through the long-standing example of the pastoral tradition and the recent, more powerful example of Rousseau, had been transformed from a medieval vice to a modern virtue and, in fact, had become the seed-bed for new inspiration:

> —Ah! better far than this, to stray about
> Voluptuously through fields and rural walks,
> And ask no record of the hours, given up
> To vacant musing, unreprov'd neglect
> Of all things, and deliberate holiday.
>
> (252-256)

And in indolence he could honorably renounce the will which the epic task demanded:

> Far better never to have heard the name
> Of zeal and just ambition, than to live
> Thus baffled by a mind that every hour
> Turns recreant to her task, takes heart again,
> Then feels immediately some hollow thought
> Hang like an interdict upon her hopes.
>
> (257-262)

But the very mention of ambition reminds us once again of the tension which plagued Wordsworth between two seemingly incompatible approaches to aesthetic creation.

In the light of such introspective passages one often wonders that the poem did not disintegrate in the process of composition, that it did not, in fact, remain a series of inspired fragments, like "The Simplon Pass" or the skating-scene, both of which Wordsworth published independently during his lifetime. And yet we also know from the very early Manuscript JJ that the idea of a longer, ambitious work was already implicit among the tentative jottings of the great spots of time of Book I:

Nor while, thou (gh) doubting yet not lost I tread
The mazes of this argument, and paint
How Nature by collateral interest
And by extrinsic passion peopled first
My mind with beauteous objects may I well
Forget what might demand a loftier song . . .

(Prel., p. 636)

What made possible the completed *Prelude,* even if *The Recluse* as a whole remained unrealized, was the fact that Wordsworth was able to draw on the resources of both the inspiration and the conscious will. *The Excursion,* quite in contrast, is an example of will-power which, instead of supplementing inspiration, has by and large replaced it. It is the peculiar triumph of *The Prelude* that, during the two periods of its composition—periods which define both the beginning and the end of his major work in all forms—Wordsworth was able to hold the two forces in balance.

2. IN SEARCH OF AN ADEQUATE LONGER FORM: WORDSWORTH'S CONTEMPORARIES AND SUCCESSORS

The fact that the Romantic age was so rich in ambitious fragments—Goethe's attempt at an *Achilleïs,* Keats's *Hyperion,* Wordsworth's *Recluse,* not to speak of poems of less lofty conception, such as Coleridge's *Christabel*—may well have something to do with the transitional nature of the age: a transition from a concept of poems as imitation of established structures to self-expressions of the individual poet, with the consequent narrowing down of the province of poetry from a wide variety of discursive forms to those few forms which could aspire to the condition either of the dreamlike or the impassioned lyric. When Keats, in answer to Leigh Hunt's question, "Why endeavor after a long Poem?" attempted to defend the form he left both the older and the newer concept of poetic structure implicit in his reply: "Do not the Lovers of Poetry like to have a little Region to wander in where they may pick and choose, and in which the images are so numerous that many are forgotten and found new in a second Reading: which may be food for a Week's stroll in the Summer? Do not they like this better than what they can read through before Mrs. Williams comes down stairs? a Morning work at most. Besides a long Poem is a test of Invention which I take to be the Polar Star of Poetry, as Fancy is the Sails, and Imagination the Rudder."[8]

The very notion of a long poem as a collection of images among which the reader may "pick and choose" need be taken only one step further to arrive at the Symbolist idea that the long poem is but a series of individual lyrics, and hence does not exist at all. Perhaps Keats was aware of the latent paradox when, at the end of his defense, he assumed the neo-classic stance, which could take for granted the high and singular accomplishment of a man who could meet the "test of Invention" necessary to successful completion of a long poem. But the above statement was made during the composition of *Endymion*; it is significant that when he announced the final abandonment of *Hyperion*, Keats stated his predicament as the inability to "make the division properly" between "the false beauty proceeding from art" and "the true voice of feeling":[9] the demands of imitation—in his case, the need to imitate Milton's language in order to sustain the style necessary for his epic structure—are rejected in favor of the demands of original expression, with the result that he is unable to complete his poem.

When A. C. Bradley surveyed "The Long Poem in the

[8] *Letters*, ed. H. E. Rollins (Cambridge, Mass., 1958), I, 170.
[9] *Ibid.*, II, 167.

Age of Wordsworth" at the beginning of this century, he concluded that the relative failure of the larger Romantic structures was a consequence of the essentially lyrical impulse which characterized the age:

"It may be suggested . . . that the excellence of the lyrical poetry of Wordsworth's time, and the imperfection of the long narratives and dramas, may have a common origin. Just as it was most natural to Homer or to Shakespeare to express the imaginative substance of his mind in the 'objective' shape of a world of persons and actions ostensibly severed from his own thoughts and feelings, so, perhaps, for some reason or reasons, it was most natural to the best poets of this later time to express that substance in the shape of impassioned reflections, aspirations, prophecies, laments, outcries of joy, murmurings of peace. The matter of these might, in another sense of the word, be 'objective' enough, a matter of general human interest, not personal in any exclusive way; but it appeared in the form of the poet's thought and feeling. Just because he most easily expressed it thus, he succeeded less completely when he attempted the more objective form of utterance."[10]

Bradley's essay is remarkable, not only for the incisive way with which he accounted for the weakness of Romantic long poems, but also for the fact that he argued for the validity of the long poem at a time when the Symbolist aesthetic—which in certain of its manifestations stands behind his own best criticism—was at its height in England: "To speak as if a small poem could do all that a long one does, and do it much more completely, is to speak as though a humming-bird could have the same kind of beauty as an eagle, the rainbow in a fountain produce the same effect as the rainbow in the sky, or a moorland stream thunder like Niagara. . . . It would be easy to show that [a long poem] admits of strictly poetic

[10] *Oxford Lectures on Poetry* (London, 1909), pp. 184-185.

effects of the highest value which the mere brevity of a short one excludes."[11]

Yet even if we grant the weakness of Romantic long poems and note the fragmentary nature of so many ambitious attempts, it is significant that the age was singularly productive in longer works, that, in fact, every major English poet from Blake through Browning—with the obvious exception of Coleridge—produced at least one, in some cases several long poems. It is also significant that most of the Romantic long poems, whether or not they succeed in their total effect, are characterized by far greater unity of conception and structure than such eighteenth-century "composite" poems—to use Wordsworth's term—as *Nights Thoughts* and *The Task*. Even a brief glance at the major poems of Thomson, Young and Cowper—as well as that anomalous modern poem, Bridges' *Testament of Beauty*—reveals a loose, episodic mixture of objective description, didactic matter, and, except for Cowper, narrative interlude. (Dr. Johnson even complained of the "want of method" in *The Seasons*.) The form of these poems, of course, ultimately derives from the *Georgics* (or, rather, the eighteenth century's conception of the form of the *Georgics*), and as a result they share far less of the spirit of classical epic than does *The Prelude*, which, for all its georgic elements, seeks to emulate, if not exactly imitate, *Paradise Lost*.

If we can speak of both the eighteenth- and nineteenth-century longer poems as uneven, we should also distinguish the nature of their unevenness. The former are uneven by virtue of a discursiveness of tone that motivates them as a whole and which is inherent in the models they seek to imitate; the latter, through the sharply varying degrees of intensity that result from a lyrical impulse which they can only partially sustain. One could, in fact, describe the

[11] *Ibid.*, p. 204.

history of the long poem since the end of the eighteenth century as a search for a form that would adequately embody—to borrow Bradley's words—those "impassioned reflections, aspirations, prophecies, laments, outcries of joy, murmurings of peace" which could not be satisfied by the limited framework of lyric and ballad. Though Bradley is doubtless right in stressing the lyrical impulse as a prime characteristic of the age, we can also, with our larger historical perspective, discern still another prevailing tendency of the age—its attempt to propound and vividly present a new world-view. And the shorter forms, however much they sought to serve this purpose (many of Wordsworth's short lyrics, for instance, "To the Cuckoo," when seen in the context of his total work, attempt to express a transcendental view of things) clearly did not suffice.

It is not merely the fact that the Romantic writers were concerned with ideas—so, indeed, are all serious poets, including the Symbolists, in their own, very indirect way—but rather, each of the Romantics, whether or not he succeeded in finding an adequate form, was concerned with a whole body of related ideas and attitudes which in their totality add up to a larger, though not necessarily consistent or even original, view of reality. When we speak of the primacy of the lyrical impulse in Romanticism we refer to the peculiar way in which the Romantics perceived the world and also to the manner in which they sought to communicate their perceptions. Yet the lyrical impulse in each of the Romantics existed side by side, and often in conjunction with, a sense of epic grandeur, the feeling that Keats, for instance, was trying to define when he wrote, "I feel more and more every day, as my imagination strengthens, that I do not live in this world alone but in a thousand worlds—No sooner am I alone than shapes of epic greatness are stationed around me, and serve my Spirit the office (of) which is equivalent to a

king's body guard."[12] Like all the Romantics at one time
or another, Keats was describing a state of mind wholly
within the area of sublimity, of *pathos* as opposed to *ethos*.
If the lyrical and epic impulses were not always compatible
in the creation of successful works of art, both nonetheless
sought expression and helped determine the particular
forms of the long poems of the age.

To return to the "objective" forms of the past was no
solution, as Keats eventually learned while struggling
with *Hyperion*. At first glance a poem like Landor's *Gebir*
seems an anomaly in its age. In its dignity and control,
its impeccably Miltonic diction, its occasional use of epic
machinery—invocation, descent to the underworld—it
would seem a serious attempt to revive not only the spirit
but the letter of classical epic. Yet, despite its claim of
ethical content and national, contemporary relevance—
"[These] twenty verses . . . describe the equality which
nature teaches, the absurdity of colonizing a country which
is peopled, and the superior advantage of cultivating those
which remain unoccupied"[13]—*Gebir* remains at bottom an
exotic Oriental tale, a romance rather than an epic, a Dido-
and-Aeneas episode (in this case, one in which the hero,
rather than abandoning the heroine, is murdered by her
servant) lifted from a still unwritten larger epic. Indeed,
in the lines preceding his hero's descent into the underworld Landor poignantly expresses the plight of a poet
who lives in an age too late to realize his highest ambitions:

O for the spirit of that matchless man
Whom Nature led throughout her whole domain,
While he, embodied, breath'd etherial air!
Though panting in the play-hour of my youth,

[12] *Letters*, I, 403.
[13] *Works*, ed. Stephen Wheeler, XIII, 48.

I drank of Avon, too, a dang'rous draught,
That rous'd within the fev'rish thirst of song—
Yet, never may I trespass o'er the stream
Of jealous Acheron, nor alive descend
The silent and unsearchable abodes
Of Erebus and Night, nor unchastized
Lead up long absent heroes into day.
When on the pausing theatre of earth
Eve's shadowy curtain falls, can any man
Bring back the far-off intercepted hills,
Grasp the round rock-built turret, or arrest
The glittering spires that pierce the brow of Heav'n?
Rather, can any, with outstripping voice,
The parting Sun's gigantic strides recall?[14]

Landor's yearning for a vanished age of poetry—though
in one sense a traditional assertion of the poet's modesty—
all too easily recalls the plight depicted by Wordsworth in
that introductory passage to *The Prelude* which describes
his troubles coming to terms with his proposed epic themes.
In both, written, as they were, within a year or two of one
another, we hear a farewell to the possibility of traditional
epic.

If the epic strain could no longer be sustained in poetry,
the less lofty demands of romance could at least provide a
form for the long poem. In romance the very need of getting one's story told made possible a structure more co-
hesive than that of the discursive eighteenth-century poems.
And by setting his romance in a distant time or place the
poet could lay the groundwork for those lyrical effects of
atmosphere which he was so bent on capturing. In romance, moreover, he could call upon a style less demanding than the sublime and, above all, one less dependent
upon Milton, whose example had determined, for better

14 *Ibid.*, p. 16.

or worse, the nature of the sublime in English. Thus, when
Scott defended the method he employed in *The Lay of the
Last Minstrel*, he made clear that his genre was one essentially different from epic or georgic: "As the description
of scenery and manners was more the object of the author
than a combined and regular narrative, the plan of the
the Ancient Metrical Romance was adopted, which allows
greater latitude in this respect than would be consistent
with the dignity of a regular Poem."[15] It is significant
that Scott came closest to the spirit and content of epic—
though not by its neo-classic definition—when he turned
away from the long poem to the novel. The so-called epics
of Southey, though endowed with a certain atmosphere
of loftiness through those violent aspects of nature which
the author was wont to evoke, are distinctly within the
realm of exotic romance, as are the less pretentious Oriental tales of his enemy Byron; indeed, the very idea of
a new epic issued regularly at four and five year intervals—
Joan of Arc in 1796, *Thalaba* in 1801, *Madoc* in 1805, *The
Curse of Kehama* in 1810, *Roderick* in 1814—is antithetical
to that conception of an epic as the single goal toward
which a poet directs his life-work. If Wordsworth sometimes approaches the forms of romance—in *The White
Doe of Rylstone*, for instance, or, on a more modest scale,
in the short narratives of *Lyrical Ballads*—one must note
the sharp distinction in language and meter between these
attempts and the ambitious, uncompleted poem of which
The Prelude is a part. It is also worth noting how rigorously he excluded the trappings of romance from his great
poem, except for the compliments he pays to older ro-
mances in Book v of *The Prelude* for the role they play
in a child's educational process.

Wordsworth dispensed not only with exotic content to
fashion his long poem, but also with myth, which made

[15] Oxford Standard Authors edition, p. 1.

possible such long poems as Blake's prophetic books and Shelley's *Revolt of Islam*. The invention of a private myth, built out of a self-enclosed world of traditional Neoplatonic symbols, gave Blake and Shelley the opportunity to voice their moral concerns—concerns as weighty as those of any epic poet of the past—with a tone of prophetic urgency, though at the obvious cost of that clarity which not only makes a long poem readable, but which can make its prophecy meaningful within the public as well as the private realm. When Wordsworth assumes the prophetic tone in *The Prelude*, he does so by means other than myth or allegory, that is, through formal rhetoric and, most conspicuously and successfully, in those culminating passages within the spots of time in which his explorations of his personal past lead naturally, and by a process of gradual intensification, into generalizations of public significance.

If there is any single longer form which is distinctly a product of the age and which could provide the cosmic scope which was once a property of epic, it is the dramatic poem—not, certainly, the dreary pseudo-Shakespearean closet drama that can be found among the works of virtually every nineteenth-century English poet, including Wordsworth, but rather the type of poem exemplified at its best in Goethe's *Faust* and Shelley's *Prometheus Unbound* and which produced a distinguished late example in Hardy's *Dynasts*. While obviously sacrificing that semblance of unity and self-containment which results from regularity of meter, the dramatic form provides a more compelling vehicle for the presentation of ideas than the more frank and open didacticism traditional to the long poem. One need only compare *Queen Mab*, which has only the rudiments of dialogue, with *Prometheus Unbound*, whose dramatic form allowed full play to Shelley's didactic and lyric, though also quite undramatic, talents. Indeed, the dramatic convention often provided an ideal outlet for an essentially lyric impulse which, not resting satisfied with the modest framework of the short poem, demanded a more comprehensive structure to express a larger vision.

In comparison with works such as *Faust* and *Prometheus*, *The Prelude* seems a peculiarly bare and restrained performance, one governed by a classical rigor which Shelley never knew and which Goethe, with his fine sense of decorum, relegated to other, less ambitious works. *The Prelude*'s bareness and restraint are even more conspicuous when we set it next to a poem to which it has more obvious affinities, Byron's *Childe Harold*, which, like *The Prelude*, could be viewed generically as an eighteenth-century loco-descriptive poem inflated by romantic introspection. But Byron's most successful approach to the longer form came neither in *Childe Harold* nor in the Oriental tales, but in *Don Juan*, which manages to entertain us throughout by that illusion of improvisation by which, to use the words of Northrop Frye, "we simultaneously read the poem and watch the poet at work writing it."[16]

In his long poem *Luise*, a work much admired by Wordsworth, the distinguished German translator of Homer, Johann Heinrich Voss, attempted to give new life to the epic by using the German hexameter line, which his readers could naturally associate with the world of epic, to focus upon the everyday details of middle-class life. The resulting form, known in Germany as the "domestic idyll," is the sort of narrative that might be created by lifting the pastoral similes out of the *Iliad* and ignoring matters of more heroic import. The greatest example of the genre, Goethe's *Hermann und Dorothea* (which Wordsworth, because of his deep prejudice against Goethe, was unable to appreciate) is in fact set during the French Revolution, whose rumbles are heard only distantly while the poet concentrates on the more stable realities of ordinary life. The

[16] *Anatomy of Criticism* (Princeton, 1957), p. 234.

genre is essentially a kind of pastoral, though, in the hands of the Germans, a pastoral not of shepherds but of small-town burghers. Its affinities are not with Virgilian epic, but with Homer, whom it tries to emulate in directness of perception and in evenness, though not loftiness, of tone. In its celebration of the ordinary rather than the extraordinary details of life it represents a full withdrawal from the world of *pathos* and a correspondingly total immersion in the world of *ethos*. Wordsworth approaches this genre at occasional moments in *The Prelude*, as in the description of the card games and other "home amusements" in Book I, and at far greater length in *The Excursion*, especially in those tedious descriptions of local families in the two books entitled "The Churchyard among the Mountains." Yet he could never successfully have sustained a longer work in the form, for the characters and incidents which most excited his imagination, though pastoral in setting, tend toward the extraordinary rather than the ordinary, toward a somber rather than a serene world. The very fact that he concentrated on solitaries, and many of the most eccentric kind, testifies to the distance he maintained from the realities of daily life.

Yet the example of domestic idyll directly inspired one of the most successful epic efforts—if one can judge by translations and the testimony of others—of the nineteenth century, the Polish national epic *Pan Tadeucz* by Adam Mickiewicz, who started out with the modest intention of imitating *Hermann und Dorothea* and gradually found himself creating a heroic poem. Mickiewicz, unlike his contemporaries in the more firmly established literary traditions, had the double fortune of a language in whose loftier reaches there were still new claims to be staked out and, second, of a burning national theme, that of liberation from Russia, for which he found fictional embodiment in a heroic interlude from the Napoleonic wars.

What ultimately gives his poem universal significance is his success in setting his heroic action against a fully realized background of everyday life: what Voss and Goethe had, so to speak, removed from Homer was now restored to the larger epic structure.

Had Coleridge had his way, still another work in German, the extended "prose poem" *The Death of Abel* by the Swiss writer Salomon Gessner, would have served Wordsworth as a model for a longer work. In 1798 the two poets, at Coleridge's instigation, set out to write a sequel to Gessner's work, calling it *The Wanderings of Cain.*

"My partner," Coleridge tells us, "undertook the first canto: I the second: and which ever had *done first*, was to set about the third. Almost thirty years have passed by; yet at this moment I cannot without something more than a smile moot the question which of the two things was the more impracticable, for a mind [Wordsworth's] so eminently original to compose another man's thoughts and fancies, or for a taste so austerely pure and simple to imitate the Death of Abel? Methinks I see his grand and noble countenance as at the moment when having despatched my own portion of the task at full finger-speed, I hastened to him with my manuscript—that look of humourous despondency fixed on his almost blank sheet of paper, and then its silent mock-piteous admission of failure struggling with the sense of the exceeding ridiculousness of the whole scheme—which broke up in a laugh; and the Ancient Mariner was written instead."[17]

Whether or not Wordsworth was capable of "imitation" or whether his taste was too "austerely pure and simple" to rework materials as sentimental as Gessner's, it is evident that *The Death of Abel*, with its far-off Biblical setting, would have provided Wordsworth with an even less

[17] *Complete Poetical Works*, ed. E. H. Coleridge (Oxford, 1912), I, 286-287.

suitable model for his talents than *Luise*. Above all, both Gessner and Voss had nothing to offer Wordsworth's heroic impulse, which, side by side with his attraction to pastoral, was to demand expression in his longer work.

The history of the long poem in England and France in the later nineteenth century is a history, if not exactly of the death of the form, at least of its gradual fragmentation. Lamartine's remarks on *Jocelyn*, which he published in 1836 as one unit in a series of never-completed long poems which were to constitute a national epic, are an attempt to redefine epic: "I looked for an epic subject suitable to our epoch," he tells us in his introduction, and what he found was an "intimate epic," the story of a Protestant pastor (as, indeed, the hero of Voss' *Luise* had been, not to speak of *The Excursion*). But *Jocelyn* is less a story than a series of lyrical meditations tied loosely together; and its subtitle, "Journal trouvé chez un curé de campagne," reveals its essentially introspective nature.

If *Jocelyn* approached the private realm, it was still possible for poets to maintain at least the semblance of a public voice by retelling traditional tales, as Tennyson's *Idylls of the King*, Morris' *Earthly Paradise*, and Hugo's *Légende des Siècles*. Of these the last-named is most self-consciously epic in intent. Drawing its tales from a large range of epochs and traditions, it is created on the assumption that a collection of small epics will somehow add up to a larger one; yet for all its pretensions it is less informed by a truly unifying idea than two other collections of poems that appeared only a few years before—*Leaves of Grass* and *Les Fleurs du Mal*.

Although Baudelaire's collection belongs primarily to the history of lyric poetry, Whitman's is characterized by a distinctly epic impulse. Its longest poem, *Song of Myself*, through its attempt to mediate between the public and private realm, its prophetic strivings, its cultivation of the

THE POSSIBILITY OF A LONG POEM

egotistical sublime, and even its organization into spots of
time, has perhaps more affinities with *The Prelude* (which
Whitman gives no evidence of having read) than any other
poem of the century. Like *The Prelude* it portrays the poet
as hero and advertises its essentially heroic argument
through its ceremonious, though also quite un-Miltonic,
language. Yet to the extent that it lacks any overt formal
structure analogous even to the chronological development
within *The Prelude*—it is less the growth than the lyrical
outpourings of the poet's mind—*Song of Myself* is yet another example of the fragmentation process that has characterized the long poem since Wordsworth's time.

Browning came to terms with the problem of form by
making his most ambitious poem, *The Ring and the Book*,
a series of thematically connected dramatic monologues.
As a result he could dispense with rhetorical connectives
as well as the embellishments of language which were traditionally the right of the poet when he spoke in his own
voice. Its affinities are less with any other long poem, past
or present, than with the modern experimental novel, as
Henry James was perhaps the first to point out.[18] If *The
Ring and the Book* failed to serve as a model for later long
poems, Tennyson's *Princess*, which includes short poems of
the highest lyric intensity interspersed within a fairly flat
narrative which is essentially a novel in meter, suggests a
method which, in one way or another, has made possible
certain long poems of our own day. The method might be
described as the alternation of various levels of intensity.

T. S. Eliot, who employs the method in *Four Quartets*,
has described it thus: "In a long poem some parts may be
deliberately planned to be less 'poetic' than others: these
passages may show no lustre when extracted, but may be
intended to elicit, by contrast, the significance of other
parts, and to unite them into a whole more significant than

[18] *Notes on Novelists* (New York, 1914), pp. 385-411.

any of the parts. A long poem may gain by the widest possible variations of intensity."[19] *Four Quartets*, of course, is a meditative poem and makes no such epic pretensions as does that other long poem of our day, William Carlos Williams' *Paterson*, which utilizes the principle of alternating intensities to the degree that its "flatter" passages often take the form of prose, and, in fact, the prose of newspaper clippings and lists of statistics.

The very notion of different levels of intensity is, of course, a consequence of the gradual narrowing down, during the nineteenth century, of what could appropriately be called "poetic." As soon as rhetoric was no longer considered poetic, it could only find its way back into poetry if the poet was willing to include the lower levels of intensity. Since the stricter adherents of Poe's theory could hardly justify their inclusion, we cannot properly speak of a Symbolist epic, as we can of a Renaissance or even Romantic epic. Yet the concept of what is poetic has radically changed during the half-century since the Symbolist aesthetic has become influential in the English-speaking countries, and since the revolution effected by Eliot and Pound our notion of what makes for high intensity has shifted from the ecstatic lyric flight which Poe called for in his essay to the tightly controlled, indeed, often somewhat "prosaic" concrete image. It is symptomatic of the modern tendency to fragmentize poetic structures that we speak of the individual image—the ideogram of Pound, or the epiphany of Joyce—as the central unit of meaning instead of the larger structure of which it is a part; indeed, Wordsworth's idea of the "spot of time" (which I shall explicate in some detail in the next two chapters), though he did not allow it to replace or distort his conception of a total poem, can be viewed as one step

[19] "From Poe to Valéry," p. 334.

on the way to the autonomous image which has been the goal of the Symbolist poet.

Despite the obstacles which Symbolist conceptions of poetic structure have set in the way of the creation of long poems, the major contemporary poets have been only slightly less deterred in their ambitions to create longer works than were their nineteenth-century predecessors. Certainly nearly all have tried their hand at a long poem, although they have often sought rather the semblance of length than actual length. *The Waste Land*, whose obscurity was early defended on grounds that Eliot had left out the rhetorical connectives which would formerly have clarified, as well as relaxed the intensity of a long poem, is perhaps the model epic within the Symbolist tradition, for within the space of 400 lines (only two or three times the length of most Wordsworthian spots of time) it presents a series of highly charged images and undeveloped dramatic situations that create the illusion of a larger vision of history. A similar illusion of amplitude was achieved by Hart Crane in *The Bridge*, which, hardly less concise but considerably more heroic in its intentions than *The Waste Land*, succeeds in uniting the introspective concerns characteristic of the modern lyric with the ceremoniousness traditional to epic. Wallace Stevens' *Notes Toward a Supreme Fiction*, though more modest in its range of interests than *The Waste Land* or *The Bridge*, also strives toward an illusion of length. It bears closer affinities to *The Prelude* than perhaps any other modern long poem, not only in its verse form and overtly didactic intent, but in its very argument for the primacy of the poetic imagination. Yet through its relatively small scope it succeeds in fusing its diverse components—fragments of memory, parables, and large blocks of discursive argument—into a far more tightly integrated whole than the much more sprawling *Prelude*, many of whose individual books are longer than Stevens' whole poem; Stevens' achievement, one might say, was to order the more loosely organized materials of most older meditative poems into a single, sustained spot of time.

If Eliot, Crane, and Stevens could create at least the semblance of a long poem by Symbolist method, Ezra Pound and St. John Perse have employed the method to create genuinely long poems. Pound, in fact, has undertaken the most ambitious epic effort of our time and, true to his Symbolist principles, has presented his view of history, both public and personal, by concentrating on certain pregnant moments which follow one another without transition, commentary, or even, for that matter, chronology. By a strange irony the boredom and relaxation of intensity which Poe and his followers deplored in the rhetoric of long poems is also inherent in the ideogrammic method of the *Cantos*; it is as though the very existence of length relaxes tension, however highly charged the components of the structure may be. But Symbolist method, like that of the dramatic poem, makes possible a vividness of presentation rarely attainable in the traditional type of long poem and thus has provided an opportunity for the return of heroic action to the long poem: such works as the *Anabasis* of Perse and the *Conquistador* of MacLeish succeed as evocation, though emphatically not as reenactment, of action.

At the present time, when we have come to recognize the limitations of the Symbolist aesthetic and, indeed, to long for a return to rhetoric and public statement, *The Prelude* can perhaps serve us as an example. Through its introspectiveness it speaks to us as a record of the modern sensibility as no earlier long poem can do; yet it is also rooted in an older rhetorical system which, however foreign to us its premises may be, may teach us how to reconcile the public and private world within a larger poetic structure and, above all, to recapture for poetry that fullness of development and presentation which, as poetic structures became more and more fragmented, passed inevitably into the domain of the novel.

CHAPTER FIVE
TIME-CONSCIOUSNESS (1)

He contracted a habit of exaggerating the importance of every-day incidents and situations.
Review of *The Prelude* in *The Examiner*, July 27, 1850.

> . . . Need I dread from thee
> Harsh judgments, if I am so loth to quit
> Those recollected hours that have the charm
> Of visionary things, and lovely forms
> And sweet sensations that throw back our life
> And almost make our Infancy itself
> A visible scene, on which the sun is shining?
>
> 1, 657-663

1. FROM SENTIMENT TO VISION

FROM our mid-twentieth century vantage-point we can
view *The Prelude* as an ancestor to those "time-books"
which Wyndham Lewis, in attacking the artistic premises
of Joyce, Proust, and Gertrude Stein, once disparaged for
their "obsession with the temporal scale," their "sick
anxiety directed to questions of time and place."[1] For it is
Wordsworth's unique experience with time (the word itself was one of his ten most frequently used, as it was not,
for instance, with Shakespeare, Milton or Pope) which has
not only determined the form of the poem, but has endowed it with that peculiar intensity which distinguishes it
at once from such a late eighteenth-century disquisition on
time as Samuel Rogers' once-celebrated *Pleasures of Memo-*

[1] *Time and Western Man* (London, 1927), p. 24.

ry (1792). When Rogers, whom time treated so gently that his life-span (1763-1855) overlapped even Wordsworth's, tries to cope with the workings of memory, he can approach them only from the outside:

> As the stern grandeur of a Gothic tower
> Awes us less deeply in its morning-hour,
> Than when the shades of Time serenely fall
> On every broken arch and ivied wall;
> The tender images we love to trace,
> Steal from each year a melancholy grace!
> And as the sparks of social love expand,
> As the heart opens in a foreign land;
> And, with a brother's warmth, a brother's smile,
> The stranger greets each native of his isle;
> So scenes of life, when present and confest,
> Stamp but their bolder features on the breast;
> Yet not an image, when remotely viewed,
> However trivial, and however rude,
> But wins the heart, and wakes the social sigh,
> With every claim of close affinity![2]

For Rogers, rooted in the preconceptions of the later eighteenth century, the pleasure of memory consists of little more than sentimental reflection: past and present meet with "a brother's warmth, a brother's smile," the images of the past "win the heart . . . wake the social sigh." Rogers does not venture beyond the confines of eighteenth-century associationism—nor, for that matter, does the Wordsworth of *An Evening Walk* and *Descriptive Sketches*. When we look at the introductory "analysis" which Rogers provided for his poem—"when ideas have any relation whatever, they are attractive to each other in the mind; and the perception of any object naturally leads to the idea of another, which was connected with it either in time or place, or

[2] *Poetical Works*, p. 27.

which can be compared or contrasted with it"[3]—its intellectual milieu seems essentially the same as that of Hartley's system, which had defined memory as "that faculty by which traces of sensations and ideas recur, or are recalled, in the same order and proportion, accurately or nearly, as they were once presented."[4] *The Pleasures of Memory*, one might say, is essentially Hartley sentimentalized by Rogers; and the contrast with Wordsworth is sharp and decisive:

> And think ye not with radiance more divine
> From these remembrances, and from the power
> They left behind? So feeling comes in aid
> Of feeling, and diversity of strength
> Attends us, if but once we have been strong.
> Oh! mystery of Man, from what a depth
> Proceed thy honours! I am lost, but see
> In simple childhood something of the base
> On which thy greatness stands, but this I feel,
> That from thyself it is that thou must give,
> Else never canst receive.
> (XI, 324-334)

The contemplation of the past, which in Rogers, in the eighteenth century, and in Wordsworth's apprentice work functioned chiefly as an occasion for pleasurable sensations, in *The Prelude* partakes of the nature of revelation. The associative process still determines Wordsworth's way of organizing his memories: one incident recalls another, but it also suggests its ultimate meaning. At innumerable spots throughout *The Prelude* the retelling of some seemingly trivial incident of childhood becomes the occasion for major poetic statement: "Oh! mystery of Man, from what a depth / Proceed thy honours" follows directly the narration of a childhood excursion to a spot where a murderer had been executed long before. If the recording of memo-

[3] *Ibid.*, p. 4.
[4] *Observations on Man* (London, 1834), p. 235.

ries in Rogers and in the early Wordsworth is largely a
pretext for observation and description, in *The Prelude*
it is a means toward positive assertion, indeed, toward an
explicit statement of values. If earlier memory poems are
centered within the human realm (in Rogers, as we remember, the past serves principally to "win the heart, and
wake the social sigh"),[5] *The Prelude* concerns itself with
individual memories only to the extent that they lead into
"deeper" explorations—explorations into the nature of
time itself and into the mysterious sources of life and
power. The difference defines emphatically what separates
the eighteenth from the nineteenth century.

2. MEMOIRS AND MEMORY

The difference between the modern "time-book" and a
conventional memoir about one's past is strikingly evident
when we compare *The Prelude* with the brief "Autobiographical Memoranda" which Wordsworth dictated a few
years before his death. The "Memoranda" consist largely
of vital statistics:

"I was born at Cockermouth, in Cumberland, on April
7th, 1770, the second son of John Wordsworth, attorney-
at-law, as lawyers of this class were then called, and law-
agent to Sir James Lowther, afterwards Earl of Lonsdale.
My mother was Anne, only daughter of William Cookson,
mercer, of Penrith, and of Dorothy, born Crackanthorp,
of the ancient family of that name, who from the times of
Edward the Third had lived in Newbiggen Hall, West-
moreland. . . .

"The time of my infancy and early boyhood was passed
partly at Cockermouth, and partly with my mother's par-

---

[5] Georges Poulet, in "Timelessness and Romanticism," indicates one passage from *The Pleasures of Memory* which anticipates a characteristic
Romantic attitude toward memory (pp. 15-16). But he also (as does
Rogers in his notes to the poem) indicates the source for Rogers' momentary transcendentalizing—John Locke.

ents at Penrith, where my mother, in the year 1778, died of a decline, brought on by a cold, the consequence of being put, at a friend's house in London, in what used to be called 'a best bedroom'. . . .

". . . I wrote, while yet a schoolboy, a long poem running upon my own adventures, and the scenery of the country in which I was brought up. The only part of that poem which has been preserved is the conclusion of it, which stands at the beginning of my collected Poems.

"In the month of October, 1787, I was sent to St. John's College, Cambridge, of which my uncle, Dr. Cookson, had been a fellow. . . .

"My Italian master was named Isola, and had been well acquainted with Gray the poet. As I took to these studies with much interest, he was proud of the progress I made. Under his correction I translated the Vision of Mirza, and two or three other papers of the Spectator, into Italian . . . ."[6]

The dozen or so pages in which Wordsworth reviews his early life in the "Memoranda" deal almost exclusively with events of a publicly verifiable nature: genealogy, matriculation date, the solid matter of names and places. Not that all the material is of a "public" nature: the friend's "best bedroom" which played so decisive a role in the family tragedy is distinctly a private affair, yet the fact that this role could be demonstrated in a courtroom, if need be, gives it a more obviously legitimate place in the memoir than a discussion of the psychological effects which we know Mrs. Wordsworth's death to have had on the family. These effects are dismissed with the lines, "My father never recovered his usual cheerfulness of mind after the loss, and died when I was in my fourteenth year, a schoolboy, just returned from Hawkshead, whither I had been sent with

[6] In Christopher Wordsworth, *Memoirs of William Wordsworth* (London, 1851), I, 6-14 *passim*.

my elder brother Richard, in my ninth year." But even this brief description of his father, to the extent that it suggests the cause of his death, retains the same solidity that his mother's cold and the friend's best bedroom had for us: private history defined by means of publicly observable phenomena.

Or one might compare Wordsworth's entrance to Cambridge as it appears in the "Memoranda" with the corresponding passage in *The Prelude*. In the former, confining himself to a single sentence, he offers concrete facts: the date (down to month and year) plus the family's connection with the college through Dr. Cookson; *The Prelude* leaves out all such details (to the disappointment of the poem's early reviewers, who thought an autobiography should offer more "information"),[7] and presents instead several pages of sights, sounds, and inward reflection. Nor do the references to his literary career in the "Memoranda" give us anything beyond outward circumstances. The fragment of his early long poem ("Dear native regions . . .") "stands at the beginning of my collected Poems," and Coleridge started the "Ancient Mariner," Wordsworth tells us, "in order to defray his part of the expense" of a tour of Devonshire. A first literary effort is thus defined in terms of its place in a table of contents, a major poem by a friend in terms not of larger meanings, nor even of literary sources, but of the economic need that occasioned the poem.

The "Memoranda" follow a thoroughly conventional method; their modern equivalent would be a sketch contributed to *Who's Who*. They are emphatically not confession but public record, the intimations not of a poet or visionary but of a public man. Their method is essentially that of the traditional memoir; Gibbon's *Autobiography*,

[7] See my article "The Reception of *The Prelude*," BNYPL, LXIV (1960), esp. pp. 200, 202, 205.

perhaps the finest earlier literary embodiment of the method in English, demonstrates how an artistically successful self-portrait can be built out of such materials, without the aid of introspective exploration. One might object, of course, that *The Prelude* is not to be taken as autobiography at all, that, to quote the subtitle tacked on by the poet's widow, its subject is properly "the growth of a poet's mind." But throughout his life Wordsworth (and his intimates as well) referred to it as "the poem on my own life," though he occasionally placed the phrase "on the growth of my own mind" in apposition. The task he set out to accomplish had no ready-made method at hand. He was less interested in revealing the "facts" of his past experience than in rendering poetically the impact and feeling of this experience. In the "Memoranda" Wordsworth needed only to assume conventional stances: what mattered about his Italian teacher was not the impact of his teaching upon a developing mind, but the fact that he had once known the poet Gray.

But it is not only in its attempt to explore the larger meanings of personal experience that *The Prelude* differs from the conventional memoir. Beyond that, it attempts to render this experience as a continuous process of growth and development, and to the degree that it seeks such a pattern it is inextricably bound up with the problem of time. The memoir is concerned with time chiefly in a mechanical sense: events follow one another because the calendar says they do. In *The Prelude* experiences are made to follow one another with a more inward inevitability; the calendar and, indeed, all publicly measurable units of time come to seem crudely inadequate within the context that the poem creates.[8]

---

[8] Roy Pascal's sensitive account of autobiography as a literary genre, *Design and Truth in Autobiography* (London, 1960), reached me after this manuscript was complete. His evaluation of Wordsworth's achieve-

3. AN EARLIER TIME-BOOK

The method which Wordsworth chose to record the evolution and significance of his experience had but one real precedent—the *Confessions* of Jean-Jacques Rousseau, together with his even more obsessively time-conscious posthumous work, the *Reveries of a Solitary Walker*, both published together in the early French edition which Wordsworth owned. The extent to which Wordsworth was aware of this precedent will always remain doubtful, for his strange silence on the subject of Rousseau has made it impossible to define the influence of the French writer upon him precisely. One finds Rousseau mentioned but twice throughout his published works: a passing reference to *Emile* in the preface to *The Borderers* in 1797 (PW, I, 345) and a disparaging allusion to the "paradoxical reveries of Rousseau" (CO, 335) in the *Convention of Cintra* pamphlet of 1809. Despite all the labors of modern scholarship, we still know incredibly little about the exact nature of Wordsworth's intellectual development in the years 1795-98, during which time the influence of the *Confessions* and *Emile* would have been at its height; as it is, most of Wordsworth's statements on his intellectual debts date from a time when his political and ideological loyalties must have clouded and, in fact, distorted his memory of those crucial early years.[9]

---

ment in *The Prelude* seems to me accurate and just: "Wordsworth is the first autobiographer to realise—and the poetic form of his autobiography is this realisation—that each man constructs out of his world a unique framework of meaningful events, and that the deepest purpose of autobiography is the account of a life as a projection of the real self (we call it personality but it seems to lie deeper than personality) on the world." (p. 45)

[9] The whole problem surrounding the Wordsworth-Rousseau relationship is taken up in some detail by two French comparatists, Henri Roddier, in *J.-J. Rousseau en Angleterre au XVIIIe siècle* (Paris, n.d.), pp. 99-104, 169, 175-177, 354, 380, and Jacques Voisine, *J.-J. Rousseau en Angleterre à l'époque romantique* (Paris, 1956), pp. 6, 202-222. Emile

I am concerned here with a single parallel between the two writers—the significance of time and memory in their autobiographical works. For both Rousseau and Wordsworth faced the task of finding a new method to render the process of their spiritual development in verbal terms —a process too complex and subjective for the methods of the conventional memoirist, yet too much contingent on the hard and fast details of everyday life to be treated in the totally inward manner of mystics such as Eckhart or St. John of the Cross. Rousseau, in fact, advertised the uniqueness of his attempt in his celebrated opening: "I have resolved on an enterprise which has no precedent, and which, once complete, will have no imitator. My purpose is to display to my kind a portrait in every way true to nature, and the man I shall portray will be myself."[10] But such an enterprise would have proved impossible if Rousseau had not possessed a unique habit of mind: the obsession to recapture past experience. "The great discovery of the eighteenth century is the phenomenon of memory," Georges Poulet tells us in his distinguished study of time in French literature, and "it is the greatness of the eighteenth century to have conceived the prime moment of consciousness as a generating moment and generative not only of other moments *but also of a self which takes shape by and through the means of these very moments.*"[11] Throughout the *Confessions* and *Reveries*, Rousseau makes repeated reference to the workings and significance

---

Legouis called Rousseau's influence "more powerful, perhaps, than any other to which he was subjected" (*Early Life of William Wordsworth* [London, 1897], p. 57), but English and American scholars, with the exception of George McLean Harper, have almost invariably described Wordsworth's intellectual milieu as though Rousseau had never existed. One suspects that they have taken too literally the dogged provincialism that marked Wordsworth's more talkative years.

[10] *Confessions*, tr. Cohen, p. 17.
[11] *Studies in Human Time*, pp. 23-24, italics mine.

of the memory process: "Now that I have passed my prime and am declining into old age, I find these memories [of early childhood] reviving as others fade, and stamping themselves on my mind with a charm and vividness of outline that grows from day to day. It is as if, feeling my life escaping from me, I were trying to recapture it at its beginnings. The smallest events of that time please me by the mere fact that they are of that time. I remember places and people and moments in all their detail. . . ."[12]

Thus far, except for the greater intensity of Rousseau's personal involvement, we have not moved very far beyond the sentimental retrospection of a Samuel Rogers. But the memory, because of the double perspective in which it sets the past, becomes a unique instrument in revealing knowledge about the self: "By surrendering myself at the same time to the memory of the impression received and the present feeling, I shall paint a double picture of the state of my soul, namely, at the moment in which the event occurred and at the moment I described it."[13] Yet the memory serves not only to reveal the self more fully than other modes of knowledge, it has also a kind of moral function in that it provides a source of strength to fortify him in his old age: "How I love, from time to time, to come upon the pleasant moments of my youth! They were so sweet! They have been so brief, so rare, and I have enjoyed them at such slight cost! Ah, their mere memory still gives my heart a pure delight, which I need in order to restore my courage and to sustain the tedium of my remaining years."[14]

Finally, the process of memory, through the chain of associations it sets into operation, serves to confound our

[12] *Confessions*, p. 31.
[13] Manuscript reproduced in the Pléiade edition of the *Confessions* (Paris, 1951), p. 756 (my translation).
[14] *Confessions*, tr. Cohen, p. 132.

ommon-sense conceptions of the nature of time. For in-
tance, on moving to the country after a long stay in Paris,
Rousseau was reminded of an idyllic experience that had
aken place long before, and this memory, in turn, recalls
he various women from different periods of his life and
rings them together in a single, powerful moment of
ime:

". . . I started remembering the dinner at the Château
e Toune and my meeting with those two charming girls,
t the same season and in country more or less similar to
he country I was in at that moment. This memory, which
as the sweeter for the innocence associated with it, re-
alled others of the same kind to me. Soon I saw all around
ne the persons I had felt emotion for in my youth: Mlle
alley, Mlle de Graffenried, Mlle de Breil, Mme Basile,
Mme de Larnage, my pretty music pupils, and even the
nticing Giulietta, whom my heart can never forget. I saw
ayself surrounded by a seraglio of houris, by my old ac-
uaintances a strong desire for whom was no new sensation
o me. My blood caught fire, my head turned despite its
rey hairs, and there was the grave citizen of Geneva, the
ustere Jean-Jacques at almost forty-five, suddenly become
nce more the love-sick swain. The intoxication that seized
ne, although so sudden and so foolish, was so strong and
asting that it took nothing less than the unforeseen and
rrible crisis it brought upon me to cure me of it."[15]

Memory has here become a creative act, fusing together
verse images of the past, substituting a wholly new order
time for the old, creating—by the energy of the emotion
releases—a type of vision which, in turn, alters the sub-
ct's present condition. With this last quotation, indeed,
e enter that area of the modern sensibility which has been
ost powerfully symbolized for us through Proust's tast-
g of the *madeleine*. To summarize, then, one can dis-

[15] *Ibid.*, p. 397.

tinguish at least four ways in which the memory function for Rousseau: (1) as an end worthy in itself, through the vivid and pleasing quality of early memories; (2) as a way of apprehending knowledge, through its ability to reveal the truth of inward states; (3) as an instrument of grace through its ability to shed the influence of an idyllic past upon an impoverished present and future; and (4) as force in the conquest of time, through its ability to fuse together events from diverse periods with imaginative power and thus to reconstitute the conventional order of time.

All these aspects of memory are implicit in *The Prelude* despite the fundamental differences between the personalities of Rousseau and Wordsworth. On a fairly obvious level, Wordsworth keeps the reader aware always of the "charm of visionary things" which the retrospective process, as he declares in the passage I have attached to the chapter as epigraph, helps to uncover. But Wordsworth attitude toward time also determined—as this and the following chapter will attempt to show—the fundamental organization of the poem, both in the basic units out of which it is composed and in its larger structure; indeed Wordsworth's characteristic mode of organization represents something unique in the history of English poetry and, from our present vantage-point, gives *The Prelude* a peculiarly modern tone. More fundamental yet, the obsession with time which underlies the work obviously proceeds from something more than a desire for technical innovation, but is itself rooted in a larger philosophical and moral quest: a quest for the restoration of the power associated with a lost or fading past. Beyond that, the obsession gives significance to that private order of time the time of personal experience, revery, intuition—which for both Rousseau and Wordsworth, serves essentially an image of timelessness to confound the pretensions of public, calendar time.

4. THE STRUCTURAL UNIT: "SPOTS OF TIME"

> ... There's not a man
> That lives who hath not had his godlike hours
> (III, 191-192)

It is characteristic of Wordsworth's retrospective method that the reader always remains aware of two points of time, the bleak, quiet present, in which the poet sits writing to Coleridge and meditating upon the epic task imposed by his ambition to create a poem on "Nature, Man, and Society," and the deep well of the personal past to which he returns again and again so that he

> might fetch
> Invigorating thoughts from former years,
> Might fix the wavering balance of my mind,
> And haply meet reproaches, too, whose power
> May spur me on, in manhood now mature,
> To honorable toil.   (I, 648-653)

This past, the quest for which in fact is the substance of *The Prelude*, is not re-created in and for itself, but only within the perspective of the present, through which alone it derives meaning. Wordsworth's method, one might say, is the antithesis of that of the historical novelist, who seeks to immerse his readers so fully in the re-created past that, if he succeeds, they lose sight of any reality outside this past. Wordsworth's past, no matter how vivid and "invigorating" it may be, never aims toward an autonomy of this sort; moreover, through the influence that the past exerts upon the present, and through his much-repeated desire to find nourishment in the past, he constantly engages in a two-way movement, back and forth, between present and past.

The characteristic form which Wordsworth developed to probe into the past is the "spot of time," a term he coined to describe two childhood incidents narrated in Book XI. The "spot of time" is defined in terms of its salutary effects upon him:

> There are in our existence spots of time,
> Which with distinct pre-eminence retain
> A vivifying Virtue, whence . . .
>   our minds
> Are nourished and invisibly repair'd. . . .
>   (XI, 258-265)

But the "spot of time" can also be viewed as a literary form—one peculiar to *The Prelude* as it is not, for instance, to *The Excursion* or, for that matter, to the contemplative poetry of the preceding century. At its simplest level the "spot" is the record of a concrete past event used to illustrate some more general statements about the past. Take, for example, the passage in which Wordsworth recaptures his moment of self-dedication to poetry:

> The memory of one particular hour
> Doth here rise up against me. In a throng,
> A festal company of Maids and Youths,
> Old Men, and Matrons staid, promiscuous rout,
> A medley of all tempers, I had pass'd
> The night in dancing, gaiety and mirth;
> With din of instruments, and shuffling feet,
> And glancing forms, and tapers glittering,
> And unaim'd prattle flying up and down,
> Spirits upon the stretch, and here and there
> Slight shocks of young love-liking interspers'd,
> That mounted up like joy into the head,

And tingled through the veins. Ere we retired,
The cock had crow'd, the sky was bright with day.
Two miles I had to walk along the fields
Before I reached my home. Magnificent
The morning was, a memorable pomp,
More glorious than I ever had beheld.
The Sea was laughing at a distance; all
The solid Mountains were as bright as clouds,
Grain-tinctured, drench'd in empyrean light;
And, in the meadows and the lower grounds,
Was all the sweetness of a common dawn,
Dews, vapours, and the melody of birds,
And Labourers going forth into the fields.
—Ah! need I say, dear Friend, that to the brim
My heart was full; I made no vows, but vows
Were then made for me; bond unknown to me
Was given, that I should be, else sinning greatly,
A dedicated Spirit. On I walk'd
In blessedness, which even yet remains.

(IV, 315-345)

On one level, at least, one could view this memory as a
sort of anecdote, called forth in the poet's mind by association and framed on each side by general commentary
about the course of his life. At bottom, however, the passage strives to accomplish more than it at first pretends, for
the anecdote itself must create the transition from the off-
handed introductory remark ("The memory of one particular hour / Doth here rise up against me") to the culminating statement ("On I walk'd / In blessedness, which
even yet remains"). By the end of the passage, with its
celebration of the ability of the past to project its powers
into the present, Wordsworth has shifted context from
casual reminiscence to religious vision.

In its whole rhetorical development the passage is typi-

cal of innumerable other "spots of time" scattered throughout *The Prelude*. Like the episode about the stolen boat
in Book I ("One evening . . . I went alone into a Shepherd's Boat") it starts out by describing a tangible world
of more or less ordinary things, in this instance a public
celebration that occurs at regular intervals, almost like a
ritual, to break the monotony of country routine. But its
ritual quality ("a *festal* company") seems strictly secular
in nature and only later in the description does the reader
even become aware of the emotional effect it has upon
Wordsworth ("Slight shocks of young love-liking . . ./
That mounted up like joy into the head / And tingled
through the veins"). The passion released here still remains essentially physical, though it points forward to the
spiritual vision encompassed in the images of the sea and
mountains, above all in the phrase "empyrean light." By
the end of the passage everything that passes through the
poet's view—fields, birds, laborers going off to their daily
routine—all are endowed with a religious aura. The passage progresses, one might say, from "trivial pleasures" to
"deeper passions" (both of these phrases are drawn from
an introductory passage to this "spot of time"—ll. 305
310); from a world of transitory things to intimations of a
more eternal realm (which includes even the "Labourer
going forth," who, in contrast to the dancers, are tied to
the recurring cycle of nature); from the language of prose
("the memory of one particular hour") through a landscape appropriate to the short lyric ("and shuffling feet,
And glancing forms, and tapers glittering") to the Miltonic
grandeur of the later lines ("Magnificent / The morning
was, a memorable pomp"). In time the passage moves from
a sense of great distance between Wordsworth's present
state and the event he is depicting ("I *had pass'd* / The
night in dancing") to a gradual apprehension of the oneness of past and present ("On I walk'd / In blessedness

which even yet remains"); moreover, what was trivial in the past—the surface gaiety of the dance—still retains its great distance in time, while the visionary experience of that night remains within him to dissolve the boundaries which the conceptualizing mind has created between present and past.

5. EMOTION REFRACTED

"In Wordsworth's most excited mood we have rather the reflexion of the flame than the authentic and derivative fire itself. Its heat and glare pass to us through some less pervious and colder lens."

Thus complained the *Gentleman's Magazine* in 1850,[16] in a review of the newly published *Prelude*. The "fire itself," so conspicuously lacking in Wordsworth's poem, was amply to be found in Shelley's work, the reviewer assured his readers. To a mid-Victorian audience, accustomed as it was to a more heightened and direct expression of emotion than Wordsworth was willing to give, *The Prelude* must have seemed a relatively tame poem, too much akin, perhaps, to the contemplative verse of the eighteenth century to thrill the reader with the impassioned sweep he so much admired in *Prometheus Unbound*.

That "less pervious and colder lens" to which the reviewer objects might be described as Wordsworth's habit of approaching the more intense areas of his experience only by first insisting on their great distance in time. One might, in fact, speak of the "spot of time" as a distancing device, a way of portraying emotion by refracting it through experiences far distant from the present. The invariably prosaic openings of the "spots":

> When summer came
> It was the pastime of our afternoons . . .

16 N.S. XXXIV, p. 460.

> Upon a small
> And rocky Island near, a fragment stood
> (Itself like a sea rock) of what had been
> A Romish Chapel . . .
>
> One Christmas-time,
> The day before the Holidays began . . .
> (II, 55-56; X, 518-521; XI, 345-346)

serve as a sort of lens through which the feelings about to
be uncovered may be refracted and brought into open
view. It is as though the poet were too reticent to release
emotions directly, as though the distancing in time and the
casualness of tone could make a deeply personal experience
less overtly and embarrassingly personal; in our own age,
indeed, the Victorian demand for the "flame itself" seems
considerably more antiquated than Wordsworth's attempt
to objectify feelings by refraction, a process which has
something in common with such modern attempts to im-
personalize emotions as we have come to characterize by the
terms *persona, mask,* and *objective correlative.* Wordsworth, in fact, is sometimes at pains to separate his past
self, which it is the object of the poem to explore, from the
present self which speaks directly to the reader:

> So wide appears
> The vacancy between me and those days,
> Which yet have such self-presence in my mind
> That, sometimes, when I think of them, I seem
> Two consciousnesses, conscious of myself
> And of some other Being.   (II, 28-33)

But if the spot of time in one sense serves to set emotion
at an appropriately classical distance, in another sense it
works to reawaken and set free long-since-forgotten feelings which, in turn, give new life and energy to the present.
Or, to put it another way, the restrained classicism that

[148]

characterizes the spot of time as a literary technique is counterbalanced through the claims which the spot of time makes for the meaningfulness of powerful feelings.

The ability of the retrospective process to help give vitality to the present through exploration of the past is at its most conspicuous, perhaps, in that spot of time in Book XI in which the poet describes his childhood visit to the scene where a murderer had once been executed. What is extraordinary about the passage is that Wordsworth does not explore merely a single past event, but that he moves through several separate points of time, each recalling the next by association and each, as it were, gathering up energy from the last. The passage starts out in the same casual way as the other spots of time:

> At a time
> When scarcely (I was then not six years old)
> My hand could hold a bridle, with proud hopes
> I mounted, and we rode towards the hills:
> We were a pair of Horsemen; honest James
> Was with me, my encourager and guide.
> We had not travell'd long, ere some mischance
> Disjoin'd me from my Comrade, and, through fear
> Dismounting, down the rough and stony Moor
> I led my Horse, and stumbling on, at length
> Came to a bottom, where in former times
> A Murderer had been hung in iron chains.
> The Gibbet-mast was moulder'd down, the bones
> And iron case were gone; but on the turf,
> Hard by, soon after that fell deed was wrought
> Some unknown hand had carved the Murderer's name.
>
> (279-294)

Thus far, we have no reason to expect anything more than straightforward narrative, something on the order of "Michael." The fussy preciseness with which Wordsworth interjects his age ("I was then not six years old"), the introduction of "honest James" as though he were already quite familiar to the reader, the painstakingness with which each of the poet's movements is recorded—all point to a prime concern with the things of this world. Only in the light of what follows would one look back on these details and speculate on more symbolic meanings: that the journey into the hills and into past time is as much a spiritual as a physical journey; and, moreover, that the story of the execution is weighted with some symbolic meaning (witness the "unknown hand," the "moulder'd" gibbet-mast, the phrase "in former times," whose plural form suggests a vast world of the past and points forward to the "times long past" a few lines later). The underlying significance of the incident becomes more evident in the lines that follow:

> The monumental writing was engraven
> In times long past, and still, from year to year,
> By superstition of the neighborhood,
> The grass is clear'd away; and to this hour
> The letters are all fresh and visible.
> Faltering, and ignorant where I was, at length
> I chanced to espy those characters inscribed
> On the green sod: forthwith I left the spot
> And, reascending the bare Common, saw
> A naked Pool that lay beneath the hills,
> The Beacon on the summit, and more near,
> A Girl who bore a Pitcher on her head
> And seem'd with difficult steps to force her way
> Against the blowing wind. It was, in truth,
> An ordinary sight; but I should need
> Colours and words that are unknown to man
> To paint the visionary dreariness
> Which, while I look'd all round for my lost Guide,

Did at that time invest the naked Pool,
The Beacon on the lonely Eminence,
The Woman, and her garments vex'd and toss'd
By the strong wind.   (295-316)

Thus far we are aware of three separate points of time: the present, from which Wordsworth looks back to his childhood and from which, in turn, a new perspective is introduced upon far earlier times. The "monumental" quality of the carved letters; the ritual of clearing away the grass (in citing local superstitions Wordsworth anticipates a device employed by novelists like Hawthorne to hint at deeper meanings which they neither wish to verify nor make too explicit); the ever-lasting "freshness" of the letters (contrasting with the "moulder'd gibbet-mast," as if to indicate the vitality latent in the seemingly dead past) —all, by the very intensity they call forth, prepare the ground (literally even) for the vision that follows. At this point the poet confronts the letters directly and, as though instinctively gathering up the energies latent within the scene, begins a new "journey," upward, to a point from which he can view the three objects—the pool, the beacon, the girl—which form the center of the vision. Yet these objects, awesome as they seem to the poet, are presented on a naturalistic level—an "ordinary sight," as Wordsworth at first puts it—and are not drawn from any recognizable tradition of symbols. If one encountered such images in the work of a conscious symbolist such as Blake or Shelley one would feel impelled to seek out a symbolic meaning for each of them. But in the present context the three images seem less significant for the individual meanings which we can assign to them than for the total effect which they produce. Through the animating medium of the wind they are fused together into a single momentous vision, which in its bleakness and fierceness seems to suggest the precariousness of human endeavor in the face of larger forces (the girl balancing the pitcher on her head is still another of Wordsworth's figures of endurance, like Margaret in *The Ruined Cottage*). Beyond that, the wind, with all the brute power which it symbolizes, sets into motion a new, even more intense movement of thought. As though having gathered something of its power within himself, Wordsworth moves forward once more to the present time in order to contemplate the past vision in still fuller perspective. Once again, in the final lines quoted, the three objects reappear, but the tone with which they are listed is more formal, almost declamatory, as if to indicate the far greater intensity with which they are now charged in his mind.

Thus far the incident is complete as it was first written, probably in 1798. But Wordsworth added still a new perspective in time in 1804, during the later stages of the poem's composition:

> When, in a blessed season
> With those two dear Ones, to my heart so dear,
> When in the blessed time of early love,
> Long afterwards, I roam'd about
> In daily presence of this very scene,
> Upon the naked pool and dreary crags,
> And on the melancholy Beacon, fell
> The spirit of pleasure and youth's golden gleam;
> And think ye not with radiance more divine
> From these remembrances, and from the power
> They left behind? So feeling comes in aid
> Of feeling, and diversity of strength
> Attends us, if but once we have been strong.
> Oh! mystery of Man, from what a depth
> Proceed thy honours! I am lost, but see
> In simple childhood something of the base

On which thy greatness stands, but this I feel,
That from thyself it is that thou must give
Else never canst receive. The days gone by
Come back upon me from the dawn almost
Of life: the hiding-places of my power
Seem open; I approach, and then they close;
I see by glimpses now; when age comes on,
May scarcely see at all, and I would give,
While yet we may, as far as words can give,
A substance and a life to what I feel:
I would enshrine the spirit of the past
For future restoration.   (316-343)

In its final development the memory of this dreary scene
is refracted through still another memory, this one benign
with "the spirit of pleasure and youth's golden gleam." To
put it another way, the memory of early love works to
transform the "visionary dreariness" of the earlier memory
into a more benign, though no less forceful power. If I
may take up once more the metaphor with which I started,
the energies latent in Wordsworth's memories are like rays
of light that pass through a prism and reveal constantly
new possibilities of color to the observing eye. But analogies will go only a short way to illuminate a process which
remains so largely implicit in the text. Wordsworth himself describes the process with deliberate imprecision: "So
feeling comes in aid / Of feeling. . . ." Thus, while reflecting in 1798 upon the meaning of his earliest memories,
he cites a particular incident which occurred when he was
six; reflection upon this incident, in turn, opens up a more
distant and impersonal past, the time of the murderer's
execution ("Times long past"); and this memory, in turn,
recalls another, much later personal memory, from his
eighteenth or nineteenth year. But if this process, on one
level, consists of a simple, though non-chronological, line

of mental associations, on another level it takes the form of a mysterious and complex transfer of power, both backward and forward, from one period of time to another: the memory of young love, though recalled by the frightening earlier childhood memory, sets this earlier memory into a new, more benign perspective and thus transforms it, while the combined effect of these memories will project into the future—a future well beyond the time of writing —to comfort the aging poet and, beyond that, through the "substance" and "life" with which they have been endowed in his poetry, to exert their effect upon readers in an even more distant future. And yet the whole process— down to the climactic statement, "Oh! mystery of Man, from what a depth / Proceed thy honours!"—seems to follow so naturally from the incident narrated off-handedly at the beginning that the reader is scarcely aware of the complexity of the thought structure into which he has been led.

In a discussion of another spot of time—the one directly following, of the poet waiting in the storm at Christmastime for the horses to fetch him home—A. C. Bradley long ago remarked, "Everything here is natural, but everything is apocalyptic. And we happen to know why. Wordsworth is describing the scene in the light of memory."[17] The writer who sets out to recapture the past can thus do two things simultaneously: on the pretext of telling the reader something about himself he can uncover an objective, tangible world and at the same time he can cast a mythical aura about it. He can reveal it in all its concrete fullness and he can use it as a symbol of still another world behind it. He can be both realist and symbolist at once.

One could speculate that Wordsworth's decision to make the recovery of his own past the subject of *The Prelude* forced him to develop that peculiar approach to metaphor

[17] *Oxford Lectures on Poetry*, p. 134.

which, in Chapter Three, I described in my discussion of his "images of interaction." Facing the dual task of retelling past events and at the same time convincing the reader of their significance, he developed a way of doing both at once: reality became symbol, concrete detail became abstraction, description became assertion, tenor and vehicle became indistinguishable. What separates *The Prelude* at once from the poems of personal or pseudo-personal reminiscence of the late eighteenth century is the fact that the individual memories and the poet's discursive comments upon them are no longer scattered about, tied to one another only by association, but rather that Wordsworth has worked out a new rhetorical form, a new genre, in fact, to fuse together concrete perception and a statement of its significance, and beyond that to make poetry assert and celebrate at the same time that it describes and analyzes. Earl R. Wasserman, in his recent attempt to define the essential difference between eighteenth- and nineteenth-century poetry, described the task of the romantic poets in the following terms:

"Largely deprived of *topoi* rich in publicly accessible values and cut off from the older conceptions of world-orders, they [the poets of the early nineteenth century] were compelled to cultivate fresh values in the objects of experience and to organize these values into a special structure within the poem so as to avail themselves of the expressive powers of a revivified vocabulary and a new syntactical system. It is, therefore, not merely in the overt statements, often disarmingly simple, but especially in the inner subtleties of their language—in the recurrences and transformations of images, in what superficially might seem only a convenient and otherwise purposeless turn of phrase, for example—that we must seek the articulation of a modern poem's fullest meaning."[18]

[18] *The Subtler Language*, pp. 251-52.

The spot of time, one might say, is that "special structure" which Wordsworth organized out of the objects of
his personal experience—a structure, moreover, which
articulates its meanings not primarily through traditional
figures of speech appealing to an outward frame of reference, but by creating its own rhetoric—for instance,
through the use of different intensities of tone at each of
the three times the images of the pool, the beacon, and the
girl with the pitcher appear—which in turn evolves its
own inner frame of reference.

The poetic values represented by the spot of time, rooted
as they are in concrete experience, have become so central
a part of modern poetic tradition that, despite the obvious
differences between the language of modern poetry and
Wordsworth's "rhetoric of interaction," we often tend to
read *The Prelude* piecemeal for its spots of time. "*The
Prelude* is at the center of our experience of Wordsworth;
at the center of our experience of *The Prelude* are those
'spots of time' where Wordsworth is endeavoring to express
key moments in the history of his imagination"[19]—thus
begins a recent psychological interpretation of these passages. To the extent that the spots of time attempt to fragmentize experience or to work toward the evocation of
pure states of being—the "trances of thought and mountings of the mind" to which Wordsworth refers at the
opening of the poem—they point forward to that conception of what was properly poetic which, in the century after
The Prelude, was increasingly to claim exclusive domain
over the province of poetry. If we have been inclined, perhaps, to lift the spots of time too readily out of their larger
context, this is not merely a sign of their special modernity,
but also, as I argued in the last chapter, of the fact that we
have lost the art of reading long poems.

[19] Jonathan Bishop, "Wordsworth and the 'Spots of Time,'" ELH, XXVI
(1959), 45.

CHAPTER SIX

TIME-CONSCIOUSNESS (2)

1. SOME STUDIES IN WORDSWORTHIAN TIME

And, as it works, th' industrious bee
Computes its time as well as we!

> Marvell's "Garden"

The thought of our past years in me doth breed
Perpetual benediction.

> "Immortality Ode"

An act of vision is no substitute. There is
no other way to solve the problem of time than
the way through physics.

> Hans Reichenbach, *The Direction of Time*

a. *Living in the Present*

THE "characters" of *The Prelude*, what few there are, can be divided according to the relationship they maintain with time. There are, first of all, those shadowy figures, like the discharged soldier, the Arab with the allegorical shell and stone, or the blind beggar on the London streets, who do not belong to the ordinary world of time. As representatives of "the utmost that we know, / Both of ourselves and of the universe," their function is to "admonish from another world" (vii, 618-622), which is, in fact, the timeless world of eternity. These figures will not concern us at this point. At an opposite extreme are those few characters, most notably Wordsworth's mother and sister, who, though part of the temporal world, are wholly in harmony with it. Thus, the poet describes his mother as one who

Was not puff'd up by false unnatural hopes;
Nor selfish with unnecessary cares;
Nor with impatience from the season ask'd
More than its timely produce: *rather lov'd*
The hours for what they are than from regards
Glanced on their promises in restless pride.

(v, 279-284; italics mine)

Satisfied as she was with her lot, making but few demands
on life, she moved along unselfconsciously with the flow of
time. Her thoughts were neither in the past nor future,
but were rooted only in the present. Dorothy, too, knew
only the present moment, and Wordsworth portrays her,
more specifically than their mother, as a part of the
natural order of things:

... Wise as Women are
When genial circumstance hath favor'd them,
She welcom'd what was given, and craved no more.
Whatever scene was present to her eyes,
That was the best, to that she was attuned
Through her humility and lowliness,
And through a perfect happiness of soul ...
For she was Nature's inmate. (XI, 205-214)

But Wordsworth, too, had once possessed this harmony
with things as they are:

I worshipp'd then among the depths of things
As my soul bade me. . . .
I felt, and nothing else; I did not judge,
I never thought of judging, with the gift
Of all this glory fill'd and satisfi'd.

(XI, 234-240)

Through the intellectualizing faculty, so he reminds us
throughout *The Prelude*, this preexisting harmony has

been destroyed; one could define the poem—indeed, all his major poems—as an attempt to restore something of this state by recapturing, in a sense even "reharnessing" the energies latent in the past. "Only through time time is conquered."

One remembers that much-explicated passage in "Tintern Abbey" in which Wordsworth recapitulates the stages of his growth, from the "aching joys" and "giddy raptures" of "thoughtless youth" (at the time he first visited the scene in 1793) to that more self-conscious state in which he hears "the still, sad music of humanity." We have been accustomed to view these stages as changes in his relationship with nature, because, after all, he describes them in those terms. But we can look at them equally as changes in his conception of time; indeed, what chiefly characterizes his earlier relationship to time (whether during childhood or as late as 1793) is the fact that he lacks any conscious conception of it. Like the fleeing animal to which he compares himself he is totally at the mercy of the present moment. His time is the time of the natural order, and he ties himself unreflectingly to its rhythm. If "Tintern Abbey" only hints at the nature of this earlier stage, the first two books of *The Prelude* recapture it in all its fullness. The very language of the early spots of time attempts to render the fullness of each present moment:

> Oh! many a time have I, a five years' Child . . .
> Made one long bathing of a summer's day,
> Bask'd in the sun, and plunged, and bask'd again
> Alternate all a summer's day . . .

> (I, 291-296)

> Oh! at that time,
> While on the perilous ridge I hung alone,
> With what strange utterance did the loud dry wind

Blow through my ears! the sky seem'd not a sky
Of earth, and with what motion mov'd the clouds!

(I, 346-350)

The first few spots of time even manage to cover the whole seasonal cycle—from the high summer of the first spot (I, 291-304); to autumn and spring in the story of the stolen bird's nest (309-350); summer (in all probability) in the episode of the stolen boat (372-427); and finally deepest winter in the ice-skating episode (452-489).

Yet, however successful Wordsworth's re-creation of his past self, we are constantly reminded of its pastness: its artistic embodiment is, after all, the spot of time, and the reader often marvels at the vividness with which events explicitly part of the distant past are made to seem present. The spot of time, by its very nature, must ultimately return the reader to the state of Wordsworth at the time he is writing his poem. Only Dorothy was able to retain her earlier relation to time during adulthood. Her real function in "Tintern Abbey," in fact, is like that of the natural scene itself, for it helps restore within the poet his earlier, lost self:

> And in thy voice I catch
> The language of my former heart, and read
> My former pleasures in the shooting lights
> Of thy wild eyes. Oh! yet a little while
> May I behold in thee what I was once,
> My dear, dear Sister!

It is no accident, of course, that Dorothy found her characteristic form of expression in the day-to-day journal entry. The mode of description exemplified by the following passage, for example, is wholly alien to her brother's art: "Went in the evening into the Coombe to get eggs; returned through the wood, and walked in the park. A duller night than last night: a sort of white shade over the blue sky. The stars dim. The spring continues to advance very slowly, no green trees, the hedges leafless; nothing green but the brambles that still retain their old leaves, the evergreens, and the palms, which indeed are not absolutely green. Some brambles I observed to-day budding afresh, and those have shed their old leaves. The crooked arm of the old oak tree points upwards to the moon."[1]

Wordsworth would have used this type of material only at the opening of a spot of time; the descriptive details would gradually have given way to reflective thought, in fact, to an attempt to apprehend a reality behind time and the present moment. The very casualness of Dorothy's art —with its random movement between tenses (as though she had no need to distinguish between past and present); the ease with which it moves from the domestic duty of getting eggs to the more lofty enterprise of nature observation—these betray a sensibility securely rooted in the present. The difference between her and her brother can be defined, perhaps, through the distinction which Schiller (who was observing the difference between himself and Goethe[2]) made between the "naïve" and the "sentimental" poet, the one who was still close to nature in all its pristine freshness and the one who was forced to make a conscious effort to apprehend nature in this condition. While Dorothy's eyes, as Wordsworth expressed it in "Tintern Abbey," still cast back "gleams / Of past existence," he himself

[1] *Journals*, ed. E. De Selincourt (London, 1952), I, 13.
[2] In a penetrating essay, "Goethe and Wordsworth: A Point of Contrast," Barker Fairley makes a central distinction between the German and the English poet by examining their attitudes toward time. Goethe's thought, says Fairley, represents "the antithesis of the Wordsworthian retrospect . . . . His life, his vision, his philosophy is rooted in the present and the past is never allowed to challenge it." (*Publications of the English Goethe Society*, N.S. X [1934], 31, 33.) One could go further and note that in his affirmation of the present, Goethe was unique among the major poets of his time.

must employ more conscious means such as retrospection to achieve the condition which is naturally hers. And if Wordsworth's art is an ancestor to the modern time-book, with its tortured and often monumental search for freshness of vision, Dorothy's is more closely akin to that of Goethe and Thoreau, whose first concern was the full and vivid apprehension of the present moment.

There is but one passage in *The Prelude* which seeks to celebrate the present, and that is the opening, in which Wordsworth rejoices at his liberation from the city in 1795 as he set out for his life of country retirement:

Oh there is blessing in this gentle breeze
That blows from the green fields and from the clouds
And from the sky: it beats against my cheek,
And seems half-conscious of the joy it gives. . . .

(I, 1-4)

Yet throughout the passage his present joy is interrupted by his consciousness of past and future—the bleak past he had experienced in the teeming city and the still uncertain but hopeful future:

What dwelling shall receive me? In what Vale
Shall be my harbour? Underneath what grove
Shall I take up my home, and what sweet stream
Shall with its murmur lull me to my rest?

(I, 11-14)

And in a later passage, when he could consider this moment as a spot of past, rather than present time, he had occasion to note its temporary aspect:

Five years are vanish'd since I first pour'd out . . .
A glad preamble to this verse: I sang
Aloud, in Dythyrambic fervour, deep
But short-liv'd uproar, like a torrent sent

Out of the bowels of a bursting cloud. . . .

(VII, 1-7)

For those cut off from the direct relation to nature that
was Dorothy's, vision is at best a short-lived thing.

And yet there exists a magnificent extended passage of
Wordsworthian blank verse which is set emphatically in
the present. I am thinking of Book One of *The Recluse*,
"Home at Grasmere," which was written in the months
following his return to the Lake District with Dorothy in
December, 1799. The work thus falls between the two
periods during which *The Prelude* was composed; yet it
is hard to imagine anything less akin to the spirit of the
longer poem. For "Home at Grasmere" is essentially a
hymn of thanksgiving, a celebration of the world into
which he had settled and which, in contrast to the world
of the past which dominates *The Prelude*, he was in the
process of discovering and experiencing even as he wrote:

> Embrace me then, ye Hills, and close me in,
> Now in the clear and open day I feel
> Your guardianship; I take it to my heart;
> 'Tis like the solemn shelter of the night.
> But I would call thee beautiful, for mild
> And soft, and gay, and beautiful thou art,
> Dear Valley, having in thy face a smile
> Though peaceful, full of gladness.

(PW, V, 317)

Instead of the driving search for lost time which motivates
The Prelude, a mood of almost total calmness governs the
lines. Words such as "calm," "soft," "beautiful," "peaceful," "gladness" are characteristic not only of this passage,
but of the whole book as well; and if the beauty which
Wordsworth depicts in *The Prelude* must there admit the
companionship of terror, the beauty retains sole dominance

in "Home at Grasmere." Even the bleaker aspects of nature seem benign here:

> The naked Trees,
> The icy brooks, as on we passed, appeared
> To question us. "Whence come ye? to what end?"
> They seemed to say; "What would ye," said the
>   shower,
> "Wild Wanderers, whither through my dark
>   domain?"
> The sunbeam said, "be happy."   (p. 319)

The "visionary dreariness" so characteristic of the landscape of *The Prelude* here gives way to something near playfulness. Unlike the benign landscapes of the longer poem, which Wordsworth treats as islands in time and which often, indeed, take the form of actual islands, the vale of Grasmere is a total and permanent world unto itself, a paradise which will withstand the pressures of time and the outside world:

> 'Tis the sense
> Of majesty, and beauty, and repose,
> A blended holiness of earth and sky,
> Something that makes this individual Spot
> This small Abiding-place of many Men,
> A termination, and a last retreat,
> A Centre, come from wheresoe'er you will,
> A Whole without dependence or defect,
> Made for itself; and happy in itself,
> Perfect Contentment, Unity entire.
>   (p. 318)

Conventional categories of time do not apply to this valley paradise, for it remains a perpetually present spot of time, one which the poet need not strive to seek out:

'Tis here,
Here as it found its way into my heart
In childhood, here as it abides by day,
By night, here only; or in chosen minds
That take it with them hence, where'er they go.

. . .

Long,
Oh long may it remain inviolate,
Diffusing health and sober cheerfulness,
And giving to the moments as they pass
Their little boons of animating thought. . . .

(pp. 317, 328)

And consequently, unlike the other poems of his major period, "Home at Grasmere" need make no real distinction between the stages of Wordsworth's growth; it celebrates neither his past self nor the present self of the "philosophic mind," toward which the "Immortality Ode" so festively builds: rather, the poet appears as one who has been no more affected by the changes of time than the vale itself. As a literary work "Home at Grasmere" reveals a considerably lower level of intensity than *The Prelude* or the ode; we miss the forward movement, the struggle toward definition, the whole larger drama of interaction—which here takes the gentle form exemplified in the line "Embrace me then, ye Hills, and close me in"—that characterizes the other poems. It is an uneven work, at its best radiating a sense of harmony and ever-present grace largely lacking elsewhere in Wordsworth's major poetry; though but a fragment of a larger work whose real nature must always have seemed uncertain to the poet, it seems to play the role of a Paradise Regained to *The Prelude*'s Paradise Lost. But it also has a rather static quality, a meditative formlessness without the rhetoric and metrical devices which might have given form to a more conventional ode

[165]

of thanksgiving; written as it is essentially in the language of *The Prelude*, it remains in a way a single sprawling spot of time. Yet, with *The Ruined Cottage*, which the poet buried in the now-forgotten pages of *The Excursion*, "Home at Grasmere" is one of Wordsworth's two neglected masterpieces. First published in 1888, under even less favorable circumstances than the posthumous *Prelude*, it remains without the critical tradition that creates and defines a place for great works in the history of our culture. But to the degree that it contains a vision of life both antithetical and complementary to that of *The Prelude*, it demands consideration in any extended discussion of the longer poem.

b. Inner and Outer

> ... And all
> That I beheld respired with inward meaning.
> (III, 128-129)

"The artificial, the merely miraculous, the event which had no inner meaning, no matter how large externally it might be, I did not care for. . . . Of more importance . . . was the birth of a habit of inner reference and a dislike to occupy myself with anything which did not in some way or other touch the soul."[3] In these words William Hale White described the powerful effect which the reading of *Lyrical Ballads*, which he had come across accidentally among a parcel of books, had had on him while he was in college. If he had not discovered the volume, he might well have experienced the same conversion a year or two later, in 1850, when *The Prelude* was published. For *The Prelude*, far more explicitly than *Lyrical Ballads*, maintains a contrast between those forms of experience which it dismisses as external and those others, inevitably more difficult to

---

[3] *Autobiography of Mark Rutherford* (London, 1881), pp. 26, 24.

achieve and describe, which it dignifies with terms such as *inner* and *inward*.

The difference between outer and inner reality in *The Prelude* is essentially the difference between two conceptions of time, the one regular and mechanical, the other unpredictable and allusive, in tune with the rhythms of nature and, indeed, with what is eternal and thus timeless. The mechanical time of the external world is the time measured in regular intervals by clocks, like "Trinity's loquacious Clock, / Who never let the Quarters, night or day, / Slip by him unproclaim'd" (III, 51-53)—an appropriate enough symbol for the external world which Cambridge represented for Wordsworth. Or in Book I, where the poet is still firmly a part of the inner world of early childhood, he is able to defy the demands of clock-time:

> It was a time of rapture: clear and loud
> The village clock toll'd six; I wheel'd about,
> Proud and exulting, like an untired horse,
> That cares not for its home.   (457-460)

For nature knows its own unmeasurable organic time, which reveals its pulse to the poet on privileged occasions, for instance, in the "faint / Internal breezes, sobbings of the place, / And respirations" (II, 128-130) which he describes after a rainstorm. In a partially rejected passage, moreover, he speaks of

> Incumbences more awful, visitings
> Of the Upholder of the tranquil Soul,
> Which regulates the motions of all life
> And tolerates the indignities of time
> Till time shall cease. . . .
>
> (*Prel.*, pp. 76-78)

Indeed, it is generally in those books that deal specifically with the external life—above all the book on Cambridge

—that he has most frequent occasion to refer to the time of nature, as in his indictment of Cambridge for tying him down to external routine, during which time "the inner pulse / Of contemplation almost fail'd to beat" (III, 337-338). While summarizing his Cambridge years, he gives us still another perspective on inward reality:

> Hush'd, meanwhile,
> Was the under soul, lock'd up in such a calm,
> That not a leaf of the great nature stirr'd.
> (III, 539-541)

Like Wordsworth's other word coinages in *The Prelude*— *under-powers* (I, 163), *under-countenance* (VI, 236, a reference to the powers latent within a single human soul, in fact, his bride-to-be), *under-thirst* (VI, 489), and *under-presence* (XIII, 71)—the "under soul," whatever its origins in the mystic tradition, is essentially a symbol of the life within: as a metaphor of direction *under* can work more powerfully than *inner*.

"A worshipper of worldly seemliness"—so Wordsworth categorizes the type of child produced by the external-minded education he condemns in Book V. *The Prelude* includes three major symbols for worldly externality— Cambridge, London, and the France of the Revolution— each of course distinguishable from the other in individual detail, yet all surprisingly similar through the problems they create in the poet's inward development. With each, for one thing, there are frequent interludes in which he retreats from the outer world, where, as at Cambridge, he turned "the mind in upon itself, / Pored, watch'd, expected, listen'd; spread my thoughts / And spread them with a wider creeping" (III, 112-114). But inevitably he is forced back into outer reality, only once more to seek out a retreat, and finally to escape from it altogether. It is noteworthy that the outer world is generally characterized by considerable turmoil and noise: the "humming sound" from the kitchens beneath the poet's room in Cambridge, the "roar" and "thickening hubbub" of the London streets (the latter perhaps echoing the "universal hubbub wild" with which Milton characterized the noises of still another "external" realm, Chaos—P.L., II, 951), and the "noisier world" of "universal ferment" and "commotions" which he entered in France. The external world has its own rhetoric as well, a rhetoric that attempts merely to list the concrete objects of this world; London is thus presented through the heaping up of detail:

> A raree-show is here
> With Children gather'd round, another Street
> Presents a company of dancing Dogs,
> Or Dromedary, with an antic pair
> Of Monkies on his back, a minstrel Band
> Of Savoyards, or, single and alone,
> An English Ballad-singer.   (VII, 190-196)

The stiffly parallel manner in which the objects are listed, each standing isolated from the last, implicitly defines their value. One notes, moreover, the total lack of interaction between poet and scene; in fact, the complex verbal machinery—the "rhetoric of interaction" described earlier in this study—which Wordsworth developed to record his inward experience is, in such passages, held totally in abeyance.

Taken as a whole, *The Prelude* can be looked upon as a struggle between both worlds, inner and outer, for primacy over its hero. As such, one can read the poem almost like a morality play, with both forces alternately triumphing in the battle which rages within the poet. The very structure of the spot of time, with its progress from publicly verifiable, external objects and events to a mysterious inward reality, seems designed to express this struggle. But the nature of this struggle is revealed even more conspicuously when we observe the sequence of the individual books of the poem, for each book concentrates primarily on but one of the two worlds. Thus, the first two, dealing with early childhood experiences, concentrate on the inner world; the book on Cambridge shifts to the outer world and is, in turn, followed by Books IV-VI, which deal largely with inward experience. The book on London shifts the reader back to external reality, while Book VIII, the "Retrospect," attempts to summarize the whole argument thus far, and attempts, in fact, to define a certain positive contribution made by the poet's outer experiences to his inward development. This book is followed by the two "outer" books on the Revolution, which culminate in an inward struggle far more intense than any occasioned by his earlier external experiences, while the three final books celebrate his triumphant restoration to the inner world.

It has often been remarked how obviously Wordsworth violates chronological order in the course of the poem: Book V, for example, legitimately belongs with the section on childhood, as do the spots of time in Book XI, while the ascent of Mt. Snowdon recorded in the last book actually preceded the period of his residence in France. But chronology, even in an autobiographical work like *The Prelude*, was necessarily subservient to the demands of its more fundamental theme. When assertions of inward power were needed to counterbalance the effects of the external world, Wordsworth did not hesitate to take them out of chronological sequence; and, given Wordsworth's theory of memory, by which early incidents gain in inward meaning through retrospection, the chronology determined by outward events was ultimately of little consequence.

c. Vaster Prospects

Beyond the confines of the personal past with which *The Prelude* is chiefly concerned, there exists a public realm of time from which Wordsworth often seeks to draw meaning. In the following passage, for instance, he compares the effect that the English national past had on him during his stay in London with his experience of nature:

> But a sense
> Of what had been here done, and suffer'd here
> Through ages, and was doing, suffering, still
> Weigh'd with me, could support the test of thought,
> Was like the enduring majesty and power
> Of independent nature; and not seldom
> Even individual remembrances,
> By working on the Shapes before my eyes,
> Became like vital functions of the soul;
> And out of what had been, what was, the place
> Was throng'd with impregnations, like those wilds,
> In which my early feelings had been nurs'd. . . .
>
> (VIII, 781-792)

Thus he feels moved and influenced not only by the memory of his private experiences, but also by that collective memory for which we commonly reserve the term history. His visit to Salisbury Plain, for example, assumes a literary form comparable to that of the more personal spot of time:

> There on the pastoral Downs without a track
> To guide me, or along the bare white roads
> Lengthening in solitude their dreary line,
> While through those vestiges of ancient times
> I ranged, and by the solitude o'ercome,
> I had a reverie and saw the past,
> Saw multitudes of men, and here and there,

A single Briton in his wolf-skin vest
With shield and stone-axe, stride across the Wold;
The voice of spears was heard, the rattling spear
Shaken by arms of mighty bone. . . .

(XII, 315-325)

The habit of being moved at the sight of ruins was scarcely new by Wordsworth's time—no more so than the habit of finding pleasure in personal memories. The poet Dyer had expostulated upon the same scene in *The Fleece* a half century before, writing of "solitary Stonehenge, gray with moss / Ruin of ages,"[4] while his *Ruins of Rome* played a notable role in establishing the cult of ruins in the eighteenth century. In later life Wordsworth praised "that noble passage of Dyer's 'Ruins of Rome,' where the poet hears the voice of Time"; this passage, which Dr. Johnson had cited with praise in his life of the poet, was remarkable, according to Wordsworth, as "a beautiful instance of the modifying and *investive* power of imagination" (*Prose Works*, III, 465; italics Wordsworth's):

The pilgrim oft
At dead of night, 'mid his oraison hears
Aghast the voice of Time, disparting towers,
Tumbling all precipitate down-dash'd,
Rattling around, loud thundering to the Moon.[5]

But except for an isolated passage like this, in which Dyer's use of the word *aghast* anticipates Wordsworth's characteristic rhetoric of interaction, the language in which eighteenth-century poets addressed public history differs from Wordsworth's as strikingly as does the language with which Samuel Rogers celebrated the pleasures of private memories: for Wordsworth succeeded in creating a language that could dramatize the process of interaction be-

4 Chalmers, *Works of the English Poets*, XIII, 229.
5 *Ibid.*, p. 224.

tween himself and the outer world, be it nature, or the memory of his earlier self encountering nature, or the relics of earlier times. It is the object of his poetry, one might say, to draw external reality into the orbit of his private world, to endow objects and events which at first seem cold and distant with inward meaning.

Within the argument of *The Prelude* public history is characterized by two forms of chronology. The first is mechanical, external, measurable by dates in the same way that the time of daily routine is measured by clocks. But there is also a second mode of historical time, unconcerned about the order of outward events and unaware of distinctions between public history and the private history of the self:

> The Human nature unto which I felt
> That I belong'd, and which I lov'd and reverenc'd,
> Was not a punctual Presence, but a Spirit
> Living in time and space, and far diffus'd.
> In this my joy, in this my dignity
> Consisted; the external universe,
> By striking upon what is found within,
> Had given me this conception, with the help
> Of Books, and what they picture and record.
>
> (VIII, 761-769)

The life of the spirit has, in fact, its own historical tradition, one that refuses to recognize common-sense distinctions between before and after. Thus, when he addresses Coleridge in Sicily, he assures his friend that despite the present degeneracy of the island, Coleridge's real affinities lie with its past greatness:

> There is
> One great Society alone on earth,
> The noble Living and the noble Dead:
> Thy consolation shall be there, and Time

And Nature shall before thee spread in store
Imperishable thoughts, the Place itself
Be conscious of thy presence, and the dull
Sirocco air of its degeneracy
Turn as thou mov'st into a healthful breeze
To cherish and invigorate thy frame.[6]

(x, 968-977)

It is significant that these attitudes toward the nature of
history were all made during the later stages in the composition of *The Prelude*. Those parts of the poem which
the modern reader generally remembers most vividly are
the personal memories, and above all those which were
written in 1798-99; of the most celebrated Wordsworthian
spots of time, only the ascent of Snowdon and the walk
home after the dance date from the time he took up the
poem once more four years later. One might conclude that
in the course of writing the poem Wordsworth's preoccupation was shifting from the more personal aspects of time to
the impersonal, from the intimate to the monumental. As
a poet he was beginning to lose touch, as it were, with the
more intimate ranges of human experience. At the end of
The Prelude his memory of the summer of 1798 has something slightly cold and official about it:

But, beloved Friend,
When, looking back, thou seest in clearer view
Than any sweetest sight of yesterday
That summer when on Quantock's grassy Hills
Far ranging, and among the sylvan Coombs . . .

[6] It is worth noting that Coleridge saw fit to repay the compliment in
1807 in the poem "To William Wordsworth: Composed on the Night after
his Recitation of a Poem on the Growth of an Individual Mind":

The truly great
Have all one age, and from one visible space
Shed influence! They, both in power and act,
Are permanent, and Time is not with them,
Save as it worketh for them, they in it.

When thou dost to that summer turn thy thoughts,
And hast before thee all which then we were,
To thee, in memory of that happiness
It will be known, by thee at least, my Friend,
Felt, that the history of a Poet's mind
Is labour not unworthy of regard.

(XIII, 390-409)

The spot of time, as a literary device which could fuse the concrete texture of past experience with a statement of its larger significance, represents but a single stage in Wordsworth's development. The later, monumental Wordsworth, the Wordsworth of the many sonnets, often has occasion to refer to time and memory, but, except for an occasional piece such as "Surprized by Joy" (composed between 1812 and 1815), we no longer find the intense explorations of private experience that set *The Prelude* off so sharply from both his earlier and later work. Time in the later Wordsworth is time with a capital T, as in the first of the *Ecclesiastical Sonnets* (1821), in which the poet "seeks upon the heights of Time the source / Of a HOLY RIVER," or in the "Mutability Sonnet," one of his most admirable later pieces, which culminates in the fine image of "the unimaginable touch of Time" (though the latter image was in fact lifted from one of his juvenile pieces ["Fragment of a 'Gothic' Tale," PW, I, 288]). In the poem entitled "Memory" (1823) he speaks on a fully impersonal level, calling memory "A pen—to register; a key—. . . a Pencil"

That smoothes foregone distress, the lines
Of lingering care subdues,
Long-vanished happiness refines,
And clothes in brighter hues.   (PW, IV, 101)

We have come back full-circle to the mode of Samuel Rogers.

Yet Wordsworth the man, if not the poet, was still capable of the type of vision he recorded with such intensity in *The Prelude*. Or so one gathers, at least, from a passage in Dorothy's 1820 "Journal of a Tour of the Continent," in which she describes the family's crossing of the Simplon: "Our eyes often turned towards the bridge and the upright path, little thinking that it was the same we had so often heard of, which misled my Brother and Robert Jones in their way from Switzerland to Italy. They were pushing right upwards, when a Peasant, having questioned them as to their object, told them they had no further ascent to make—'The Alps were crossed!' The ambition of youth was disappointed at these tidings; and they remeasured their steps with sadness. At the point where our Fellow-travellers had rejoined the road, W. was waiting to shew us the track, on the green precipice. *It was impossible for me to say how much it had moved him, when he discovered it was the very same which had tempted him in his youth. The feelings of that time came back with the freshness of yesterday,* accompanied with a dim vision of thirty years of life between."[7] The words that failed Dorothy in the lines I have italicized, no doubt also failed her brother, who was by now content to keep his private visionary experiences to himself.

d. From Time to Eternity

The notion that there exist two distinct realms—the realm of observable, transitory things and the realm of eternal forms—and that these can be distinguished by such terms as *time* and *eternity*, has remained a persistent element in Western thought since Plato. The classic statement of this distinction occurs in the cosmological discussion in the *Timaeus*: "When the father who had begotten [the world] saw it set in motion and alive, a shrine brought into

[7] *Journals*, II, 260-261.

being for the everlasting gods, he rejoiced and being well pleased he took thought to make it yet more like its pattern. So as that pattern is the Living Being that is for ever existent, he sought to make this universe also like it, so far as might be, in that respect. Now the nature of that Living Being was eternal, and this character it was impossible to confer in full completeness on the generated thing. But he took thought to make, as it were, a moving likeness of eternity; and, at the same time that he ordered the Heaven, he made, of eternity that abides in unity, an everlasting likeness moving according to number—that to which we have given the name Time" (Cornford translation). Whether we employ the specifically Christian dichotomy of the realms of Nature and Grace, or the more secular terms *appearance* and *reality*, or *being* and *becoming*, we are still reworking the metaphor suggested by Plato; and the history of this dichotomy and of our changing terminology is, in one sense, the history of the fortunes of Platonism.

Among the many images that Eternity has assumed in various periods, the Romantic image is unique, according to Georges Poulet, for the degree to which it grows directly out of the poet's everyday experience in the temporal realm. "The Romantics," writes Poulet, "did not want to describe in their poems an ideal world or the abstract existence of God. They wanted to express their own concrete experiences, their own immediate realities, and to reflect in their poetry not the fixed splendor of God's eternity but their own personal confused apprehension, in the here and now, of a human timelessness. They took hold of the idea of eternity; but they removed it from its empyrean world into their own. In brief, paradoxically, they brought Eternity into Time."[8]

Thus, Wordsworth grounds his image of a timeless realm in the natural world, above all, in the lakes and hills with

[8] "Timelessness and Romanticism," p. 7.

which he portrays the self in interaction. As with Rousseau, nature acts as a kind of catalyst to lead him into a contemplative state whereby he is gradually removed from the distractions of the temporal realm. This state, moreover—call it revery, contemplation, trance—is in itself a kind of suspension of ordinary time; not only is the self protected from worldly distractions, but it loses track of the units of time-measurement which have given the temporal realm its very name. "What exactly does one experience in a state such as this?" asks Rousseau in a famous passage in the *Reveries* describing the intimations of eternity which he received while watching the lapping of waves on the Lac de Bienne. "Nothing outside oneself," he replies, "nothing except for oneself and one's own being; as long as that state of being lasts, one is sufficient unto oneself, like God."[9] In their moments of deepest insight, then, the natural realm for whose celebration both Rousseau and Wordsworth are so justly famed is only a means to an end—an end which ultimately denies the meaningfulness of the whole visible world, whether it be the generally benign realm of external nature or the coldly mechanical world which for Rousseau was symbolized by Paris and for Wordsworth by Cambridge and London. When crossing the Simplon, for instance, Wordsworth affirms his fealty to a world well beyond nature:

> In such strength
> Of usurpation, in such visitings
> Of awful promise, when the light of sense

[9] *Confessions*, Pléiade edition, p. 702 (my translation). Rousseau's succeeding line, "*Le sentiment de l'existence* dépouillé de toute autre affection est par lui-même un sentiment précieux de *contentement* et de *paix*," may well have been echoed by Wordsworth in these lines:

> I was only then
> Contented when with bliss ineffable
> I felt *the sentiment of Being* spread
> O'er all that moves, and all that seemeth *still*. . . .
> (II, 418-421, italics mine)

Goes out in flashes that have shewn to us
The invisible world, doth Greatness make abode,
There harbours whether we be young or old.
Our destiny, our nature, and *our home*
Is with infinitude, and only there. . . .

(VI, 532-539; italics mine)

Yet a close reading of Wordsworth reveals a certain discrepancy, even during his major period, between his conceptions of the eternal realm. At times he seems content to regard nature as an image of eternity, at others, as in the lines above, to insist on the inadequacy of nature except as a means beyond itself. Among recent students of Wordsworth, David Ferry has best succeeded in defining this dual view of nature: "Intervening between the objective eternal world and man is the perishable natural scene, which though it can be a symbol for eternity is nevertheless subject to change. The problem of the man who desires to be 'in eternity' (before he actually dies) come down to this: he must somehow get past or go through his own temporal passions, and past or through the temporal natural scene. He must reduce his common passions to the smallest part of the mind and look at nature as it were *sacramentally*, regarding it in the mode of eternity, responding insofar as he can only to its harmonious relations, to those things which appear least accidental and which most easily can be symbolic of eternity."[10]

Had Wordsworth been wholly content with this sacramental view of nature, one for which visible nature sufficed as an image of eternity, the result might have been a less intense type of poetry, one focusing upon the individualities of landscape and rural life (as in many of his shorter poems, or in the depiction of the country festival that opens Book VIII of *The Prelude*); its chief tensions might then

[10] *The Limits of Mortality* (Middletown, Conn., 1960), p. 29.

have derived from the conflict—exemplified in the Cambridge and London books—between the life of solitude in nature and the more "external" life of society. But, as Ferry points out, Wordsworth's sacramental view at times gives way to a more radical view, the mystical:

"Even a sacramentalist view, even a view which is more or less satisfied with the natural scene as a symbol for the eternal, is to a degree destructive of the ordinary natural scene and the ordinary passions, since it tries to concentrate only on those aspects of things which can most readily stand for the eternal. Such a view at least *tends* toward the minimization of a complex sensuous and emotional texture in poetry. But a literally mystical view is more destructive than that: it is destructive of poetry itself, for it is destructive of all articulation. It is an experience of the unutterable, the immediate experience of *that for which there is no image*."[11]

One must remember, of course, that *The Prelude*, unlike the *Timaeus* or a theological work, is not a body of metaphysics which contents itself with setting down a clear and self-consistent image of reality. Indeed, the very qualities that give it individuality as a poem—the struggle toward definition, the constant intensification of language, the recurring spots of time—these are above all a record of search and struggle toward goals which remain ultimately dim and which are even in certain respects contradictory with one another. Those who try to boil down Wordsworth's philosophy—his concepts of nature and imagination, his politics and pantheism—from a study of *The Prelude* are usually defeated by the fact that what seems at first a body of doctrine is actually a record of the *process toward* doctrine. At best we can say that the process takes us from the temporal to the eternal realm, and by routes which we must not try too hard to reconcile.

[11] *Ibid.*, pp. 32-33.

e. Time the Restorer

Concerned though it is with the past, *The Prelude* is also in a sense directed toward the future. In one respect this is evident from the title itself, which the poet's widow, viewing the poem as introductory to his great uncompleted work, bestowed upon it. Whatever the many possible reasons that he was unable to carry out his epic ambitions, one thing remains clear—he was unable to start his larger poem before coming to terms with his past self:

> Meanwhile, my hope has been that I might fetch
> *Invigorating* thoughts from former years,
> Might fix the wavering balance of my mind,
> And haply meet reproaches, too, whose power
> May spur me on, in manhood now mature,
> To honorable toil.   (I, 648-653)

The word *invigorating* is characteristic; it is but one of several more or less synonymous words:

> One end hereby at least hath been attain'd,
> My mind hath been *revived*. . . .   (I, 664-665)

> Thus did I steal along that silent road,
> My body from the stillness drinking in
> A *restoration* like the calm of sleep. . . .
>   (IV, 385-387)

> To the *reanimating* influence sweet
> Of memory, to virtue lost and hope . . .
>   (Rejected MS passage, *Prel.*, p. 423;
>   italics mine in each quotation)

Behind these terms there stands a common metaphor—the memory works as a vital force to bring the sick or disturbed poet back to health. In addition, the memory acts as a kind of storehouse to nurture the poet in bad times, and thus

enables him to draw on his past inner life while subjected
to the meaningless social whirl of Cambridge:

> . . . Having in my native hills given loose
> To a Schoolboy's dreaming, I had rais'd a pile
> Upon the basis of the coming time,
> Which now before me melted fast away,
> Which could not live, scarcely had life enough
> To mock the Builder. (III, 434-439)

The effects of Cambridge upon him were thus so adverse
that the storehouse gave out, although when he later looks
back at the Cambridge experience he finds that it, too, may
help replenish the storehouse—"Yet something to the
memory sticks at last, / Whence profit may be drawn in
times to come" (III, 667-668).

To think of memory as a storehouse is perhaps to make
it seem too passive, too mechanical. For Wordsworth it was
obviously something more than a repository for dead
images, for through it the power latent in past experiences
could be transferred to the present and future. An adequate
explanation of the Wordsworthian memory might do well,
in fact, to resort to images such as the dynamo and the
powerhouse. The exact process by which power is transferred is made to seem as mysterious as, for instance, the
workings of electrical energy:

> There are in our existence spots of time,
> Which with distinct pre-eminence retain
> A vivifying Virtue, whence . . .
> > our minds
> Are nourished and invisibly repair'd. . . .
> > (XI, 258-265)

Wordsworth supplies many explanations like this one, but
the word "invisibly" defines the nature of the process as
explicitly as any, for it excludes the possibility of any more

precise account. As in Proust, the memory, for all that is said about it, plays a mysterious role analogous to that of grace in Christian thought: its workings are ultimately beyond the control of man, who at best can set himself in the frame of mind by which it may most propitiously exercise its effects.[12]

On various occasions in *The Prelude* there recurs an image of an evil present sandwiched in between a glorious past and a millennial future:

> If in these times of fear,
> This melancholy waste of hopes o'erthrown,
> If, 'mid indifference and apathy
> And wicked exultation, when good men,
> On every side fall off we know not how. . . .
>
> (II, 448-452)

The impoverished quality of the present does not apply merely to the poet's personal condition, but is inherent

---

[12] If the memory of the past was largely beneficent for Wordsworth, it had a wholly opposite function for Coleridge. Such, at least, was the contention of De Quincey, who in his *Literary Reminiscences*, tried to account for Coleridge's failure to return to the Lake District after his departure in 1810. I refer to De Quincey not because I have any faith in the accuracy with which he can depict the workings of Coleridge's psyche, but because the dialectic in which he accounted for Coleridge's absence shows his complete immersion in Wordsworth's theory of the restorative effects of memory (it is worth noting that his essays on Wordsworth's life, written two decades after his rupture with the poet, show that he retained much of the still unpublished *Prelude* by heart): "What might be his reason for this eternal self-banishment from scenes which he so well understood in all their shifting forms of beauty, I can only guess. Perhaps it was the very opposite reason to that which is most obvious: not possibly because he had become indifferent to their attractions, but because his undecaying sensibility to their commanding power, had become associated with too afflicting remembrances, and flashes of personal recollections, suddenly restored and illuminated—recollections which will

> 'Sometimes leap
> From hiding places ten years deep,'

and bring into collision the present with some long-forgotten past, in a form too trying and too painful for endurance (*Literary Reminiscences*, I, 227)."

within the whole public realm. The lost paradise, more-over, is not merely the poet's lost childhood vision, but a condition from which all mankind has fallen. And the future "restoration" which he foresees resulting from the recapture of past vision is not merely the recovery of his mental health, but a condition toward which he and Cole-ridge can lead other men:

> Then, though, too weak to tread the ways of truth,
> This Age fall back to old idolatry,
> Though men return to servitude as fast
> As the tide ebbs, to ignominy and shame
> By Nations sink together, we shall still
> Find solace in the knowledge which we have,
> Bless'd with true happiness if we may be
> United helpers forward of a day
> Of firmer trust, joint-labourers in a work . . .
> Of their redemption, surely yet to come.
> Prophets of Nature, we to them will speak
> A lasting inspiration. . . .
>
> (XIII, 431-443)

"Old idolatry . . . redemption . . . Prophets of Nature"—the Biblical overtones hardly surprise us in these, the closing lines of the poem. Throughout the work the spots of time, which opened so matter-of-factly as accounts of private ex-perience, culminated in references to the Apocalypse, the Empyrean, and other images traditionally associated with eternity. Autobiographical though *The Prelude* is, Words-worth's private vision shifts constantly, if almost imper-ceptibly, into public vision. Coleridge, in fact, in reporting the original plan for *The Recluse* as a whole, noted that Wordsworth was to reveal "a redemptive process in opera-tion, showing how this idea . . . promised future glory and restoration."[13]

13 *Table-Talk*, July 21, 1832.

The pattern of fall and redemption which lurks beneath the surface of the poem becomes especially evident when Wordsworth has occasion to echo Milton. Take, for instance, the line "The earth is all before me," which we encounter on the opening page of *The Prelude*. In *Paradise Lost*, coming as it does in the final lines of the poem, the line carries with it all the symbolic overtones that derive from man's journey from Eden to the new world which the Archangel had pointed out to Adam; if the line in one sense refers to the personal future of Adam and Eve, the reader is also much aware that they represent mankind in general and involve all human destiny in their personal destiny. In Wordsworth our response is of a different sort. At first we are charmed by the way Wordsworth has transferred its awesome meanings to the personal level (it is as though a later composer had used the major theme of Beethoven's "Ode to Joy" for a set of intimate piano variations). But as we read further we become aware that the world in which Wordsworth rejoices after leaving the big city is not merely the private pastoral world in which he will attempt to write poetry and recapture his early visionary powers; it is also the world which he, as "Prophet of Nature," will help lead out of its old idolatries. When looking back at the personal history he has traversed in the course of the poem, he even invokes the public, Miltonic tone:

> Anon I rose
> As if on wings, and saw beneath me stretch'd
> Vast prospect of the world which I had been
> And was.   (XIII, 377-380)

The image recalls the traditional figure of the world as a stage on which all mankind enacts its destiny; as Michael reveals the vast prospects of the future to Adam, so Wordsworth's poem has revealed a symbolic and exemplary past.

The Romantic dialectic, it has often enough been said, transfers paradise from its set, theologically determined locale to other settings, most notably the natural landscape and the mind of the child. Rousseau's *Confessions* is neatly divided into two halves—the first detailing the paradise of Rousseau's youth in Mme de Warens' pastoral world, the second, the urban hell in which he is trapped in his post-lapsarian state. The fall, which occurs at the end of the first half, is due, characteristically, not to any failing in Rousseau himself, but to his betrayal by Mme de Warens and her new caretaker, whose liaison serves symbolically to eject the hero from his former mistress' garden. Words-worth's fall, though more inward, is as little concerned with the free choice of good and evil as Rousseau's: it is simply the loss of childhood vision—"The things which I have seen I now can see no more." The *Confessions*, despite momentary idylls in the second half—Rousseau's infatu-ation with Mme d'Houdetot, for instance, or his island solitude on the Lac de Bienne—is essentially a vision of paradise lost; only in the later *Reveries*, a kind of prose poem consisting of a series of spots of time, does Rousseau approach the area of paradise regained. *The Prelude*, how-ever, attempts both at once: from the early books of child-hood paradise he descends to the unholy depths of Cam-bridge, London, and revolutionary France, but in the final books, through his return to the pastoral world of child-hood, his cultivation of memory, and his act of creating poetry out of his retrospective vision, he is able to recover something of the power of the past. With paradise restored, after *The Prelude* no other installment of Wordsworth's projected long poem—his "pictures of Nature, Man and Society"—was either necessary or possible.

The late Professor Reichenbach was perhaps right when he lumped together past philosophies of time as "documents of emotional dissatisfaction,"[14] but his reason for dismissing them in itself indicates why they have been so powerful a stimulus for literature at all times. It was the achievement of both Rousseau and Wordsworth to bring together what are essentially two separate philosophies of time—first, the doctrine of the dual realms, time and eternity, which they in turn fused with their philosophy of memory, itself a part of a larger philosophy of history implicit in their work.

To recapitulate, then: the Wordsworthian time-book is grounded in the Platonic doctrine of varying degrees of reality, each characterized by its own order of time. From this base Wordsworth developed his distinctions between the time of the secular world and that of nature, and between secular time and the timelessness of eternity. Once we understand these distinctions we can distinguish the "characters" in his poems according to the varying orders of time to which they belong and we can also discern the process by which Wordsworth in *The Prelude* indicates his shifts from one order to another in the course of his life. His concept of memory, deriving from eighteenth-century preoccupations with association and given a certain stature by his own memory of childhood vision, becomes the instrument he employs to move from the temporal order to the timeless. In terms of this central underlying metaphor *The Prelude*, then, is less a "document of emotional dissatisfaction" than a celebration of Wordsworth's conquest of time.

Of all the time themes traditional to Western literature, only the *carpe diem* motif is notably missing in Wordsworth. But one would scarcely expect to find it in a poet so bent on eternity and hostile to the secular world. Even the Lucy poems, despite their elegiac tone, can be shown to poise between a feeling of regret at earthly loss and a feel-

---

[14] *The Direction of Time* (Berkeley and Los Angeles, 1956), p. 5.

ing of the essential rightness of Lucy's place among the "rocks, and stones, and trees." It is significant that Wallace Stevens' "Sunday Morning," the greatest embodiment of the *carpe diem* theme in our time, is in its rhetoric and its apprehension of nature the most Wordsworthian of modern poems, though its argument for the self-sufficiency of the temporal world is distinctly antithetical to the central argument of *The Prelude*.[15]

2. THE LARGER STRUCTURE: REPETITION

I propose to look at each spot of time throughout *The Prelude* as a repetition of the last, in fact, to look at the poem as saying essentially the same thing again and again. From beginning to end Wordsworth is constantly at work finding new ways to invoke the inexpressible. There is no real progression in *The Prelude*, but only restatements of the poet's efforts to transcend the confines of the temporal order.

The spots of time I described in preceding sections are those based on Wordsworth's earlier experiences in nature, and, to a lesser degree, those motivated by his contemplation of larger human history. But eternity is revealed in innumerable guises throughout the poem. For one thing, it manifests itself in the various solitaries who people the work: the discharged soldier, the lone shepherd whose presence the poet has felt "as of a Lord and Master; or a Power / Or Genius, under Nature, under God, / Presiding" (VIII, 393-395), or the blind beggar on the London

---

15 It is of interest that a passage from "Sunday Morning" has been shown to "derive" from one of the few passages in which Wordsworth celebrates the self-sufficiency of the present—the "prospectus" at the conclusion of "Home at Grasmere" (see J. V. Cunningham, "The Poetry of Wallace Stevens," *Poetry*, LXXV [1949], 162-163). I might add, parenthetically, that in a lovely late poem, "Look at the fate of summer flowers. . ." (PW, II, 31-32), Wordsworth employs the traditional language and imagery of the *carpe diem* convention to assert the *meaninglessness* of the temporal world and thus turns the convention brilliantly against itself.

streets on whom the poet gazed "as if admonish'd from another world" (VII, 622). Comparable in method to those
spots of time built around Wordsworth's interaction with
nature, a whole group of passages is devoted to his meetings
with solitaries. The temporal world is transcended in still
other ways in *The Prelude*, for instance, through the study
of geometry:

> And specially delightful unto me
> Was that clear Synthesis built up aloft
> So gracefully, even then when it appear'd
> No more than as a plaything, or a toy
> Embodied to the sense, not what it is
> In verity, an independent world
> Created out of pure Intelligence.
>
> (VI, 181-187)

But eternity need not be invoked only in the more fully
developed spots of time: a momentary image, a passing allusion to things "gleaming," "flashing," "radiant" will
suddenly shift the narrative into a new, more elevated
frame of reference; or even in the repetition of the word
again in "Tintern Abbey"—recurrences which aroused the
criticism of that perfectionist Tennyson[16]—one finds still
another Wordsworthian strategy to suggest a mode of experience beyond that of the everyday world.

The reader does not normally object to Wordsworth's
frequent violation of the chronology of events in his life,
for the visionary experiences he depicts are ultimately not
very different from one another. There is no reason, for
instance, to believe that the spots of time that fill the first
two books are in anything approaching chronological order.
For the sake of Wordsworth's more fundamental purposes
the ascent of Mt. Snowdon in the last book might just as
well have changed places with the crossing of the Simplon,

[16] *Alfred Lord Tennyson: A Memoir by His Son*, II, 70.

for both occurred within a year of one another. Nor does Wordsworth hesitate to repeat part of a narrative if he can thereby build still another climactic moment: the famous passage starting "Bliss was it in that dawn to be alive" (x, 693-728) comes near the end of Wordsworth's narrative of his period in France, in fact, in the midst of the story of his disillusionment. It serves in one sense merely to summarize what was told before; but its deeper function is to recapture the jubilant mood that had marked Wordsworth's first sight of revolutionary France during his trip to the Alps ("France standing on the top of golden hours, / And human nature seeming born again"—vi, 353-354). The later passage not only repeats, but attempts to repeat with a higher measure of intensity than before (in something like the same way, Thomson, in the "Hymn" which he attached to *The Seasons*, had attempted both to recapture and intensify what he had celebrated earlier in his poem).

It can be said of *The Prelude* that it follows three separate principles of organization. The most obvious of these is that of the conventional memoir: the events of the author's life in more or less chronological sequence. It was on this level that the later nineteenth century read *The Prelude*, when it read it at all; and valuable as the poem may have been in filling in hitherto unknown areas of Wordsworth's life, through its casualness about the poet's more "external" experiences and its general lack of system ("Two winters may be pass'd / Without a separate notice" —vi, 25-26), one scarcely wonders that it seemed unsatisfactory as a whole. The second principle is the one Wordsworth himself was most fully aware of: the threefold pattern of early vision, loss, and restoration, which, on one level, he saw rooted in the actual chronological pattern of his life, but which on another level followed the traditional cycle of paradise, fall, and redemption. The third principle is repetition. As a pattern controlling the poem it stands at odds with the other two, for, unlike both of them, it recognizes no beginning, middle, or end. Restoration comes again and again, if also in unpremeditated fashion, and it is always followed by a period of lower intensity, when the eternal realm seems momentarily forgotten. From the standpoint of repetition the concluding lines, in which Wordsworth and Coleridge set out to redeem a fallen world, seem merely tacked on, for there is no real conclusion; the process of invoking the inexpressible might as well go on indefinitely. In contrast to a work like *The Divine Comedy*, in which the surface narrative stands in harmony with its deeper emotional pattern (Dante could well afford to suggest four levels of meaning to his work), *The Prelude* shows deep strains between its stated intentions and what it is actually doing poetically. As each spot of time takes the form of a struggle toward definition, so the poem as a whole reveals a struggle to be unified and complete; and as the rhetoric with which the poet struggles to define the inexpressible often gives the reader the illusion that his definitions are complete, so these repeated definitions throughout the poem convince the reader that he has completed a larger experience.

The repetitive pattern should perhaps be called a pattern of alternation—between moments of high and low intensity, between fealty to the demands of "inner" reality and eternity and the demands of the "external" world. The pattern is revealed in innumerable ways throughout the poem, sometimes even in quick summary fashion:

> No otherwise had I at first been moved
> With such a swell of feeling, follow'd soon
> By a blank sense of greatness pass'd away . . .
>
> (VIII, 742-744)

or in his contrast of his Cambridge experience, with its "inner falling-off," the "vague / And loose indifference, easy likings, aims / Of a low pitch" (III, 331-333), and his return to the Lake District during his first summer vacation, when "restoration came, / Like an intruder, knocking at the door / Of unacknowledg'd weariness," followed by "hopes and peace / And swellings of the spirits" (IV, 146-148, 152-153). But the difference is not simply one between two places—Cambridge and the Lake District, or London and the Alps—and what they can do for Wordsworth; it is as much something within the poet himself, his way of looking at things at different times. In an epic simile he compares his experiences in London to those of a traveller inspecting a cave: at one moment "the scene before him lies in perfect view, / Exposed and lifeless, as a written book" (VIII, 726-727). But if he looks long and hard enough, it may take on new life for him:

> But let him pause awhile, and look again
> And a new quickening shall succeed, at first
> Beginning timidly, then creeping fast
> Through all which he beholds.
>
> (VIII, 728-731)

Though London, in terms of the larger argument of the poem, represents the betrayal of the spiritual life, it too has its moments of illumination—inspired at this point by Wordsworth's sense of its past greatness—alternating with moments of emptiness.

The process of alternation is more than a method of literary composition. Basically, it is something rooted in the Romantic sensibility: "Having two natures in me, joy the one / The other melancholy" (X, 869-870), Wordsworth declares at one point, echoing that far more memorable passage from "Resolution and Independence," "We Poets in our youth begin in gladness; / But thereof come in the end despondency and madness." And we do not have to look very widely within the literature of the age to discover innumerable other declarations of the poet's or, indeed, life's divided nature—for instance, Faust's pronouncement, "Zwei Seelen wohnen, ach!, in meiner Brust," or Hölderlin's more indirect approach to this dichotomy in his best-known shorter poem, "Hälfte des Lebens," where he contrasts an image of perfection and fulfillment —symbolized by swans floating upon a lake in summer— with a lonely winter scene. The dichotomy can take other forms besides that of melancholy and joy—the earthly and the infinite (the Faustian formulation), the lifeless and vital, the prosaic and the poetic (a combination that is present, as we have seen, in the language of each spot of time), disintegration and unity, listlessness and inspiration. One could, in fact, speak of a kind of manic-depressive movement which lurks beneath the surface—and often on the surface—of much Romantic art. "In truth, I never wrote anything with so much glee," Wordsworth once said of the composition of "The Idiot Boy." Though we are accustomed to approach *The Prelude* in loftier terms, we cannot ignore its attempt to restore the manic—as well as the mantic—side of life.

The repetitive method is by its nature hostile to any canons of economy in art. To repeat means also to accumulate. The difference between a single spot of time, or a single poem like "Tintern Abbey," and *The Prelude* as a whole is more than a difference in degree; the accumulation, one after another, of visionary moments produces an illusion of heroic enterprise that no work of narrower breadth can match. Wordsworth, who, as Coleridge has reminded us, was not always aware of the nature of his work, expressed some worry about the poem's lack of economy as he approached the last stages of composition: "This might certainly have been done in narrower compass by a man of more address, but I have done my best. If, when the work shall be finished, it appears to the judicious to have redundancies, they shall be lopped off, if possible; but this is very difficult to do, when a man has written with thought; and this defect, whenever I have suspected it or found it to exist in any writings of mine, I have always found incurable. The fault lies too deep, and is in the first conception" (co, 441). Trained as he was in an older rhetorical system, Wordsworth naturally thought of his "redundancies" as faults, though he was shrewd enough to recognize that they were intrinsic to the poem ("in the first conception").

Our own age has reasserted the principle of economy, and as a result we have found ourselves at pains to make our criticism account for even those works in the Romantic tradition which we most admire. The repetitive method, the constant alternation of sharply opposed levels of intensity—these are central to Romantic art, to works as diverse as *Moby Dick*, the poems of Whitman, the major novels of D. H. Lawrence, and, if I may turn to another art-form, to the Wagnerian music-dramas and the symphonies of Anton Bruckner. The Romantic composer, in fact, has had one crucial advantage over the writer: he could invoke the inexpressible without, like Wordsworth, having to declare that his art by its very nature lacks the means to do so, or, like Shelley and so many others, having to create a private symbolism for the task; yet our frequent uneasiness with nineteenth-century music—its expansiveness, its constant straining for the heroic—is rooted in the same cause as our uneasiness with Romantic literature. Modern criticism has often proved ingenious at reconciling Romantic literary structure with economy—we have found a dramatic function for the whaling treatises that fill up so much of *Moby Dick*; we have learned to look at *Women in Love* primarily as a novel of character and

manners in the "great tradition"; and we have even found
a meaningful line of development within *Song of Myself*,
a work which carries the twin principles of repetition and
alternation to a far extreme, and one which lacks even the
chronological outer plot of *The Prelude*.[17]

But criticism can only justify according to the preconceptions of its own time, and nineteenth-century literature,
however ingenious our justifications, has tenaciously re-
sisted these preconceptions. For one thing, it is hard to
"analyze" (the very word is inimical to the nature of Romantic art) a work like *The Prelude* or *Song of Myself*
without constant reference to its larger religious purpose;
unlike a Shakespearean play or a poem by Donne, there is
no easily discernible line between the poem as object and
the poem as a means toward persuasion (including self-
persuasion). The particular task faced by Wordsworth and
his contemporaries—in contrast to earlier poets—is well
defined in the following statement by Wasserman:

"Wordsworth's persistent private faith in some spirit
deeply interfused in all creation did not itself constitute
meaningful order, but only the ground for possible order,
since man must recurrently wed himself by the imagination with the one pervading spirit. For there to be a
meaningful whole the nineteenth-century poet—although
a common body of private beliefs may run through all his
utterances—must make it be his own willful creative act,
*and yet the creative act must forever be renewed; for in
the intervals between imaginative experiences there is, for
Wordsworth as for Coleridge, only the chaos of aimless and
bewildering multiplicity that parades before the passive
senses,* and for Keats and Shelley only the unreality of flux

---

[17] I refer to three well known and distinguished interpretations, those,
respectively, of F. O. Matthiessen (*American Renaissance* [New York,
1941], p. 416), F. R. Leavis (*D. H. Lawrence: Novelist* [London, 1955], pp.
146-196), and James E. Miller, Jr. (*A Critical Guide to "Leaves of Grass"*
[Chicago, 1957], pp. 6-35).

and mutability. No longer can a poem be conceived of as a reflection or imitation of an autonomous order outside itself. The creation of a poem is also the creation of the cosmic wholeness that gives meaning to the poem, and each poet must independently make his own world-picture, his own language within language."[18]

Wasserman's distinction between the poem that reflects or imitates an order outside itself and one that creates its own order is similar to Kierkegaard's famous distinction—found in his work entitled *Repetition*—between the processes of recollection and repetition. Kierkegaard speaks, of course, not of art but life, of mental habits, processes within the mind: his book, significantly, is subtitled "An Essay in Experimental Psychology." Recollection for Kierkegaard is essentially a passive thing, a habit of mind suitable to those who live in a stable and ordered universe; he associates it specifically with the mind of ancient Greece. But recollection is not enough for the modern world, which demands a more creative act, namely repetition, an act which involves a constant reordering of the universe.

"Repetition and recollection are the same movement, only in opposite directions; for what is recollected has been, is repeated backwards, whereas repetition properly so called is recollected forwards. Therefore, repetition, if it is possible, makes a man happy, whereas recollection makes him unhappy. . . ."

"When the Greeks said that all knowledge is recollection they affirmed that all that is has been; when one says that life is a repetition one affirms that existence which has been now becomes."[19]

Kierkegaard's little book is a kind of dialogue with himself, sometimes whimsical, at other times assuming a tone

[18] *The Subtler Language*, p. 186, italics mine.
[19] *Repetition*, tr. Walter Lowrie (Princeton, 1941), pp. 3-4, 34.

of near-frenzy. It emanates directly from a personal problem—the author's efforts to come to terms with himself after he has broken with his fiancée. He journeys to Berlin to the haunts of his student days to recapture past happiness; but his relatively passive efforts prove insufficient to accomplish what he calls a true repetition—that is, a restoration in his present state of the blessedness of the past. For repetition, to Kierkegaard, is an action which takes place in the ethical and the religious realms, a kind of rebirth that must re-create the whole order of things. But explicating any single Kierkegaardian idea inevitably gets one involved in the larger movement of Kierkegaardian dialectic, and I shall go no further here. I have introduced his concept of repetition because I think it shares something of the moral atmosphere of *The Prelude*. For the repetitive pattern of *The Prelude* is no mere accident, nor is it the result of carelessness: Wordsworth the poet knew better what he was doing than Wordsworth the self-critic. Had he persisted in his earlier plans to retell an older story—of Mithridates, Odin, Gustavus Vasa, or "some British theme, some old / Romantic tale, by Milton left unsung" (i, 179-180)—he would have been essentially practicing recollection, not repetition. When he played with the possibility of concocting an original narrative— "some Tale from my own heart" (i, 221)—he quickly recognized that "the whole beauteous Fabric seems to lack / Foundation, and, withal, appears throughout / Shadowy and unsubstantial" (i, 226-228). But the repeated invocations of past vision in *The Prelude* are something other than inventions or imitations (terms drawn directly from the older rhetoric) of past actions; they are above all an attempt to re-create and restore, by verbal means, a past order which can give substance to the future.

3. THE PRELUDE AND THE TIME-BOOK TRADITION

It is possible to view much of the significant literature of the last century and a half as a series of attempts to break down the reader's conception of the external world as a solid entity whose essential nature both poet and reader could take for granted. As such, the obsession which so many writers have had with time is explicable through the peculiar opportunities which literature affords its creators to use time as a means of breaking down an older conception of the world, or creating a new one. In a literary work, one might say, time can serve to qualify place; the visual arts, which must do without the temporal perspective, have found other, equally radical means to accomplish the same thing.

But if the exploration of time has consorted well with the nature of literary composition, it has also proved appropriate for fulfilling at least part of the larger task which literature has taken upon itself—to assert the meaningfulness of subjective experience in a coldly mechanical Newtonian universe that conceives of time in absolute, measurable units marching on in relentless succession and unaffected by human thought and activity. That Newton himself conceived of two orders of time—the one personal and subjective, the other absolute and unrelated to the human realm—is of course immaterial here. Once the absolute conception of time had come to seem the truer and, indeed, common-sensical version of reality, it became the task of literature to defend and explore the opposite version. If the various time-philosophies from Locke to Bergson could approach subjective time only on the theoretical level, imaginative literature could apply to the task its ability to apprehend the world in all its concrete fullness. Moreover, the dissolution of the traditional literary genres and the increasing eccentricity of structure in literary works during the last century have proved coincidental with, perhaps have even resulted from, the development of time-consciousness among writers. *The Prelude*, to the extent that it attempts to confound the reader's ordinary sense of time, differs from such a radically contemporary work as *The Sound and the Fury* less in kind than in degree. But literary history does not, of course, show any single line of "progress" in the break-down of time-relationships: *Tristram Shandy*, the first of the great time-books, is by no means the least radical in method.

The prevalence of autobiography (the first recorded use of the word was by Southey in 1809) and autobiographical fiction among the literary genres since the eighteenth century is no doubt closely connected with the attempts of writers to explore the nature of time. To ask which came first—the motive to record and re-create the self or to break the time barrier—is useless, for the two motives are part of a single, driving preoccupation which has engaged the modern mind. From a more simple-minded point of view it seems only natural that any attempt to record one's past should raise questions about the nature of time and change; and it seems only appropriate, for instance, that St. Augustine should have devoted a section of his *Confessions* (Chapter XI) to a disquisition on time. Personal experience, when used explicitly as the raw material of literature, is rarely present for its own sake alone. For Rousseau and Wordsworth it served as a convenient vehicle for what was essentially a religious and philosophical purpose; for many modern writers it has served chiefly to foster the illusion that the written word could render the feel of things themselves. In our own time, though writers have often sought masks through which to filter their experience, we have come to view personal experience as a kind of *donnée* from which the writer starts, as at an earlier time he had started not from experience, but from a plot he was adapting, or from a conventional conception of the particular genre—with its given rules and forms—which he had chosen to work. One of Ezra Pound's admirers, in trying to defend the coherence of the *Cantos*, has described it as a kind of autobiography, "a Guide to Kulchur, yes, but . . . also a history of how Pound got kulchured—a kind of *Prelude*, though lacking that poem's chronological arrangement, narrative continuity, and retrospective-meditative character."[20] And even when we speak of writers like Faulkner, who have chosen a more explicitly fictional garb than have modern poets, we are accustomed to describe their settings, symbols, and characters as elements of their "personal vision."

If the writer's personal experience has come to seem the factor controlling a work's larger form (or even its lack of form), the peculiar texture of his experience—the feel of things as he experiences them—has given license to the mannerisms which make up his personal style. We often explain the tortured, eccentric quality of so much modern literature by stressing the writer's attempt to be faithful to the intricacies of his experience. The literature of personal experience possesses its own set of conventions as emphatically as did the literature composed within the classical system of rhetoric. Thus, the absence of syntactical connectives in Symbolist poetry and the violation of commonsense chronology in modern fiction can be taken as literary conventions as one once accepted the strict separation of comic and tragic elements, or the refusal to let characters of high station speak of trivial things. (One might note that the neo-classical imitator of epic had a ready-made departure from conventional time structure, namely the Homeric-Virgilian flashback; but from the standpoint of the modern time-book the epic flashback, though employed

[20] Clark Emery, *Ideas into Action: A Study of Pound's Cantos* (Coral Gables, Florida, 1958), p. 114.

with the greatest finesse by such poets as Milton and Pope, was scarcely suited to the exploration of subjective experience.) In a late version of the Preface to *Lyrical Ballads* Wordsworth states that the purpose of the poems in the volume "is to follow the fluxes and refluxes of the mind when agitated by the great and simple affections of our nature" (PW, II, 388n.). Like so many writers after him, Wordsworth had recourse to an expressive theory to justify the eccentricities of his style.[21] *The Prelude*, too, attempts to follow the "fluxes and refluxes of the mind," though it reveals a mind considerably more complex than that of *Lyrical Ballads*. The shifts of tone within each spot of time, the continual gliding into and out of the past, in fact, the whole rhetoric of interaction which he developed —all these are an attempt to render the illusion of a mind intensely engaged in the process of contemplation.

To the degree that it seeks to imitate the structure of experience *The Prelude* is a distinctly modern work, one that stands more at the head than at the tail-end of a tradition. I do not of course speak of tradition in the literal sense, for of all the major poems in English, *The Prelude*— withheld as it was during the first half century after its composition—has doubtless been the least influential. Yet much that was revolutionary in it was transmitted through "Tintern Abbey," the "Immortality Ode," and such a spot of time as the ice-skating episode, which Wordsworth allowed into print during his lifetime. And though *The Prelude* created no line of descent as striking as those that emanated, say, from *The Divine Weeks* or *Cooper's Hill*, in its impulse to explore man's relationship to time, it anticipates much that we have come to find significant in

---

[21] And like at least one important writer before him. In a fragment originally intended as part of his *Confessions*, Rousseau wrote: "My irregular and artless style, sometimes swift and sometimes diffuse, sometimes sober and sometimes rash, sometimes serious and sometimes gay, will itself be a part of my history" (Pléiade edition, p. 756).

various literary forms since its composition. In its spots of time, for instance, *The Prelude* presides, as it were, over a whole line of shorter poems, from "Dover Beach" to "Among School Children," which run the gamut from casual personal revery to major poetic statement. More distantly perhaps it is related to that major strain in the lyric poetry of the nineteenth century which yearns for the return of a lost past or rebels against the encroachments of the temporal world upon the human sensibility; whether they seek escape in the exotic East or in an idyllic medieval past—images from which the realistic-minded Wordsworth kept himself singularly free—many of the finest lyrics from "Kubla Khan" to those that make up *The Wind among the Reeds* are centrally involved with the meaning of time.

If *The Prelude* is related at one extreme to the lyric genres, at the other it shares many of the concerns which later became the property of the novel. Some years ago, before the recent revival of George Eliot, a critic suggested that we seek out the significance of her achievement through the work of one of her most fervent admirers, Marcel Proust.[22] What he meant essentially was that through our experience with Proust we might view her early novels as attempts to recover a lost past. In perhaps the same way we can approach *The Prelude* through the perspective of George Eliot (who often had occasion to declare her affinities with Wordsworth, though his work had already had its major effect on her before the publication of *The Prelude*). When we look at the opening pages of *The Mill on the Floss* (a book over which Proust claimed to have wept profusely),[23] we are aware of the past

22 Franklin Gary, "In Search of George Eliot," *Symposium*, IV (1933), 182-206.

23 "Il n'y a pas de littérature qui ait sur moi un pouvoir comparable à la littérature anglaise et américaine. L'Allemagne, l'Italie, bien souvent la France me laissent indifférent. Mais deux pages du Moulin sur la Floss me font pleurer" (quoted by Robert de Billy in *Marcel Proust: Lettres*

slowly coming into focus, of memory in the process of re-creating an otherwise lost world:

"Just by the red-roofed town the tributary Ribble flows with a lively current into the Floss. How lovely the little river is, with its dark, changing wavelets! It seems to me like a living companion while I wander along the bank and listen to its low placid voice, as to the voice of one who is deaf and loving. I remember those large dipping willows. I remember the stone bridge.

"And this is Dorlcote Mill. I must stand a minute or two here on the bridge and look at it, though the clouds are threatening, and it is far on in the afternoon. Even in this leafless time of departing February it is pleasant to look at —perhaps the chill damp season adds a charm to the trimly kept comfortable dwelling house, as old as the elms and chestnuts that shelter it from the northern blast. . . .

"The rush of the water, and the booming of the mill, bring a dreary deafness, which seems to heighten the peacefulness of the scene. They are like a great curtain of sound, shutting one out from the world beyond. And now there is the thunder of the huge covered waggon coming home with sacks of grain. That honest waggoner is thinking of his dinner, getting sadly dry in the oven at this late hour; but he will not touch it till he has fed his horses—the strong, submissive, meek-eyed beasts, who, I fancy, are looking mild reproach at him from between their blinkers, that he should crack his whip at them in that awful manner, as if they needed that hint! See how they stretch their shoulders up the slope towards the bridge, with all the more energy because they are so near home. Look at their grand shaggy feet that seem to grasp the firm earth. . . ."

et Conversations [Paris, 1930], p. 181). See also Walter A. Strauss, *Proust and Literature* (Cambridge, Mass., 1957), p. 174, and L. A. Bisson, "Proust, Bergson, and George Eliot," MLR, XL (1945), 108.

If *The Prelude* employed memory as a means for transcending the temporal world, for George Eliot, as, indeed, for most novelists who drew on the world of their childhood, memory could help re-create this world in all its detail. Through their reliance on concrete detail, and the methods intrinsic to prose, the great autobiographical novels of the nineteenth century could depict the process of growing-up in a manner far different from that of *The Prelude*. But in our own century Joyce's attempt in his *Portrait* to make style mirror the process of growth, or Proust's to render the mysteries inherent in the recovery of the past, remind one that the "fluxes and refluxes of the mind" of which Wordsworth spoke could be embodied in the form of the novel. And it is perhaps not a coincidence that *The Prelude* had to wait until the twentieth century, the great age of the time-book, to achieve its major acclaim.

CHAPTER SEVEN

THE SOCIAL DIMENSION (1):
VISIONARY ALOOFNESS

Of more than Fancy, of the Social Sense
Distending wide . . .
> Coleridge, "To William Wordsworth:
> Composed on the Night after His
> Recitation of a Poem on the Growth
> of the Individual Mind"

Although he [Wordsworth] was known to the world
only as a poet, he had given twelve hours thought to the
conditions and prospects of society, for one to poetry.
> Recorded by Orville Dewey,
> *The Old World and the New*

1. SPECTATOR AB EXTRA

Scarcely of the household then
Of social life, I look'd upon these things
As from a distance, heard, and saw, and felt,
Was touch'd, but with no intimate concern.
(VI, 693-696)

THE notion that Wordsworth lacked real sympathy with human beings, despite his protestations about "love of nature leading to love of mankind," has recurred frequently among his critics. In its most contemporary form it is argued persuasively by David Ferry, whose recent study of Wordsworth, *The Limits of Mortality*, is built on the thesis that "his genius was his enmity to man, which he mistook for love."[1] But even at the time *The Prelude* ap-

[1] P. 173.

peared, one of its first reviewers complained of an "absence of deep and vital sympathy with men, their works and ways,"[2] while a year before, Walt Whitman, perhaps trying to define the difference between himself and a poet with whom he had more in common than he would have liked to think, jotted down these words: "Wordsworth lacks sympathy with men and women—that does not pervade him enough by a long shot."[3]

But the classic statement of this sentiment was made by Coleridge in two of his discussions of Wordsworth in *Table Talk*. "Although Wordsworth and Goethe are not much alike to be sure, upon the whole, yet they both have this peculiarity of utter non-sympathy with the subjects of their poetry. They are always, both of them, spectators *ab extra*,—feeling *for*, but never *with*, their characters."[4] Although Coleridge recognized this as a limitation in Wordsworth's range as a poet, he by no means took it as a weakness. One could even argue that Coleridge's influence during the years of their friendship was directed toward cultivating those powers of philosophical detachment whose absence he must have deplored in many of Wordsworth's more colloquial poems: "I think Wordsworth possessed more of the genius of a great philosophic poet than any man I ever knew, or, as I believe, has existed in England since Milton; but it seems to me that he ought never to have abandoned the contemplative position which is peculiarly—perhaps I might say exclusively—fitted for him. His proper title is *Spectator ab extra*."[5]

This image of a poet who was too aloof to sympathize adequately with his characters is obviously at odds with Wordsworth's conception of himself. It is hard to reconcile,

2 *Gentleman's Magazine*, N.S. XXXIV, 460.
3 *Complete Writings* (New York, 1902), VII, 98.
4 *Table Talk*, February 16, 1833.
5 *Ibid.*, July 21, 1832.

for one thing, with the complaint he makes in the Preface to *Lyrical Ballads* about poets who "separate themselves from the sympathies of men" (PW, II, 387), or the impassioned argument, in his letter to Fox in 1801, that his poems seek to "excite profitable sympathies in many kind and good hearts" (EL, 262). Indeed, there is no major English poet whose work is so full of the case histories of ordinary men, above all, of course, in *Lyrical Ballads* and *The Excursion*; and although *The Prelude*, in its very conception, concentrates on the poet himself, at least a third of it is concerned not with his relation to external nature, but to the world of men. In most of the preceding chapters I have explored that side of the poem which deals with the interaction of the self with nature, for it was in his attempt to apprehend this relationship in verbal terms that Wordsworth developed what today seems most conspicuously unique in his contribution to the language and structure of poetry. But when we come across such lines as these from *The Prelude*:

> I took the knife in hand
> And stopping not at parts less sensitive,
> Endeavoured with my best of skill to probe
> The living body of society
> Even to the heart. . .   (X, 873-877)

in such lines we are aware of a wholly different area of experience which Wordsworth stressed as influential upon the "growth of his mind." Indeed, when we read these lines out of context, we feel we have virtually entered the domain of Balzac, who, employing a similar metaphor, declared himself a "doctor of social medicine."[6]

Yet to mention Balzac is at once to call attention to the

---

[6] *Oeuvres complètes*, ed. M. Bouteron and H. Longnon (Paris, 1946), XVII, 17; see also the extended discussion of this remark by Harry Levin, "Toward Balzac," *Direction*, III (1947), 25-41.

very real and large gap which separates Wordsworth from the world of the realistic novel. The difference is not fundamentally one between poet and novelist: one can always point to Crabbe (as Wordsworth's early reviewers were wont to do) as a poet who could people a rich and objective world of human beings. Rather, it is the distinction which, I think, Keats was trying to make when he contrasted the true "poetical Character" with the Wordsworthian mode:

"As to the poetical Character itself, (I mean that sort of which, if I am any thing, I am a Member; that sort distinguished from the wordsworthian or egotistical sublime; which is a thing per se and stands alone) it is not itself—it has no self—it is every thing and nothing—It has no character—it enjoys light and shade; it lives in gusto, be it foul or fair, high or low, rich or poor, mean or elevated . . . . A Poet is the most unpoetical of any thing in existence; because he has no Identity—he is continually in for —and filling some other Body—The Sun, the Moon, the Sea and Men and Women who are creatures of impulse are poetical and have about them an unchangeable attribute—the poet has none."[7]

This is only to say that in Wordsworth it is the poet, not the characters, who claims identity; or, to put it another way, Wordsworth's characters do not have an objective existence of their own, but rather, their identity seems swallowed up either by the poet's own or by that of the external universe (in the poetry of interaction the difference is not always discernible). Consider the description of the discharged soldier:

> He was alone,
> Had no attendant, neither Dog, nor Staff,
> Nor knapsack; in his very dress appear'd

[7] *Letters*, ed. Rollins, I, 386-387.

A desolation, a simplicity
That seem'd akin to solitude. Long time
Did I peruse him with a mingled sense
Of fear and sorrow. From his lips, meanwhile,
There issued murmuring sounds, as if of pain
Or of uneasy thought; yet still his form
Kept the same steadiness; and at his feet
His shadow lay, and mov'd not.   (IV, 415-425)

"A ghost was never ghostlier than he," A. C. Bradley once remarked of the soldier.[8] But he is also something more than a ghost: in one sense, as I shall elaborate later, he is a projection of the poet's own personality, an embodiment of certain potentialities within himself which the poet chooses to confront and transform, while in still another sense he is an aspect of nature with which, like the huge cliff in the episode about the stolen boat (the cliff, like the soldier, had called forth thoughts of "darkness, call it solitude, / Or blank desertion . . ."), the poet's sensibilities interact.

Wordsworth's most memorable "characters"—the soldier, the leech-gatherer, Margaret in *The Ruined Cottage*, the various eccentrics who people *Lyrical Ballads*—are obviously not, then, the fully rounded personages that the reader encounters in Crabbe or the nineteenth-century novelists, and it is small wonder that critics have noted something unusual in his approach to character. Yet these characters scarcely add up to a society as such; Wordsworth's treatment of them is intrinsically different from his treatment of society as a whole. It is in his picture of society, in fact, that Wordsworth's role can most properly be termed *spectator ab extra*:

What Crowd
Is yon, assembled in the gay green Field? . . .

8 *Oxford Lectures on Poetry*, pp. 137-138.

Though but a little Family of Men,
Twice twenty, with their Children and their Wives,
And here and there a Stranger interspers'd.

(VIII, 4-9)

The crowd picnicking at the foot of Mount Helvellyn is
seen from a distance, with a degree of condescension almost
unbearable to the modern reader. The individuals among
them are essentially types, each with his predetermined
place in the general order of things:

Hither, too,

From far, with Basket, slung upon her arm,
Of Hawker's Wares, books, pictures, combs, and pins,
Some aged Woman finds her way again,
Year after year a punctual Visitant!
The Showman with his Freight upon his Back,
And once, perchance, in lapse of many years
Prouder Itinerant, Mountebank, or He
Whose Wonders in a cover'd Wain lie hid.
But One is here, the loveliest of them all,
Some sweet Lass of the Valley, looking out
For gains, and who that sees her would not buy?

(VIII, 27-38)

The ideal society of dalesmen which he pictures here—
The Excursion is virtually an extension of this passage
from *The Prelude*—has the air of something abstract and
preconceived: his way of apprehending society, one might
say, stands at an opposite pole from that of the great realist
novelists, who, however doctrinaire their theories of society, were able to create the dual illusion of a living social
organism made up of fully individualized, vital parts. It is
a tribute, for instance, to Balzac's grasp of the actual world
of men that, despite his avowed conservatism, his portrait
of society could gain the admiration of Marxist critics;

[210]

Wordsworth's portrait of society, on the other hand, must stand or fall by one's degree of assent to his theories.

2. COMMUNION WITH SOLITARIES

> I prized such walks still more; for there I found
> Hope to my hope, and to my pleasure peace,
> And steadiness; and healing and repose
> To every angry passion. There I heard,
> From mouths of lowly men and of obscure
> A tale of honour; sounds in unison
> With loftiest promises of good and fair.
>
> (XII, 178-184)

The central character throughout Wordsworth's work is the solitary; there is probably no other major writer whose *dramatis personae* are all so much alike. "In my treatment of the intellectual instincts affections & passions of mankind," Wordsworth once wrote to Crabb Robinson, "I am nobly distinguished by having drawn out into notice the points in which they resemble each other, in preference to dwelling, as dramatic Authors must do, upon those in which they differ."[9] Though Wordsworth was perhaps not entirely aware of it, the point in which the characters he chose to write about most resemble one another is their isolation—be it spiritual or physical—from any organized human context. I do not refer merely to the most famous solitaries—the soldier, the leech-gatherer, Lucy, the heroes and heroines of *Lyrical Ballads*—but to those with briefer, less conspicuous roles to play: the blind beggar on the London streets; the "Girl who bore a Pitcher on her head / And seem'd with difficult steps to force her way / Against the blowing wind" (XI, 306-308); the lone, Quixote-like figure in the dream allegory of the shell and stone. Even

[9] *Correspondence of Henry Crabb Robinson with the Wordsworth Circle*, ed. E. J. Morley (Oxford, 1927), I, 273.

the poet's intimates are viewed as solitaries: Michel Beau-puy, garrisoned among the Royalist officers at Blois, was "of other mold, / A Patriot, thence rejected by the rest / And with an oriental loathing spurn'd" (IX, 294-296); Dorothy is depicted communing only with nature; the most extensive passage on Coleridge pictures him in Sicily, "a lonely wanderer . . . by pain / Compell'd and sickness" (X, 984-985). The poet's beloved schoolmaster, William Taylor, is eulogized at his lone grave, with lines from Gray's "Elegy" engraved on the tombstone; Milton is re-membered for having "stood almost single, uttering odious truth" (III, 285); while the celebrated image of Newton "voyaging through strange seas of Thought, alone" (III, 63 [1850])—for Wordsworth doubtless the highest com-pliment that could be paid to artist or thinker—would scarcely have been thought so flattering among Newton's Augustan admirers a century before. The flora and fauna of Wordsworth's poetic world—the butterfly, cuckoo, the celandine, all of them apostrophied in the singular; the albatross which he donated to Coleridge's greatest poem; "the single sheep, and the one blasted tree" (XI, 378) in the spot of time centering around his father's death—these hold their place among his solitaries as surely as the human inhabitants.

At the center of this world, of course, stands the most important solitary of them all, the poet himself—for it is from him that all the rest emanate and derive their being. They are all, in one way or another, projections of his own self, his hopes, fears, and depths of despair and they re-ceive only so much characterization as Wordsworth needs to portray his own subjective states. The shadowy, insub-stantial quality of Wordsworth's solitaries was, of course, recognized from the first. Jeffrey, with his usual Augustan bias, had written as early as 1808 that Wordsworth's char-acters were formed "upon certain fantastic and affected

peculiarities in the mind or fancy of the author," and, referring to "The Thorn," had complained, "He has con-
trived to tell us nothing whatever of the unfortunate fair
one, but that her name is Martha Ray; and that she goes
up to the top of a hill, in a red cloak, and cries 'O
misery!' "[10] It is hardly necessary today to defend a writer
for creating characters out of his "inner" world. But what
is peculiar about Wordsworth's way of creating them is that
he never allows them even to *seem* wholly independent
entities. It is, in fact, characteristic of Wordsworth that
when he undertook to analyze the workings of the poetic
imagination he did not use one of his landscapes as an example, but rather that passage from "Resolution and Independence" in which the leech-gatherer is compared
successively to a huge stone, a sea-beast, and a cloud: "The
stone," wrote Wordsworth in a passage I quoted in an
earlier chapter, "is endowed with something of the power
of life to approximate it to the sea-beast; and the sea-beast
stripped of some of its vital qualities to assimilate it to the
stone," while the leech-gatherer himself "is divested of so
much of the indications of life and motion as to bring him
to the point where the two objects unite and coalesce in
just comparison" (PW, II, 438).

One could add innumerable examples to the one that
Wordsworth chose, for instance, the discharged soldier with
his ghost-like qualities, or the shepherd seen through the
fog "like an aerial Cross, / As it is stationed on some spiry
Rock / Of the Chartreuse" (VIII, 408-410). Not only does
Wordsworth create solitaries out of non-human objects,
but he insists on interchanging these with his human solitaries. None of his figures is allowed to remain independent in itself, but it must inevitably dissolve into, or stand

[10] In John Wain, *Contemporary Reviews of Romantic Poetry* (London,
1953), pp. 57, 56.

as a symbol of, some other being: thus, Lucy asumes the
qualities of a goddess, Dorothy becomes a part of the nature
with which she communes (XI, 208-221), and the identi-
fication which the blind beggar displays becomes "a type,
/ Or emblem, of the utmost that we know, / Both of ourselves and of the universe" (VII, 617-619).

Although there is little enough of drama, in the usual
sense, in Wordsworth, one can distinguish a dramatic element in the various confrontations between the poet and
his solitaries. For one thing, these confrontations are part
of the whole interaction process with which *The Prelude* is
centrally concerned: just as he portrays the interaction between the poet and external nature, and between the various objects of nature, so he portrays a kind of interaction
between the poet and his solitary figures. As I suggested in
the last chapter, one could speak of his confrontations with
the soldier and the blind man as spots of time, in much the
same way that one speaks of the ice-skating passage or the
lines on the Simplon Pass. The encounter with the blind
man, for instance, develops in the same form as the other
spots of time:

> Lost
> Amid the moving pageant, 'twas my chance
> Abruptly to be smitten with the view
> Of a blind Beggar, who, with upright face,
> Stood propp'd against a Wall, upon his Chest
> Wearing a written paper, to explain
> The story of the Man, and who he was.
> My mind did at this spectacle turn round
> As with the might of waters, and it seem'd
> To me that in this Label was a type,
> Or emblem, of the utmost that we know,
> Both of ourselves and of the universe;
> And, on the shape of the unmoving man,

His fixèd face and sightless eyes, I look'd
As if admonish'd from another world.

(VII, 608-622)

Similarly to his other memories, Wordsworth moves from prosaic statement to a larger poetic assertion, from the "real" world of the London streets to the beggar's symbolic meaning, with all its transcendental connotations. What makes the passage particularly dramatic is the fact that as a result of the chance encounter the poet undergoes an inward development: lost as he is in the hubbub of the big city, he starts out in a state of relative unawareness, is snared unexpectedly into a new experience ("abruptly . . . smitten") and gradually finds his circle of awareness widened until it reaches universal proportions. But it is only the poet, not the beggar, who undergoes change; the beggar is only functional, and once he has fulfilled his brief purpose, the poet can move on to other matters. Wordsworth's peculiar way of utilizing characters can perhaps be set in relief if we compare him once more to Keats. I quote again from the letter on the "poetical character": "When I am in a room with People if I ever am free from speculating on creations of my own brain, then not myself goes home to myself: but the identity of every one in the room begins to press upon me that, I am in a very little time annihilated." Wordsworth, in sharp contrast to Keats, is never annihilated; indeed, his identity becomes all the more firmly grounded as a result of his confrontations with others.

Throughout the poet's encounters with solitaries, both in *The Prelude* and his other verse, the reader is rarely allowed to forget the role played by the narrator-poet. And in one sense we could look at these encounters as unique experiments in the use of point of view.[11] In "We Are Seven,"

11 At least two recent critics have, in fact, called attention to *Lyrical*

for example, the girl's doggedly persistent faith becomes moving only through the battle in semantics which she carries on with the narrator. In "Simon Lee," the narrator must even perform a strenuous physical act to bring the old man's emotions into focus. The almost ephemeral Lucy would disappear entirely without the narrator's far more substantial presence ("And oh, the difference to me!"). Like so many modern novelists Wordsworth plays the role of reflector, at once keeping us at a distance from his characters, and providing us with only those details necessary to evoke the desired emotional response from the reader. His reflector role is ideally suited, moreover, to evoking that sense of mystery with which he tries to surround his solitaries:

> I wish'd to see him move; but he remain'd
> Fix'd to his place, and still from time to time
> Sent forth a murmuring voice of dead complaint,
> Groans scarcely audible . . .   (IV, 429-432)

> And as I looked around, distress and fear
> Came creeping over me, when at my side,
> Close at my side, an uncouth shape appeared
> Upon a dromedary, mounted high.
> He seemed an Arab of the Bedouin tribes. . . .
>   (V, 73-77 [1850])

The reflector technique also provides the poet with a way of introducing a new situation. It helps create the necessary suspense, for one thing, and it ensures a bridge between the real world of the reader and the subjective, eccentric world of the solitary. "I saw an aged Beggar in my walk," he starts "The Old Cumberland Beggar" and only

---

Ballads as precursors of the dramatic monologue: see Langbaum, *The Poetry of Experience*, esp. pp. 71-72, and Stephen M. Parrish, "Dramatic Technique in 'Lyrical Ballads'," PMLA, LXXIV (1959), 85-97.

gradually, with an almost classical reticence, does he approach the old man's inner world. In "Michael," although the narrator plays no role in the main story, his lengthy monologues at the opening and close place the characters in a far different perspective than they would otherwise have for the reader. *The Ruined Cottage*, like *Wuthering Heights* and some of Conrad's narratives, has a double reflector: the poet first encounters the pedlar, who, in turn, introduces the still more remote world of Margaret. An even more distinct anticipation of modern narrative technique becomes evident when we note Coleridge's inability to appreciate "The Thorn" because of the unappealing quality of the narrator of that poem: "It is not possible to imitate truly a dull and garrulous discourser," he wrote, "without repeating the effects of dullness and garrulity."[12] In depicting his encounters with solitaries Wordsworth employed something perhaps analogous to what we today call a mask—a speaking voice chosen for its appropriateness to each poetic occasion. Wordsworth himself was quite explicit in a note describing the voice of the narrator of "The Thorn": "a Captain of a small trading vessel . . . who being past the middle age of life, had retired upon an annuity . . . to some village or country town of which he was not a native . . ." (PW, II, 512). But even when the poet masks as his own narrator he exploits sharply varying tones of voice: the subdued, almost impersonal tone which relates the tale of "Michael," for instance:

> If from the public way you turn your steps
> Up the tumultuous brook of Green-head Ghyll,
> You will suppose that with an upright path
> Your feet must struggle . . .

[12] *Biographia Literaria*, ed. Shawcross (London, 1907), II, 36. A rigorous application of Coleridge's principle would rule out much of the significant poetry and fiction since 1900—for instance, "Prufrock," *Ulysses*, *The Sound and the Fury*.

is different from the candid, manic-depressive tone which sets the scene for the meeting with the leech-gatherer:

> I was a Traveller then upon the moor;
> I saw the hare that raced about with joy;
> I heard the woods and distant waters roar;
> Or heard them not, as happy as a boy.

But even within the confines of *The Prelude* we can distinguish a gradation of voices, ranging from the invocatory enthusiasm of these lines:

> Ye Visions of the hills!
> And Souls of lonely places! can I think
> A vulgar hope was yours when Ye employ'd
> Such ministry . . .   (I, 491-494)

to the quiet solemnity which governs his meeting with the soldier:

> I return'd
> The blessing of the poor unhappy Man;
> And so we parted. Back I cast a look,
> And linger'd near the door a little space;
> Then sought with quiet heart my distant home.
> (IV, 500-505)

In language and tone the passage about the soldier is, in fact, far closer to "Michael" than it is to most other parts of *The Prelude*. For the tones of voice which Wordsworth assumes in his meetings with solitaries are often different from those with which he confronts the natural world. His stance with the solitaries is less presumptuous, for one thing, than with the non-human objects of nature. He is more modest, more passively receptive in their presence: the Wordsworth who meets the leech-gatherer is one caught unstably between the poles of joy and despair, and the Wordsworth who passes by the blind beggar in *The*

Prelude allows himself to be "admonished from another world." Moreover, although he may idealize his solitaries, he does not deify them as he does natural objects, nor does he approach them with the rapture that often characterizes his communings with nature.

But the meetings with solitaries are also communions of a sort. They are essentially different from the encounters between people that one finds, say, in Crabbe or Jane Austen. Rather, they are a kind of ritual, a drama of gesture and atmosphere; in the soldier episode, for instance, the reader's eye goes back and forth between the boy and the soldier as they enact their ritual:

> And now,
> Subduing my heart's specious cowardise
> I left the shady nook where I had stood,
> And hail'd him. Slowly from his resting-place
> He rose, and with a lean and wasted arm
> In measur'd gesture lifted to his head,
> Return'd my salutation; then resum'd
> His station as before.   (IV, 433-440)

Conversation is kept to a minimum: for Lewis Carroll to parody "Resolution and Independence" successfully he had merely to lift the few spoken words—"How is it that you live, and what is it you do?"—out of their highly ritualized context. In fact, it was Wordsworth's singular accomplishment in these encounters that he could bestow a measure of dignity upon figures who, in any other context, might have seemed ridiculous or, at best, inconsequential. "Demeanor calm . . . solemn and sublime" (IV, 472-473) are the words used to characterize the soldier; the leech-gatherer, despite his feebleness, spoke his words "in solemn order . . . choice word and measured phrase, above the reach / Of ordinary men; a stately speech"; even the eccentric heroine of the poem "The Sailor's Mother," who insists on carrying her dead son's caged bird while she goes begging on the roads, is described as "majestic in her person, tall and straight; / And like a Roman matron's was her mien and gait." One must never make the mistake, as did Wordsworth's earlier critics, of demanding verisimilitude between the solitaries and their prototypes in the real world; they are above all components of a poetic world, and as such they have no existence apart from it.

3 . SKIRTING TRAGEDY

In terror,
Remembered terror, there is peace and rest.
(*Borderers*, ll. 1468-1469)

As parts of a poetic world, the solitaries belong to the private, inner world of the poet, and it is through them that he is able to postulate at least the possibility of tragic events. Writing of "Resolution and Independence," G. S. Fraser has commented, "What Wordsworth had met with . . . , what awed and terrified him in the old leech-gatherer, was a dream image of *himself*; of himself as a lonely, patriarchal, godlike figure. Wordsworth looked in men, as he looked in nature, for a mirror; for a satisfactory reflection, or phantasmal embodiment, of his own predicaments."[13] The solitaries, to put it simply, helped Wordsworth overcome his own anxieties. "One sheds one's sicknesses in one's books," said D. H. Lawrence, and the statement is more or less applicable to any Romantic writer. Wordsworth projected his own fears in his solitaries, and in the leech-gatherer, for instance, his particular fear of "solitude, pain of heart, distress, and poverty." His usual strategy, after introducing them in their lowly state, is to enter into a ritual game with them, discovering and sharing a certain

[13] "Common Speech and Poetic Diction in Wordsworth," *Tribute to Wordsworth*, ed. M. Spark and D. Stanford (London, 1950), p. 174.

awesomeness which they reveal in the very intensity of their degradation. Figures who at first seem examples of the direst possibilities within life gradually emerge as models of endurance and even holiness. And by the time Wordsworth is done with them he has himself been raised to a higher, calmer state, as, after the episode with the soldier, he is ready, figuratively, to "seek with quiet heart his distant home."

> There I found
> Hope to my hope, and to my pleasure peace,
> And steadiness; and healing and repose
> To every angry passion—   (XII, 178-181)

thus he writes of his walks along the public roads meeting "strolling Bedlamites" and "uncouth vagrants." This is not to say that Wordsworth lacked what Henry James called the "imagination of disaster," the ability to "see life as ferocious and sinister."[14] The possibility, at least, of disaster is a central element in Wordsworth's vision. In the traditional emphasis upon his "wise passivity" and all the other platitudes with which his poetry has been surrounded, one often forgets that he is also a poet of terror and gloom, of the "visionary dreariness" which he invokes in his visit to the scene of the murderer's execution, with its

> Naked Pool,
> The Beacon on the lonely Eminence,
> The Woman, and her garments vex'd and toss'd
> By the strong wind. . . .   (XI, 313-316)

There is actually much in this mode in *The Prelude* and *Lyrical Ballads*, but we all too easily overlook it, perhaps because it avoids what is merely thrilling or sinister or grue-

[14] Quoted by Lionel Trilling in his study of *The Princess Casamassima*, *The Liberal Imagination* (New York, 1953), p. 67.

some. We know with what contempt Wordsworth looked upon the Gothic horrors in the popular literature of his time and how rigorously he kept them out of his own work. The bleakness and terror in Wordsworth never exist for themselves alone, but are inseparable from that sense of religious awe with which he invests them. Yet the very presence of this awe also works to transform them, to lift his visions of gloom and devastation to a less negative level. One can discern a certain "brinkmanship" in which Wordsworth engages, whereby he leads the reader to the edge of the abyss, only to reveal the saving hand of a higher power. His image of the boy virtually hanging from the cliff is, I think, emblematic of this habit:

> Oh! when I have hung
> Above the raven's nest, by knots of grass
> And half-inch fissures in the slippery rock
> But ill sustain'd, and almost, as it seem'd,
> Suspended by the blast which blew amain,
> Shouldering the naked crag; Oh! at that time,
> While on the perilous ridge I hung alone,
> With what strange utterance did the loud dry wind
> Blow through my ears! the sky seem'd not a sky
> Of earth, and with what motion mov'd the clouds!
>
> (I, 341-350)

One marvels at the poise (both physical and literary) with which he balances two seemingly opposed forces, the dangers ("fissures . . . slippery rock . . . naked crag . . . blast . . . hung alone") and the higher Providence which manifests itself in the inspiring wind, terrifying yet majestic, and the enraptured tone of the final lines.

Though capable of evoking the darker side of life, Wordsworth refuses to remain absolute for death. The classic instance of this refusal is his memory of the sight of a drowned man:

At length, the dead Man, 'mid that beauteous scene
Of trees, and hills and water, bolt upright
Rose with his ghastly face; a spectre shape
Of terror even, and yet no vulgar fear,
Young as I was, a Child not nine years old,
Possess'd me; for my inner eye had seen
Such sights before, among the shining streams
Of Fairy Land, the Forests of Romance:
Thence came a spirit hallowing what I saw
With decoration and ideal grace;
A dignity, a smoothness, like the works
Of Grecian Art, and purest Poesy.   (v, 470-481)

The grotesqueness of the dead man's gesture is swallowed
up as it were by the loveliness of the surrounding context.
The "inner eye" which has created this context is similar
in its workings to the "internal Being" in the following
passage, from the "Essay upon Epitaphs":

"It is to me inconceivable, that the sympathies of love
towards each other . . . could ever attain any new strength
. . . after we had received from the outward senses the impression of death . . . if the same were not counteracted by
those communications with our internal Being, which are
anterior to all these experiences, and with which revelation
coincides, and has through that coincidence alone . . . a
power to affect us. I confess, with me the conviction is
absolute, that, if the impression and sense of death were
not thus counterbalanced, such a hollowness would pervade the whole system of things, such a want of correspondence and consistency, a disproportion so astounding be-
twixt means and ends, that there could be no repose, no
joy" (PW, v, 446).

The essay dates from 1810, by which time the pantheism
which had informed *The Prelude* was fast being assimilated into Christian doctrine. But the sentiment is still

much the same: revelation merely "coincides" with it, for the "internal Being" by its very nature will perform its task of conciliation and renewal. The possibility of a tragic world is emotionally intolerable to him. "Such a hollowness would pervade the whole system of things . . . that there could be no repose, no joy"—Wordsworth's seems less a will to believe, than a will to create repose and joy.

Wordsworth's conciliating tendency, his habit of resolving harsher chords into less discordant ones, derives not so much from his later Christianity as from the Rousseauism which stands at the base of his best work. In the *Recluse* fragment of 1800, written at the height of his faith in nature's processes, he postulates a pleasure principle that governs his experience with the more dreadful aspects of life:

> Yea to this hour I cannot read a tale
> Of two brave Vessels matched in deadly fight,
> And fighting to the death, but I am pleased
> More than a wise man ought to be. I wish,
> Fret, burn, and struggle, and in soul am there;
> But me hath Nature tamed, and bade to seek
> For other agitations, or be calm;
> Hath dealt with me as with a turbulent Stream,
> Some nursling of the mountains, whom she leads
> Through quiet meadows, after he has learnt
> His strength, and had his triumph and his joy,
> His desperate course of tumult and of glee.
>
> (PW, V, 337)

We recognize the familiar formula of *pathos* changing to *ethos*. What is perhaps most striking about Wordsworth's theory is that the attainment of *ethos* does not exclude the possibility of experiencing *pathos*: one may revert vicariously to the mode of *pathos* through one's reading or

memory of the past (by writing *The Prelude* and by reading it, both he and the reader can have the best of both
worlds at once). The world of tragic and fearsome things,
he declares in lines following those quoted above,

> Of foes
> To wrestle with, and victory to complete,
> Bounds to be leapt, darkness to be explored,
> All that inflamed thy infant heart, the love,
> The longing, the contempt, the undaunted quest,
> All shall survive—though changed their office, all
> Shall live,—it is not in their power to die.

Wordsworth's theory of tragedy is perhaps not so far removed from Aristotle's as one might think: the *katharsis*
which for Aristotle occurred within the audience as a result
of the tragic events enacted on the stage, for Wordsworth
becomes a process ("though changed their office, all / Shall
live") enacted within the poet himself.

There was one brief moment in Wordsworth's life when
he came close to writing in the tragic mode. I refer to the
period of his retreat from Godwinism, when the optimistic
intellectual system toward which he had been so passionately committed broke down for him and the reconciling
influence of Nature had not yet filled the gap. Such a period of breakdown might have been the ideal breeding-
ground for tragedy; it is a pity that so little poetry of the
first order came out of it. And although Wordsworth later
wrote of this period in *The Prelude* with great distinction,
it had by then lost its tragic bite: the darker emotions,
when recollected in tranquility, assume a new perspective
altogether.

The darkness of this short period—which extends roughly from late 1795 to early 1797—is actually revealed in only
three works. The first of these is the revisions he made late
in 1796 to *Guilt and Sorrow*, changing its hollowly opti-

mistic ending to an uncompromisingly tragic one, with a final image of the hero dangling from the scaffold and gazed at by "dissolute men unthinking and untaught" (PW, I, 127n). But *Guilt and Sorrow*, even in this second and best version (the version usually printed contains the intolerable revisions made by Wordsworth in his old age), is hardly a successful poem. Although its characters are all solitaries of one sort or another, Wordsworth had not yet worked out a technique appropriate to his talents; above all, the discomfort he must have felt narrating action (his hero's initial crime is disposed of with the line "He met a traveller, robbed him, shed his blood"—p. 98) shows through from beginning to end because of the event-laden story he has chosen to tell.

The Borderers, subtitled tragedy, still reads as an impressive work once we grant Wordsworth's total lack of dramaturgy. Its impressiveness stems from the quality of its verse (higher than that of most of the better known nineteenth-century closet dramas) and from the genuine atmosphere of gloom with which Wordsworth has managed to pervade the whole; its tragic resolution, moreover, is unmitigated. Its hero and its villian, though not fully realized dramatically, are both alter-egos to the poet, and they are solitaries as well, though not of the lowly kind that Wordsworth later learned to use with such undisputed success; when the two confront each other in their great third act scene the verse burns with a dusky glow which he was never quite to recapture:

> Action is transitory—a step, a blow,
> The motion of a muscle—this way or that—
> 'Tis done, and in the after-vacancy
> We wonder at ourselves like men betrayed:
> Suffering is permanent, obscure and dark,
> And shares the nature of infinity.

(PW, I, 188)

But the one truly great work of Wordsworth's dark period is without question *The Ruined Cottage*. Coleridge once called this work "the finest Poem in our Language, comparing it with any of the same or similar Length,"[15] and although his judgments on nearly all the rest of the Wordsworth canon have been vindicated by time, this poem has remained largely neglected. The reason, of course, is clear: *The Ruined Cottage* was incorporated by Wordsworth into *The Excursion* and its tragic impact muted down by the conciliatory context with which he surrounded it. Indeed, an independent, early version was first made available in 1949, and then only in a fine-print appendix to the De Selincourt-Darbishire edition (PW, V, 379-399). My purpose here is merely to call attention to some of Wordsworth's additions and revisions as an example of the way in which he came to skirt the tragic consequences of his material. It is of interest, for instance, that the first lines which he composed, in late 1795, were those relating Margaret's catastrophe, with its note of inexorable doom (I quote only the end of the passage):

> And so she lived
> Through the long winter, reckless and alone;
> Till this reft house, by frost, and thaw, and rain
> Was sapped, and, when she slept, the nightly damps
> Did chill her breast, and in the stormy day
> Her tattered clothes were ruffled by the wind
> Even at the side of her own fire. Yet still
> She loved this wretched spot, nor would for worlds
> Have parted hence, and still that length of road
> And this rude bench one torturing hope endeared,
> Fast rooted at her heart; and here, my friend,
> In sickness she remained, and here she died,
> Last human tenant of these ruined walls.

> (PW, V, 399)

[15] *Collected Letters* (Oxford, 1959), IV, 564.

The words "The End," appended to this line in an early manuscript, add to the resounding finality of the last line. But in succeeding versions Margaret's tragedy declines in importance in inverse proportion as the role of the pedlar, who narrates her tale, increases. For the pedlar is still another of Wordsworth's masks, this one a Wordsworth who knew only the benign in nature and had escaped the burdens of despair; and Margaret's story reaches us only after being filtered, as it were, through the pedlar's increasingly optimistic point of view. By 1798 Wordsworth felt the need to add lines such as the following to the ones above:

> Be wise and chearful, and no longer read
> The forms of things with an unworthy eye.
> She sleeps in the calm earth and peace is here.
> I well remember that those very plumes,
> Those weeds and the high spear-grass on that wall,
> By mist and silent rain-drops silvered o'er,
> As once I passed, did to my mind convey
> So still an image of tranquillity,
> So calm and still, and looked so beautiful,
> Amid the uneasy thoughts which filled my mind,
> That what we feel of sorrow and despair
> From ruin and from change, and all the grief
> The passing shews of being leave behind
> Appeared an idle dream that could not live
> Where meditation was.   (PW, V, 403)

With minor revisions the poem stood resolved in this way when it became part of *The Excursion* in 1814. The additional lines, especially the image of the spear-grass and mist, are lovely in themselves and provide a cool, elegiac close to the stark tale narrated earlier; but we must also recognize that they (plus other additions to the pedlar's role) have created a new poem altogether and, above all, a poem of an entirely different genre, as different from the poem which Coleridge first read in 1797 as the *King Lear* of Nahum Tate is from Shakespeare's tragedy. But those familiar with *The Excursion* in its final and standard version may remember still another perspective placed upon Margaret's tragedy: in 1845 Wordsworth added these lines:

> Nor more would she have craved as due to One
> Who, in her worst distress, had ofttimes felt
> The unbounded might of prayer; and learned, with
>   soul
> Fixed on the Cross, that consolation springs,
> From sources deeper far than deepest pain,
> For the meek Sufferer.   (PW, V, 39)

If the Wordsworth of the Great Decade, having turned his back to tragedy, could rest satisfied with pantheistic consolations, the aged poet laureate felt compelled to affix an explicitly Christian seal to Margaret's sufferings.[16]

But the type of transformation to which Wordsworth subjected his materials was not peculiar to him. This tendency to seek a dimension beyond tragedy, to absorb the tragic occurrences of life, however real they may seem momentarily, within a higher, more beneficent way of seeing things, is at the root of most Romantic art. Like *The Ruined Cottage*, Goethe's portrayal of another lowly woman named Margaret was subjected to additions which totally altered the perspective through which her tragedy made itself felt. Thus, the *Urfaust*, the earliest surviving fragment of Goethe's greatest work, concludes with the uncompromising judgment "Sie ist gerichtet!" ("She is condemned!") pronounced by Mephistopheles on the help-

[16] For a more detailed examination of the development of *The Ruined Cottage* and its later fortunes, see the notes to the critical edition—PW, V, 7-40, 376-415—as well as Miss Darbishire's essay, " 'The Ruined Cottage' and 'The Excursion,' " *Essays, Mainly on the Nineteenth Century, Presented to Sir Humphrey Milford* (London, 1948), pp. 1-13.

less heroine. A later, more mature Goethe, one whose faith in the ultimate benevolence of nature had become more firmly rooted, was able to interject a voice from above with the words "Ist gerettet!" ("She is saved!") to counterbalance and transcend Mephistopheles' pronouncement; indeed, in the final version of *Faust* the reader need only turn the page from Gretchen's tormented monologues to find Faust "bedded on flowery turf" and surrounded by a chorus of soothing spirits who, shifting gears as it were from tragedy to a less absolute genre, enjoin him to forget the past and contemplate nature with its inexhaustible and ever-renewing energies. When one attacks Goethe, as did Erich Heller in an acute and influential essay,[17] for his failure to carry a potentially tragic situation to its ultimate consequences, one attacks the whole Romantic *ethos*. As a moral judgment made in an age with an almost compulsive demand for tragic vision, Heller's attack may be relevant enough; as criticism of art it is somehow beside the point. The art that emanates from the Rousseauistic strain in European thought—a tradition that holds together such diverse personalities as Wordsworth, Goethe, Tolstoy, and D. H. Lawrence—starts frankly from the premise that the tragic view of life is too narrow to account for the manifold possibilities open to men. Within this art the tragic view is often re-created movingly and persuasively, but it is never allowed the last word. At best it remains a momentary thing, the reverse, one might say, of the temporary bliss with which Shakespeare teased Lear and Cordelia in the otherwise tragic world of the play. The "visionary dreariness" that Wordsworth saw in all its vividness provides the basis for his "future restoration"; the impact of Anna Karenina's personal tragedy is finally absorbed within the higher contemplations of Tolstoy's alter-ego Levin.

---

[17] "Goethe and the Avoidance of Tragedy," *The Disinherited Mind* (Cambridge, 1952), pp. 29-49.

The anti-tragic view, when reduced to a set of cold abstractions, may well be bound to a specific time and place, in many ways incompatible with our own. As art, at its greatest it evinces the same power to convince—though with less blinding intensity—than its currently more fashionable alternative.

CHAPTER EIGHT

THE SOCIAL DIMENSION (2): THE
NON-VISIONARY BOOKS

1. THE JUVENALIAN SPIRIT

He truly is alone . . .
He by the vast Metropolis immured.
"Home at Grasmere," ll. 593, 597

TAKEN by itself, "Residence in London" is one of the least impressive books in *The Prelude*. Its importance becomes evident only when it is viewed within the larger scheme of the poem, for, together with Cambridge and revolutionary France, London is one of Wordsworth's images of the deceptive "outer" life which distracts him in his spiritual journey. Regardless of the actual facts of Wordsworth's life, it is basic to the poem's design that imagination must first be impaired before its triumphant restoration at the end of the poem. The imagination, in fact, remained "asleep" during Wordsworth's London sojourn:

Amid my sobs and tears
It slept, even in the season of my youth:
For though I was most passionately moved
And yielded to the changes of the scene
With most obsequious feeling, yet all this
Pass'd not beyond the suburbs of the mind.
(VII, 501-506)

The modern city, with its noise and restlessness, its false spectacles, squalor, and perversities, could penetrate only to the "suburbs of the mind": the true city of the mind, to extend Wordsworth's metaphor, could be stirred only by non-urban sights and experiences. Yet it was necessary for Wordsworth to come to terms with the meaning of the city in order to fulfill the epic-didactic task which he had set for himself. The condemnation of cities was originally to be relegated to a later portion of *The Recluse*, if we accept the testimony of Coleridge, who in his last years tried to recapitulate the plan for Wordsworth's vast uncompleted poem: ". . . Then he was to describe the pastoral and other states of society, assuming something of the Juvenalian spirit as he approached the high civilization of cities and towns, and opening a melancholy picture of the present state of degeneracy and vice; thence he was to infer and reveal the proof of, and necessity for, the whole state of man and society being subject to, and illustrative of, a redemptive process in operation. . . ."[1]

We know that the books on London and France were not originally planned for *The Prelude*, which, up to a relatively late date in its composition, was to consist of only the first four books and the present conclusion, plus individual passages now incorporated in the intervening books. Yet one speculates that Wordsworth, occupying himself with *The Prelude* while awaiting the strength and inspiration he needed to launch his larger philosophical poem, gradually adapted some of his plans for *The Recluse* to the needs of his more modest poem. As such, *The Prelude* increased in richness and scope, while *The Recluse* was drained of much of its lifeblood. If his autobiographical poem could not take up the "high civilization of cities and towns" in general, it could at least speak of the one great city which Wordsworth knew through personal ex-

[1] *Table Talk*, July 21, 1832.

perience and which could amply provide that "melancholy picture of the present state of degeneracy and vice" which the "Juvenalian spirit" by tradition demanded. Moreover, London and the French Revolution presented Wordsworth with images of hell embodying an appropriate stage in his spiritual journey from the lost paradise of childhood to the paradise regained with which the poem concludes. One wonders, in fact, how much flatter and more impoverished *The Prelude* would have seemed if he had stuck to his earlier plan of shifting directly from the adolescent exultations of Book IV to the restoration which he celebrates in the final book; for all its lofty passages—and most of the great spots of time had been composed before Wordsworth decided to include London and the Revolution—one would have noted a narrowness of emotional range, a monotony of loftiness such as one feels in reading a work like *Prometheus Unbound*.

Yet throughout Book VII Wordsworth maintains a stance of almost total aloofness from the urban inferno which he describes. Quite in contrast to those parts of the poem which deal with his experiences in nature, he does not celebrate his interaction with the outer environment, but insists, instead, on his alienation from it. "The face of every one / That passes by me is a mystery" (VII, 596-597), he notes with pain at one point. But his approach to this mystery is far different from his approach to the mysteries posed by Mt. Snowdon and the Simplon Pass, for in the book on London, except for his encounter with the beggar, he does not attempt to come fully to terms with the mystery, to explore the mysterious processes of interaction with an object which can never quite define. Wordsworth's characteristic language of personal vision is scarcely to be found in "Residence in London"; instead, the poet rigorously maintains his role of *spectator ab extra*:

> Now homeward through the thickening hubbub,
>   where
> See, among less distinguishable Shapes,
> The Italian, with his frame of Images
> Upon his head; with Basket at his waist
> The Jew; the stately and slow-moving Turk
> With freight of slippers piled beneath his arm.
> Briefly, we find, if tired of random sights . . .
>
> (VII, 227-233)

At such times the poet sounds curiously like a tourist guide. His technique throughout the book, in fact, is descriptive, consisting largely of a catalogue of sights and sounds— "Here this . . . there that": one is reminded of *An Evening Walk* and *Descriptive Sketches*, both of which reveal a poet adept in the Augustan art of complex and precise description:

> Here, plots of sparkling water tremble bright
> With thousand thousand twinkling points of light;
> There, waves that, hardly weltering, die away,
> Tip their smooth ridges with a softer ray;
> And now the whole wide lake in deep repose
> Is hushed, and like a burnished mirror glows . . .
>
> (PW, I, 15)

If one compares these two passages, one notes the superiority of the couplet to blank verse in controlling the tone of such descriptive passages; with its long-standing tradition of metrical and syntactical variations—note the sharply contrasting effects he achieved in the third and fifth lines of the second passage—the couplet, one speculates, might have provided Wordsworth with a more subtle and appropriate medium for his vision of the outer world. Consider these two urban scenes, the first from *The Prelude*

[236]

the second from a poem more strictly in the Juvenalian spirit, Johnson's *London*:

> Private Courts,
> Gloomy as Coffins, and unsightly Lanes
> Thrill'd by some female Vender's scream, belike
> The very shrillest of all London Cries,
> May then entangle us awhile,
> Conducted through those labyrinths unawares
> To privileg'd Regions and inviolate,
> Where from their airy lodges studious Lawyers
> Look out on waters, walks, and gardens green.
>
> (VII, 196-204)

> Prepare for death, if here at night you roam,
> And sign your will before you sup from home.
> Some finery fop, with new commission vain,
> Who sleeps on brambles till he kills his man;
> Some frolick drunkard, reeling from a feast,
> Provokes a broil, and stabs you for a jest.
>
> (*London*, ll. 224-229)

Wordsworth's lines, when lifted out of their context, rise little beyond the monotony of guidebook prose ("belike / The very shrillest of all London Cries"); and the same slightly disdainful tone governs his description of the vendor's scream and the lawyers gazing out of the Inns. Johnson's tone is all suppleness; the dire injunction "Prepare for death" rudely interrupts the urban routine of going out to sup, while the "frolick" drunkard's jesting stab hits the reader with a sudden, grim wryness. Johnson's verse, in short, is marked by a complexity of attitude unknown to Wordsworth, and his criticism of the social order—the essence of the Juvenalian attitude—does not, for Johnson at least, exclude the possibility of wit. Wordsworth, to be sure, had once tried his hand at Juvenalian imitation. In 1795, with the collaboration of his Cambridge friend Francis Wrangham, he had started an imitation of Juvenal's eighth satire, which, directed as it is against hereditary nobility, was an appropriate enough topic for him at that time. But the verse lacks Johnson's control, as the following passage, one of Wordsworth's contributions to the uncompleted project, will testify:

> Are these the studies that beseem a prince?
> Wedged in with blacklegs at a boxer's show
> To shout with transport o'er a knock-down blow,
> Mid knots of grooms the council of his state
> To scheme and counter-scheme for purse and plate.
> Thy ancient honours when shalt thou resume?
> Oh! shame! is this thy service boastful plume?
>
> (PW, I, 305)

When writing in the Augustan mode, Wordsworth was obviously more comfortable with the subject matter offered by *An Evening Walk* than by the social vision demanded in Juvenalian imitation.

It appears, then, that there was something more basic than verse form involved in the weakness of Wordsworth's picture of London. For one thing, Wordsworth was temperamentally adverse to satire. "I have long since come to a fixed resolution to steer clear of personal satire," he wrote to Wrangham in 1806 to explain his refusal to allow publication of their Juvenalian imitation (CO, 142). But his antipathy quite obviously extended beyond personal satire. To the degree that satire demands irony, or cynicism, or a sense of the absurd, it was as foreign to him as the tragic mode. On the few occasions in which he indulged in satire, one is aware of a deliberate heaviness, as in his portrait of a worldly London preacher:

[238]

There have I seen a comely Bachelor,
Fresh from a toilette of two hours, ascend
The Pulpit, with seraphic glance look up,
And, in a tone elaborately low
Beginning, lead his voice through many a maze,
A minuet course, and winding up his mouth,
From time to time into an orifice
Most delicate, a lurking eyelet, small
And only not invisible, again
Open it out, diffusing thence a smile
Of rapt irradiation exquisite.

(VII, 546-556)

The mock-Miltonic language of this parody retains little of the playful quality which one finds in Cowper, who had made this type of satire his own, but, in its context, helps to create the image of a grotesque, almost perverse urban world which constantly threatens the private world of the poet. Indeed, the detachment which Wordsworth so often asserts throughout the book on London has nothing in common with the self-assured, imperious detachment traditional to the satirical mode; rather, it is the detachment of the private self fighting to preserve its identity.

Wordsworth's condemnation of the city, moreover, does not issue from someone intimately in touch with the pulse of urban life, as were Juvenal and Johnson, but from an outsider whose knowledge of the city often betrays a certain simple-mindedness. Aubrey de Vere recalls the following anecdote about the poet:

"Wordsworth, despite his dislike to great cities, was attracted occasionally [to London] in his later years. . . . But he complained bitterly of the great city. It was next to impossible, he remarked, to tell the truth in it. 'Yesterday I was at S____ House; the Duchess of S____, showing me the pictures, observed: "Here is the portrait of my brother" (naming him), "and it is considered very like." To this I assented, partly perhaps in absence of mind, but chiefly, I think, with an impression that her Grace's brother was probably a person whose face every one knew or was expected to know; so that, as I had never met him, my answer was in fact a lie! It is too bad that, when more than seventy years old, I should be drawn from the mountains to London in order to tell a lie!' "[2]

The dogged naïveté that informs this passage issued from a stubborn pride in the mountain stronghold with which he identifies himself in the last sentence and which, with its associations of plain living and high thinking, confers upon him the right to denounce the whole of civilized urban life. Throughout "Residence in London" he reminds the reader of the distance he is trying to maintain from the corruption he sees around him: "A Traveller from our pastoral hills" (VII, 414) . . . "a transient visitant" (VII, 74), he calls himself, while throughout the book—for instance, by comparing the mother and child he saw in a theatre with the country lass Mary of Buttermere and her child (VII, 346-411)—he sustains a rigid contrast between pastoral virtue and urban vice.

In its approach to the city, "Residence in London" is characteristic, in varying ways, of both eighteenth- and nineteenth-century poetry. To the degree that it attempts to describe the intricacies of city life it looks back to the long line of Augustan city poems, whether in the breezy "georgic" manner of Swift and Gay or the caustic Juvenalian manner of Johnson. Judged in the light of this tradition, it seems a rather weak performance, for it lacks the wit, the complexity of attitude, and that intimate sense of

[2] "Recollections of Wordsworth," *Essays, Chiefly on Poetry* (London, 1887), II, 292-293.

the daily trivialities of urban life which only the confirmed city-dweller can know.

At other moments, however, we note a conception of the city that looks forward to the literature of the nineteenth century, as in these lines:

> When the great tide of human life stands still,
> The business of the day to come unborn,
> Of that gone by, lock'd up as in the grave . . .
> At late hours
> Of winter evenings when unwholesome rains
> Are falling hard, with people yet astir,
> The feeble salutation from the voice
> Of some unhappy Woman, now and then
> Heard as we pass . . .   (VII, 630-632, 635-640)

Within the broad limits of this conception the city appears as a mysterious entity, often dreamlike and fantastic, housing within itself a horde of lonely, suffering beings. The city, in short, assumes a consciously symbolic role—and often, indeed, it becomes grotesquely symbolic of hell, or of the whole multitude of evils in the modern world. In this role, it has served as one of the most powerful and inexhaustible symbols in post-Romantic literature. Within the novel its symbolic potentialities encompass the fog of Dickens' London and the searing summer heat of Dostoevsky's Saint Petersburg; in poetry one need only mention the infernal cities invoked by Baudelaire, Thomson, and the early Eliot.

In the first half of "Residence in London," with its guidebook method, Wordsworth was still reworking eighteenth-century materials; but in the second half, in the mad hysteria of Bartholemew Fair, for instance, he anticipates this symbolic conception of the modern city. Yet he does little more than anticipate; one need only compare his lines on prostitution:

> A Traveller from our pastoral hills,
> Southward two hundred miles I had advanced,
> And for the first time in my life did hear
> The voice of Woman utter blasphemy;
> Saw Woman as she is to open shame
> Abandon'd and the pride of public vice.
> Full surely from the bottom of my heart
> I shudder'd . . .   (VII, 414-421)

with these from Baudelaire:

> A travers les lueurs que tourmente le vent
> La Prostitution s'allume dans les rues;
> Comme une fourmilière elle ouvre ses issues;
> Partout elle se fraye un occulte chemin,
> Ainsi que l'ennemi qui tente un coup de main;
> Elle remue au sein de la cité de fange
> Comme un ver qui dérobe à l'Homme ce qu'il mange.
>
>   ("Le crépuscule du soir")

It is hardly fair, I think, to note with what concreteness and symbolic power Baudelaire has invested his subject. Wordsworth's genius was incapable of such effects. Objects that aroused his distaste also inhibited his imagination. The blind beggar, whom he could assimilate within his private world of solitaries, leaves a powerful impression; the prostitute, whom he could not so assimilate, is dismissed with the usual platitudes. The literature of social observation cannot afford to make such distinctions.

But this is only to say that Wordsworth has only a peripheral relationship to the social strain in literature. Like Balzac's Rastignac and Flaubert's Frédéric Moreau, the protagonist of *The Prelude* starts out as that archetypal figure in modern literature whom Lionel Trilling once described as the Young Man from the Provinces.[3] In the many nineteenth-century novels of which he is the hero, he seeks his way in the world of the big city, at the same time serving as a naïve reflector of the various layers of society through which he moves. But Rastignac, vowing to make war on the city on its own terms, is a more useful subject for the social analyst than the young Wordsworth, who, after a few months of viewing urban corruption, reaffirms his provincial integrity and leaves town. As it is, his later report on London remains but a brief, undramatic interlude surrounded by massive, memorable images of nature.

2 . SINCERE PASTORAL

Praise of the pastoral life stands on the other side of the coin from rejection of the city. It is appropriate, then, that Book VIII, "Love of Nature Leading to Love of Mankind," is devoted to the affirmation of pastoral values. In one sense, of course, the whole of *The Prelude*, since it claims the primacy of Nature over Art and Society, can be viewed as a version of pastoral. But in Book VIII Wordsworth is centrally concerned with man and society in a natural setting.

Unlike most of the great pastoral poets, Wordsworth actually grew up in a pastoral society—not, of course, the idealized society of nonchalant, piping shepherds celebrated by the pastoral tradition, but one of hard-working, "rude and homely" shepherds who spend their energies coping with the quite un-Arcadian fogs and storms which regularly beset his native domain. Everyone who has been in the Lake District is aware of the prominent role that shepherds and their flocks play in the landscape; indeed, the lone, bleating sheep is often the only living creature the traveller meets among the crags and on the summits

[3] *The Liberal Imagination*, pp. 67-73.

after he has left the inhabited valleys. Wordsworth thus had a ready-made pastoral image for his autobiographical poem, and he exploited it to the full.

There are three distinct types of pastoral described in Book VIII, each distinguished from one another by a different degree of artificiality. The first of these, and the one he most uncompromisingly rejects, is literary pastoral, the type which treats of

> A Corin of the groves, who lives
> For his own fancies, or to dance by the hour
> In coronal, with Phillis in the midst.
>
> (VIII, 420-422)

He rejects not so much the pastoral of the ancient poets—he even praised Theocritus for his naturalness (CO, 78)—but rather the pastoral of the rococo, which, removed as it was from its country roots, for Wordsworth's generation was typified by the academic pastorals of the Augustans and the *hameau* of Versailles to which the court of Louis XVI repaired for a frolicsome relief from courtly burdens.

The second type of pastoral was real enough—the shepherd's life which he had himself observed from the walls of Goslar:

> Telling there his hours
> In unlaborious pleasure, with no task
> More toilsome than to carve a beechen bowl
> For Spring or Fountain.   (VIII, 342-345)

Nature was benign here, work reduced to a minimum, and the whole mode of life idyllic without seeming artificial or literary; or, rather, Wordsworth conceives the pastoral life he observed during his brief German sojourn within the conventional Arcadian archetype (note the "beechen bowl"), though without the literary embellishments with which it had become associated over the centuries. But like all things of the external world, the pastoral realm he saw near Goslar was meaningful and real to Wordsworth only to the extent that it could interact with his own sensibilities. In this respect it was deficient, for although it was a place "where Fancy might run wild" (VIII, 326), it could not stir his deeper imaginative faculty. In preference to this benign form of pastoral, he invokes the harsher pastoral of his native territory:

> Yet hail to You,
> Your rocks and precipices, Ye that seize
> The heart with firmer grasp! Your snows and streams
> Ungovernable, and your terrifying winds,
> That howl'd so dismally when I have been
> Companionless, among your solitudes.
> There 'tis the Shepherd's task the winter long
> To wait upon the storms. . . .   (VIII, 353-360)

Quite in contrast to the older literary tradition, Wordsworth here locates pastoral in the realm of *pathos* rather than *ethos*. But this is "true" pastoral, as he saw and experienced it; indeed, its only connection to literary pastoral is its concentration on the "simpler" forms of social life and, in particular, on a sheep-raising economy. In the interest of truth and sincerity, the image of a long-past Golden Age toward which literary pastoral yearns to return is rigorously excluded from Wordsworth's pastoral. Even his native region had once known customs which might have created such an image for him:

> Of maids at sunrise bringing in from far
> Their May-bush, and along the Streets, in flocks,
> Parading with a Song of taunting Rhymes,
> Aim'd at the Laggards slumbering within doors. . . .
>   (VIII, 193-196)

But sincerity compelled him to reject such folk memories:

> This, alas!
> Was but a dream; the times had scatter'd all
> These lighter graces, and the rural ways
> And manners which it was my chance to see
> In childhood were severe and unadorn'd. . . .
>
> (VIII, 203-207)

Sincerity, perhaps, but one suspects the determining factor was the fact that Wordsworth's childhood imagination, or, more precisely, his later memory of his childhood imagination, was more powerfully excited by the "severe and unadorn'd" than by reports he had heard of the English rural golden age:

> But images of danger and distress,
> And suffering, these took deepest hold of me,
> Man suffering among awful Powers, and Forms;
> Of this I heard and saw enough to make
> The imagination restless. . . .
>
> (VIII, 211-215)

To exemplify the sort of pastoral experience which stirred him in childhood he follows the above passages (though he removed it from the 1850 text) with his conception of a pastoral poem, "The Matron's Tale" of the sheep and boy lost in the fog. Like "Michael," which bears the designation "A Pastoral Poem" and of which it was apparently first intended to form a part, "The Matron's Tale" is written largely in Wordsworth's lean-and-spare blank verse style, a style appropriately symbolized in Arnold's touchstone, "And never lifted up a single stone." The Miltonic catalogue of local place-names with which the tale opens:

> Thence up Helvellyn, a superior Mount
> With prospect underneath of Striding-Edge,

And Grisdale's houseless Vale, along the brink
Of Russet Cove, and those two other Coves,
Huge skeletons of crags . . .   (VIII, 238-242)

stands in severe contrast to the idyllic Arcadian places of
conventional pastoral. But if Wordsworth throughout the
tale insists on the harsh, unlovely aspects of Lake District
pastoral life, the tale also reveals his habit of skirting the
tragic. Even as we approach the end, the boy is seen "Right
in the middle of the roaring Stream, / Now stronger every
moment and more fierce" (VIII, 305-306). Yet in the final
lines he effects a quick transformation:

The sight was such as no one could have seen
Without distress and fear. The Shepherd heard
The outcry of his Son, he stretch'd his Staff
Towards him, bade him leap, which word scarce said
The Boy was safe within his Father's arms.
                                        (VIII, 307-311)

As usual, Wordsworth has moved from *pathos* to *ethos*,
from near-tragedy to the unmistakable showing-forth of
Providence. Nor need we take his bareness of style or his
insistence on local realism as signs that the tale has no
meaning beyond itself. Just as we perceive Biblical overtones in the mess of pottage which Michael and his family
so modestly consume, so the progress of "The Matron's
Tale," as Abbie F. Potts has argued in her comprehensive
study of the relation of *The Prelude* to earlier literary traditions, by analogy imitates the pattern of Christian redemption.[4]

The central argument around which *The Prelude*'s pastoral book—doubtless the most discursive section of the
poem—is built is the exaltation of mankind, and, in par·

[4] *Wordsworth's Prelude: A Study of Its Literary Form*, pp. 14n., 114,
239, 330, 342.

ticular, that segment of mankind whom Wordsworth had seen around him during childhood. Yet as one reads Book VIII closely one is aware that the love of mankind toward which the love of nature has led does not include the love of lowly men in general, but only a single type, the solitary. Wordsworth's memorable affirmation—

> Thus was Man
> Ennobled outwardly before mine eyes,
> And thus my heart at first was introduc'd
> To an unconscious love and reverence
> Of human Nature— (VIII, 410-414)

is preceded directly by one of his confrontations with solitaries:

> When I have angled up the lonely brooks
> Mine eyes have glanced upon him, few steps off,
> In size a giant, stalking through the fog,
> His Sheep like Greenland Bears; at other times
> When round some shady promontory turning,
> His Form hath flash'd upon me, glorified
> By the deep radiance of the setting sun:
> Or him have I descried in distant sky,
> A solitary object and sublime,
> Above all height! like an aerial Cross,
> As it is stationed on some spiry Rock
> Of the Chartreuse, for worship. (VIII, 399-410)

The shepherds of earlier pastoral poetry were much allegorized, as we know; but I can think of none who possessed quite the titanic qualities—his pagan form of a giant mixes unselfconsciously with his Christian role as a huge cross—with which Wordsworth invests this solitary shepherd. Less even than the leech-gatherer and Wordsworth's other solitaries, he seems to have no real roots in the world of everyday things. He is a grand imaginative construct, but no man; yet this is Wordsworth's example of the being who led him to the love of mankind. Significantly, Wordsworth writes "mankind," not "men," in the 1805 title; what Mme Roland wrote of his one-time leader Brissot—that he knew man, but not men[5]—can be said equally of Wordsworth. "He substituted one kind of pastoralism, one kind of idealization and simplification, for another," David Ferry concludes in his Wordsworth study,[6] which is itself a demonstration of the poet's fundamental unfriendliness to men and all mortal things. Next to Crabbe's uncompromising attitude, for instance, Wordsworth's anti-pastoralism seems curiously half-hearted. All his claims notwithstanding, the sincere pastoral which Wordsworth thought he had substituted for that of literary artifice was itself an artifice, though of a boldly original kind.

Wordsworth idealizes not only his individual shepherds, but the whole society of dalesmen who, in their ordered, traditional way of living, are contrasted with the brute masses of the city. In the preceding chapter I spoke of the high degree of detachment which Wordsworth, in his role of *spectator ab extra*, displays in his formal picture of the summer festival on Helvellyn at the opening of Book VIII. Whenever he has occasion to discuss this society as a whole, he treats it as a collection of long-since-determined types, each with his assigned place:

> Why should I speak of Tillers of the soil?
> The Ploughman and his Team; or Men and Boys
> In festive summer busy with the rake . . .
> The Quarry-man, far heard! that blasts the rock,
> The Fishermen in pairs, the one to row,
> And one to drop the Net. . . .   (VIII, 498-506)

[5] ". . . il juge bien l'homme et ne connaît pas du tout les hommes" (*Mémoires de Madame Roland*, ed. Cl. Perroud [Paris, 1905], I, 197).
[6] *Limits of Mortality*, p. 138.

THE SOCIAL DIMENSION (2)

At first sight one takes Wordsworth's manner to be simply
the traditional one of generalizing about each link in the
closely tied chain of society. Yet I think he also betrays a
peculiarly modern form of pastoralism in speaking of his
dalesmen. Thus, when he characterizes a family farm as
"the home and ancient Birth-right of their Flock" (VIII,
263) or describes the Lake District as one

> Which yet
> Retaineth more of ancient homeliness,
> Manners erect, and frank simplicity,
> Than any other nook of English Land,
> (IX, 217-220)

he displays the same zeal for rootedness that has stirred the
conservative imagination of so many poets down to the
present day. It is essentially the same form of pastoralism,
for instance, that we discern behind Yeats' prayer that his
daughter

> Live like some green laurel
> Rooted in one dear perpetual place. . . .
> And may her bridegroom bring her to a house
> Where all's accustomed, ceremonious . . .
> ("A Prayer for My Daughter")

or the tradition-conscious society which T. S. Eliot advo-
cates in his later writings. With its recurrent vocabulary of
words such as *roots, ancient, birth-right, custom,* it is an
attitude less directly related to any older conservatism than
to the type we associate with Burke, whom Wordsworth, in
a late addition to *The Prelude,* had described in terms
applicable to the social theories which emerge from Book
VIII:

> While he forewarns, denounces, launches forth,
> Against all systems built on abstract rights,
> Keen ridicule; the majesty proclaims

Of Institutes and Laws, hallowed by time;
Declares the vital power of social ties
Endeared by Custom. . . .   (VII, 523-528 [1850])

Although Book VIII was composed in 1804, when Wordsworth, his conservatism already fairly rooted, was sealing
his friendship with Sir George Beaumont, the social sentiments in this book are but an extension of those expressed
in his famous letter to Fox four years before, when he complained of the "rapid decay of the domestic affections
among the lower orders of society. . . . Parents are separated from their children, and children from their parents;
the wife no longer prepares with her own hands a meal for
her husband, the produce of his labour" (EL, 260-261). The
attempt to remodel a disintegrating social structure by
pleading a return to traditional domestic relationships is
of the essence of modern conservatism.

Although Wordsworth claimed to transform and refine
the meaning of pastoral, his conception in one respect
repudiates the very nature of the pastoral ideal. "The psychological root of the pastoral," writes Renato Poggioli in
his penetrating analysis of the transformations which the
form has undergone, "is a double longing after innocence
and happiness, to be recovered not through conversion or
regeneration, but merely through a retreat."[7] Wordsworth's
storm-battered shepherds have little leisure for retreats;
true pastoral, one suspects, must reside elsewhere within
the Wordsworthian world. In writing of Rousseau's *Reveries*, Poggioli distinguishes a new role that pastoral assumed in the Romantic period:

"As the pastoral poet replaces the labors and troubles of
love with an exclusive concern for the self, he changes into
a new Narcissus, contemplating with passionate interest
not his body but his soul. At this point, he deals only, in

[7] "The Oaten Flute," *Harvard Library Bulletin*, XI (1957), 147.

Whitman's words, with 'the single, solitary soul,' and the pastoral becomes the poetic vehicle of solipsism. . . . What Rousseau terms 'rêverie' is a state of passive introspection, by which the pastoral psyche reflects its shadow in nature's mirror, fondly and blissfully losing its being within the image of itself."[8]

By this definition, Wordsworth himself emerges as the shepherd of his poem; and during those mystic moments

> In which the heavy and the weary weight
> Of all this unintelligible world,
> Is lightened,

he finds an inward Arcadia as blissful as, though less heavily peopled than, that of the older pastoral poets.

3 . THE POETRY OF REVOLUTION

> But these are things
> Of which I speak, only as they were storm
> Or sunshine to my individual mind,
> No further.   (x, 103-106)

a. Finding a Style

Once Wordsworth had decided that his experiences in the French Revolution were necessary to the design of *The Prelude*, he was faced with the problem of finding a language appropriate to these experiences. The rhetoric which he had developed for the early books to celebrate the interaction of man and nature was useless for the revolutionary books. The Revolution, after all, was an extension of the season in Hell which he depicted in "Residence in London"; his task was not to celebrate, but to elegize, condemn, and, as it turned out, to dramatize. The spot of time, the struggle toward definition, the use of breezes and water to probe the mysterious interconnections within the

---

[8] *Ibid.*, pp. 166-167.

whole natural world—these characteristic devices were of no avail in his picture of the Revolution. Throughout Books ix and x (the latter comprises Books x and xi in the 1850 version) there are but two passages which we could call spots of time: his fearsome night in Paris after the September Massacres (x, 38-82) and his reception of the news of Robespierre's death (x, 516-567); for the rest he was forced to depend on a manner distinctly different from that of the other books.

The drama of the revolutionary books is obviously not drama in the usual sense. The reader is shown scarcely any of the actual day-by-day events of the Revolution, and the books have doubtless disappointed those who have sought in them the usual color of narrative history. Indeed, Wordsworth is at his weakest when he starts to chronicle; a passage such as the following is no more than undistinguished prose:

> The Men already spoken of as chief
> Of my Associates were prepared for flight
> To augment the band of Emigrants in Arms
> Upon the borders of the Rhine, and leagued
> With foreign Foes mustered for instant war.
>
> (ix, 183-187)

For depicting detail a method such as Carlyle's has the indisputable advantage; I quote at random from his account of the September Massacres:

"Man after man is cut down; the sabres need sharpening, the killers refresh themselves from wine-jugs. Onward and onward goes the butchery; the loud yells wearying down into bass growls. A sombre-faced shifting multitude looks on; in dull approval, or dull disapproval; in dull recognition that it is Necessity. 'An *Anglais* in drab greatcoat' was seen, or seemed to be seen, serving liquor from his own dram-bottle;—for what purpose, 'if not set on by Pitt,'

Satan and himself knew best! Witty Dr. Moore grew sick on approaching, and turned into another street.—Quick enough goes this Jury-Court; and rigorous. The brave are not spared, nor the beautiful, nor the weak. Old M. de Montmorin, the Minister's Brother, was acquitted by the Tribunal of the Seventeenth; and conducted back, elbowed by howling galleries; but is not acquitted here. Princess de Lamballe has lain down on bed: 'Madame you are to be removed to the Abbaye.' 'I do not wish to remove; I am well enough here.' There is a need-be for removing. She will arrange her dress a little, then; rude voices answer, 'You have not far to go.' She too is led to the hell-gate. . . ."[9]

Wordsworth was too reflective to indulge in such details in his poem. Significantly, he was never on the spot during the Massacres; he arrived in the capital well over a month later, and had left for England long before the actual Reign of Terror had begun. When he writes of violence he views it with a decorum which, in fact, eschews all detail:

> Domestic carnage now filled all the year
> With Feast-days; the old Man from the chimney-nook,
> The Maiden from the bosom of her Love,
> The Mother from the Cradle of her Babe,
> The Warrior from the Field, all perish'd, all. . . .
>
> (X, 330-334)

Yet such generalization is not altogether typical of Wordsworth's approach to the Revolution; his characteristic mode stands somewhere between the two extremes—the accumulation of chronicled detail and its larger, symbolic reverberations. Blake's prophecy, *The French Revolution*, attempts to capture only the reverberations, with the result that the actual world of men and events dissolves into an apocalyptic vision:

[9] *The French Revolution*, Centenary Edition (New York, n.d.), III, 29.

Then the ancientest Peer, Duke of Burgundy, rose
   from the Monarch's right hand, red as wines
From his mountains; an odor of war, like a ripe
   vineyard, rose from his garments,
And the chamber became as a clouded sky; o'er the
   council he stretch'd his red limbs,
Cloth'd in flames of crimson.   (ll. 83-86)

For Blake, and to a large degree for Carlyle, whose details
are counterbalanced by constant evocations of the hellish
aspects of the events he is describing, only a single, bom-
bastic tone is possible. In Wordsworth, on the other hand,
the events are filtered through a reflective mind:

>   'Twas in truth an hour
> Of universal ferment; mildest men
> Were agitated; and commotions, strife
> Of passion and opinion fill'd the walls
> Of peaceful houses with unquiet sounds.
> The soil of common life was at that time
> Too hot to tread upon. . . .   (IX, 163-169)

The violence of the events is everywhere apparent in
Wordsworth's account; imagery of noise, storm and earth-
quake is as pervasive here as in Blake and Carlyle. But it
is violence seen from a distance, muted down, reflected
upon. For one thing, the temporal perspective works here
less to reawaken past emotion than to subdue it (note, for
instance, how the phrase "at that time" counterbalances
the brusque "too hot"). Behind the events one feels a controlling intelligence at work interpreting them through a
perspective hallowed by long rhetorical tradition: the
changes affecting France are viewed as *ethos* giving way to
pathos. "Mildest," "peaceful," and "common life" are set
in contrast to "passion," "agitated," and "commotions,"
and behind these last two words one hears the Latin *agitare*

and *commovere*, the traditional attributes of *pathos*. But if the distancing that Wordsworth achieves serves to subdue the harsh immediacy of the events, it also endows them with a certain legendary quality, making the men whom Wordsworth had seen in the convention halls but a dozen years before seem like ancient figures who long ago had finished playing their roles in an ever-recurring pattern:

> The land all swarm'd with passion, like a Plain
> Devour'd by locusts, Carra, Gorsas, add
> A hundred other names, forgotten now,
> Nor to be heard of more, yet were they Powers,
> Like earthquakes, shocks repeated day by day,
> And felt through every nook of town and field.
>
> (IX, 177-182)

Although we distinguish an attitude of detachment, it is the detachment of an elegiac poet, of one who strains to view events which have moved him through an appropriately larger perspective.

It is well known that Wordsworth dealt with the Revolution in three of his longer works. In the first of these, *Descriptive Sketches*, written well before his disillusionment, he is uncomplicatedly exultant:

> —Tho' Liberty shall soon, indignant, raise
> Red on his hills his beacon's comet blaze;
> Bid from on high his lonely cannon sound,
> And on ten thousand hearths his shout rebound;
> His larum-bell from village-tow'r to tow'r
> Swing on th' astounded ear it's dull undying roar.
>
> (PW, I, 88)

But in *The Prelude* and *The Excursion* the joy is only the first movement in a longer cycle which takes him through the depths of despair and thence back to the restoration of his powers. In *The Prelude* the cycle starts in Book VI when Wordsworth, on his first trip to France, joins the festivities celebrating the first anniversary of the Bastille: "France standing on the top of golden hours, / And human nature seeming born again" (VI, 353-354); and the cycle is only partly completed in Book X, for its real end is properly the resolution and conclusion of the poem as a whole. In *The Excursion* the cycle encompasses principally Books III and IV, called respectively "Despondency" and "Despondency Corrected." But in *The Excursion* Wordsworth was no longer able to recapture his attitudes toward the Revolution with the intensity he had achieved in *The Prelude* only a few years before. In the later poem the Revolution is experienced not by the poet himself, but by one of his masks, the despondent Solitary. The essential quality of Wordsworth's achievement in the revolutionary books of *The Prelude* can best be suggested if we set corresponding passages from the two poems next to one another. Each of these passages attempts to record his inner conflict after his initial shock at the excesses of the Revolution, but while he still attempts to uphold its ideals. I quote first from *The Prelude*:

> An active partisan, I thus convoked
> From every object pleasant circumstance
> To suit my ends; I moved among mankind
> With genial feelings still predominant;
> When erring, erring on the better part,
> And in the kinder spirit; placable,
> Indulgent oft-times to the worst desires
> As on one side not uninform'd that men
> See as it hath been taught them, and that time
> Gives rights to error; on the other hand
> That throwing off oppression must be work
> As well of licence as of liberty;
> And above all, for this was more than all,

> Not caring if the wind did now and then
> Blow keen upon an eminence that gave
> Prospect so large into futurity,
> In brief, a child of nature, as at first,
> Diffusing only those affections wider
> That from the cradle had grown up with me,
> And losing, in no other way than light
> Is lost in light, the weak in the more strong.
>
> (x, 737-757)

I have quoted at length because the passage is essentially an argument—an argument within the poet's mind—and one whose shifts and waywardings are discernible only in a larger segment. One's first impression is perhaps the high concentration of mental energy within these lines. Through the frequent transitions—"as on the one side," "and above all," "in brief"—plus the qualifications— "when erring, erring on the better part," "for this was more than all"—even before one has determined the meaning of each twist and turn of thought, one is aware of his deep inner turmoil, though also of a determined effort at precision, as though the precision with which he analyzed the turmoil could, in effect, help to contain it. There is nothing "poetic," in the nineteenth-century sense, about the passage, nothing, for instance, comparable to the major spots of time and the invocations to nature. Nor does it utilize the language of concrete, visible objects which our own century has come to demand in poetry. The concreteness in these lines inheres rather in the precision with which he portrays the mental process; and it is a concreteness of movement rather than of things, and, as in the later Henry James, it is achieved to a great degree by the accumulation of transitions and qualifications which guide the stream of thought.

I turn next to a comparable passage from the Solitary's
Tale in *The Excursion*:

> For rights,
> Widely—inveterately usurped upon,
> I spake with vehemence; and promptly seized
> All that Abstraction furnished for my needs
> Or purposes; nor scrupled to proclaim,
> And propagate, by liberty of life,
> Those new persuasions. Not that I rejoiced,
> Or even found pleasure, in such vagrant course,
> For its own sake; but farthest from the walk
> Which I had trod in happiness and peace,
> Was most inviting to a troubled mind;
> That, in a struggling and distempered world,
> Saw a seductive image of herself.
>
> (III, 793-805)

Here he attempts to use the same rhetorical method to record his inner turmoil—one notes the transitions of
thought: "nor scrupled to proclaim," "not that I rejoiced,"
"but farthest"—yet he captures only faintly the tensions of
the earlier poem. The fullness and variety which marked
his earlier portrayal of intense mental process are missing
in the later passage. One feels that he is condensing the
process, as in the clumsy locution, "Farthest from the
walk . . . / Was most inviting to a troubled mind." The
language betrays a relentlessly Miltonic quality: "inveter-
ately usurped upon, / I spake with vehemence," "a struggling and distempered world," and it lacks that delicate
balance between the heavy, Latinate word and the short,
informal word or phrase which marked the lines from *The
Prelude*—

> Not caring if the wind did now and then
> Blow keen upon an eminence that gave

Prospect so large into futurity—

(X, 750-752)

in which the off-handed "now and then" and the unexpectedly concrete "blow keen" set up a base for the grand
abstractions that follow. Through his failure to reproduce
the inner argument in all its freshness and richness, one
suspects that by the time he got to *The Excursion* he had
begun to lose touch with his earlier experience, that the
gates of memory were already closing for him ("I see by
glimpses now; when age comes on, / May scarcely see at
all"). Moreover, his doctrinal purposes in *The Excursion*
prevented him from treating "despondency" with full
imaginative power, for he was quite obviously in a hurry
to get on with "despondency corrected."

Above all, the lines from *The Excursion* lack the peculiarly dramatic quality which characterizes the revolutionary books in *The Prelude*. The drama does not, as I
have stressed, lie in the excitement of outer event, for it is
a drama within the poet's mind, one that exerts its impact
rhetorically by means of its syntactical action rather than
by plot or interchange of dialogue. It is a type of poetry
ideally suited to the discussion of ideas: Wordsworth's reactions to Godwinian rationalism come forward with the
same dramatic force, and, indeed, are part of the same continuing monologue, as his reactions to an actual scene such
as Louvet's accusation of Robespierre. The revolutionary
books are dramatic in still another sense, in that Wordsworth succeeds in rendering the quality of his inner
struggle at *each* stage within the long cycle; emotions and
attitudes that were obviously foreign to him at the time of
writing are recollected in their immediacy, while in *The
Excursion* they seem to reecho only as reconsidered passion,
recollected in perhaps too rigidly imposed a tranquillity.

As biographical documents the books on the Revolution have received ample, though sometimes also misguided attention; as poetry they have been virtually ignored. Perhaps their justest appreciation was made by John Morley in 1888 when he pointed to "their strenuous simplicity, their deep truthfulness, their slowfooted and inexorable transition from ardent hope to dark imaginations, sense of woes to come, sorrow for human kind, and pain of heart. . . . The story of these three Books has something of the severity, the self-control, the inexorable necessity of classic tragedy, and like classic tragedy it has a noble end."[10] It might also be said that they represent a type of poetry unique in the literature of the last 300 years—a type perhaps best described by the "direct sensuous apprehension of thought" which Mr. Eliot once affected to see no later than the Metaphysicals, though the diction and the sentiments have little enough in common with Metaphysical verse. As the monologue of a single intelligence coming to grips with the constantly changing relationships of a group of attitudes, the poetry of these books stirs the reader with something of the power that we admire in the dramatic language of Shakespeare and Chapman. Its language of argument has been found, moreover, to derive partly from Wordsworth's reading of Samuel Daniel.[11] In only one other work, in the very Elizabethan speeches of Oswald in *The Borderers*, from which, indeed, he borrowed several lines for Book x (see *Prel.*, p. 606), did Wordsworth successfully write this type of verse. Since it is not characteristic of the language, or even of the subject matter, which

[10] In Macmillan edition of *Complete Poetical Works of William Wordsworth* (London, 1898), p. liii.

[11] See Joan Rees, "Wordsworth and Samuel Daniel," N&Q, N.S. VI (1959), 26-27, and Cecil C. Seronsy, "Daniel and Wordsworth," SP, LVI (1959), 187-213. Seronsy discusses Daniel's influence on Wordsworth in general, but his conclusions seem to me especially relevant to the verse of the books on the Revolution.

established his reputation, it has long remained neglected for want of appropriate admirers.

b. *The Unpolitical Poet*

For all the space that Wordsworth devotes to the Revolution and its aftermath—virtually a fourth of the poem—*The Prelude* has as little real concern with politics as perhaps any longer work in our literature. By politics in a literary work I do not mean merely the expression of a particular set of moral convictions about how society should be run—Wordsworth possessed such convictions amply and did not hesitate to voice them in his work—but something more comprehensive. For politics, in literature as in life, involves all the complexities of human behavior as manifested in the public realm. It involves, for instance, any choice between alternatives—often a choice among evils—made by anyone empowered to exercise choice. It involves, as well, the manipulation of other men for desired ends, the exercise of influence and the whole intricate relationship between a leader and those who follow him. When moral convictions enter the domain of politics their role is less interesting in isolation than in their relation to the larger complex—for instance, the discrepancy between what should be and what is, or the transformation of these convictions into workable action. By this larger definition a work such as *Paradise Lost* is profoundly political in a way that *The Prelude* is not. Satan's Council in Hell, for instance, explores the problems of political leadership with the same incisiveness as, say, Shakespeare's *Julius Caesar*, while the whole drama of the Fall is a model of the conflict between theoretical conviction and the human entanglements created by the pressure of actual experience.

Wordsworth's incapacity for dramatic interchange between characters would preclude the treatment of politics as I have tried to define it. And when he entered the political arena in *The Prelude* he could approach it only in a limited and special way. The peculiar quality of Wordsworth's political commitment is suggested in his description of his first trip to France, when he and his companion sail down the Rhône with a group of delegates returning from the festivities commemorating the fall of the Bastille:

> In this blithe Company
> We landed, took with them our evening Meal,
> Guests welcome almost as the Angels were
> To Abraham of old. The Supper done,
> With flowing cups elate, and happy thoughts,
> We rose at signal giv'n, and form'd a ring
> And, hand in hand, danced round and round the
>   Board;
> All hearts were open, every tongue was loud
> With amity and glee; we bore a name
> Honour'd in France, the name of Englishmen,
> And hospitably did they give us hail
> As their forerunners in a glorious course,
> And round, and round the Board they danced again.
>
> (VI, 401-413)

As poetry, these lines brilliantly celebrate a moment of communion between the poet and people. Their closest literary prototype is, perhaps, that scene in *Anna Karenina* in which the landowner Levin, after joining his peasants in the work of harvest, communes with them in their revels. Wordsworth sustains a tone of rapture throughout the passage; words and images suggesting a state of mania abound: "blithe," "flowing cups," "happy thoughts," "danced round and round," "glee," the last of these being a term which Wordsworth often used to suggest a kind of childlike non-responsibility. Yet the frenzy is kept within bounds: the Biblical-pastoral simile of the angels visiting Abraham at once sets up and limits the perspective in which it may be viewed. As a romantic response to public events, this passage, like the more celebrated one beginning "Bliss was it in that dawn to be alive," is doubtless unsurpassed among poetry of its kind; but it also betrays the sensibility of an enthusiast, of one who can generate strong feelings—whether of hope or despair—toward events, but who also stands essentially outside the complex process by which these events are brought about.

One feels the same distance between the poet and the historical process even after Wordsworth had gained his knowledge of revolutionary ideals under the tutelage of Michel Beaupuy. For what Beaupuy gave him was above all a sense of ideals and principles, but not the political realities which lurk beneath them. The "hunger-bitten" girl who elicits Beaupuy's comment, "'Tis against *that* / Which we are fighting" (IX, 518-519), suggests the quality of the sentiments which passed between the two men: on a poetic level she is an acceptable enough addition to the Wordsworthian collection of solitaries, but the reader is also struck by the naïveté with which Wordsworth expects him to accept her as a political emblem. As with the Girondins to whom he so naturally attached himself, Wordsworth's notions about the Revolution are strongly colored by analogies from ancient history.

> Such conversation under Attic shades
> Did Dion hold with Plato, ripen'd thus
> For a Deliverer's glorious task—
>
> (IX, 414-416)

Thus he describes his relationship with Beaupuy; and a similarly Plutarchian context is invoked when he portrays his reactions to Jacobin tyranny:

I called to mind those truths . . .
. . . to Harmodius known
And his Compeer Aristogiton, known
To Brutus, that tyrannic Power is weak,
Hath neither gratitude, nor faith, nor love,
Nor the support of good or evil men
To trust in, that the Godhead which is ours
Can never utterly be charm'd or still'd. . . .

(x, 159-172)

Wordsworth makes stirring enough verse out of the Revolution, but, trapped as he is by the black-and-white moral absolutes which govern his perspective, he is unable to engage in that free play of the intellect which can make critical distinctions between men's motives and take into account the ambivalences in human behavior. It is indicative of Wordsworth's historical imagination that the epic themes which he proposed at the opening of *The Prelude* —Gustavus Vasa, Sertorius, Mithridates, De Gourges, Wallace—are all, in one way or another, concerned with the subject of oppression and liberation. Had he carried out any of these themes, one can well imagine the heroic enthusiasm with which he would have sought to embody it; but one can also imagine what difficulty he would have had coping with the less lofty aspects of his heroes—for instance, their problems in manipulating rival factions among their men.

I have tried to describe what I take to be a limitation in Wordsworth's range of perception—a limitation that shows up whenever he attempts to comment on the social or political scene. Consider, for instance, his tract *The Convention of Cintra*, written in 1809 to protest the compromise reached by Wellington and his officers with the Napoleonic forces on the Peninsula. The *Convention* conveys something of the same excitement as the books in

The Prelude on the Revolution. But since Wordsworth conceived of politics only in terms of abstract principles, the excitement emanates not from the intellectual play with which he might have explored the gap between principles and actualities, but from the energetic and lofty rhetoric with which he praises the oppressed and denounces tyrants and compromisers. Wordsworth interprets events within as rigorously moralistic a framework as that of any of the ancient historians he so much admired.[12] The oppressed Spaniards become the heroes of his tract:

"A people, whose government had been dissolved by foreign tyranny, and which had been left to work out its salvation by its own virtues, prayed for our help. . . . They had spoken of unrelenting and inhuman wrongs; of patience wearied out; of the agonizing yoke cast off; of the blessed service of freedom chosen; of heroic aspirations; of constancy, and fortitude, and perseverance; of resolution even to the death; of gladness in the embrace of death; of weeping over the graves of the slain, by those who had not been so happy as to die; of resignation under the worst final doom; of glory, and triumph, and punishment" (*Prose Works*, I, 111).

Even Coleridge, who greatly admired the Cintra tract, thought this account of Spanish nationalism "somewhat too much *idealized*."[13] Coleridge also, for that matter, considered the tract "almost a self-robbery from some great philosophical poem,"[14] which was only to say that it shared in the same "poetical" conception of politics as the revolutionary books of *The Prelude* or the treatment of poli-

12 Jane Worthington's study, *Wordsworth's Reading of Roman Prose* (New Haven, 1946), gives ample evidence of the profound effect that Plutarch and the Roman historians had on his way of looking at history and politics. See particularly the chapter entitled "Roman Influence on Wordsworth's Political Thought," pp. 19-42.

13 *Collected Letters* (Oxford, 1959), III, 216, italics Coleridge's.

14 *Ibid.*, p. 214.

tics we might have found in some later, uncompleted part of *The Recluse*. There are long stretches in the *Convention* in which Wordsworth quite loses track of the peculiarities of time and place, and in which we, in fact, become aware that the political and military situation he started from was but a metaphor to help him launch out on a more pressing concern, the exploration of an emotional pattern that proceeds from despondency to the attainment of spiritual power:

"—Despair thinks of *safety*, and hath no purpose; fear thinks of safety; despondency looks the same way:—but these passions are far too selfish, and therefore too blind, to reach the thing at which they aim; even when there is in them sufficient dignity to have an aim.—All courage is a projection from ourselves; however short-lived, it is a motion of hope. But these thoughts bind too closely to something inward,—to the present and to the past,—that is, to the self which is or has been. Whereas the vigour of the human soul is from without and from futurity,—in breaking down limit, and losing and forgetting herself in the sensation and image of Country and of the human race; and, when she returns and is most restricted and confined, her dignity consists in the contemplation of a better and more exalted being, which, though proceeding from herself, she loves and is devoted to as to another" (I, 115-116).

The pattern, as it emerges here, is similar to the one we find in *The Prelude* and *The Excursion*: it is essentially the journey of the soul—individual or collective—from the confinement of despair and false allegiances to the freedom of higher spiritual commitments. It hardly matters, ultimately, whether this commitment is directed toward the imagination, as in *The Prelude*, or toward "country and the human race," as in the passage above; what matters is the peculiarly spiritual nature of the commitment and its basic antipathy to other, less spiritual commitments. Indeed, on close examination Wordsworth's notorious conservatism does not really look much different from his early liberalism; in the abstract quality of its thought the "Apology for the French Revolution" of 1793, for instance, has far deeper affinities with *The Convention of Cintra* than Wordsworth would have liked to admit.[15]

In his penetrating study *Politics and the Novel*, Irving Howe has defined the political novel—as practiced, for instance, by Stendhal, Dostoevsky, and Joseph Conrad—as one that aims "to show the relation between theory and experience, between the ideology that has been preconceived and the tangle of feelings and relationships he [the author] is trying to present."[16] In a sense this is the very conflict that Wordsworth attempts to portray in "Residence in France," yet the experience that, for Wordsworth, comes in conflict with the theory of the French revolutionists and Godwin is not, as in the novelists whom Howe discusses, experience in a concretely embodied world, but the private, inward experience of a single intelligence, one guided wholly by abstract principle and spiritual perception. Thus, the "tangle of feelings and relationships," which in such works as *The Charterhouse of Parma* and *Nostromo* encompasses a whole spectrum of attitudes and actions represented within the imaginary commonwealths of these two books, in *The Prelude* is reduced to the tangle of Wordsworth's personal feelings.

Although Wordsworth purports to treat a political and historical theme, his picture of England and France in the early 1790's is essentially a metaphor he employs to motivate a private spiritual struggle within himself. We all too easily misunderstand his treatment of the Revolution if we

---

[15] The essential continuity of Wordsworth's political thought is convincingly demonstrated in F. M. Todd's survey of his political attitudes, *Politics and the Poet* (London, 1957).

[16] *Politics and the Novel* (New York, 1957), p. 22.

expect it to yield the same rich insights into the nature of political man which we find in the realistic fiction that has flourished so imposingly since Wordsworth's time. The characteristic achievement of this realistic tradition, as Lionel Trilling has reminded us in many essays, has been to project a convincing image of society and, above all, to explore the tensions between society and the private self. In *The Prelude* this social dimension is largely missing, or, more precisely, it exists only as a shadowy and negative force against which the self struggles and which it ultimately transcends. In its almost exclusive concern with the self and the life of the spirit, *The Prelude*'s real affinities are not with the realistic tradition, but with works such as *Faust, Either-Or,* and *Prometheus Unbound.* And like these works, it is motivated by perhaps the central informing idea in the serious literature of the early nineteenth century: the restoration of faith—in God, Nature, the mind of man, or whatever—after the ideals of the secular world have been found wanting. Less panoramic in scope and more classical in spirit than these other works, *The Prelude* sticks close to its central theme; and what view it gives of the external world is strictly subordinated to the requirements of this theme. To put it another way, throughout *The Prelude* the external world is rarely dwelt upon for its own sake—as it is in the realistic novel— but it is projected in the poem only in order that it may be transcended, or swept up by the unifying spirit that rolls through all things.

The limitations we see in the range of the poem also suggest limitations within the "character" Wordsworth in his role as hero of his poem. When the world of men and politics became too much for him—as it inevitably must in a character with so rigid an integrity—he asserted the primacy of the private sensibility, which, in the final books of the poem, emerges heroic and triumphant. Like

Yeats in his tower poems of the 1920's he comes to view the tragic realm beneath him with a stoic detachment granted only to those who feel themselves elected to a self-enclosed world of contemplation. It is significant, I think, that he saved the ascent of Mt. Snowdon, which, chronologically speaking, should have come earlier in the poem, for the last book, at which point it could serve as a symbol of his proud separation from the teeming world below. The poem's resolution corresponds to what Northrop Frye, in his conspectus of archetypal literary patterns, calls the *"penseroso* phase of romance . . . the end of a movement from active to contemplative adventure."[17] But the earlier adventure in which Wordsworth had engaged in the poem is scarcely active in the usual sense of the word. Though he was close at hand during the greatest public events of his time, his role remained that of *spectator ab extra*; and if at one point he dreamed of becoming a leader to save the Revolution, his plan, though eloquently put (x, 129-158), never got beyond the stage of contemplation. What battles he knew took place within the mind itself; his victories were those of the higher over the lower phases of the mind.

From our present vantage-point, after a century in which the contemplative stance came increasingly to confine itself to the realm of aesthetic sensation, we reserve the right at times to detach ourselves from the spell cast by Wordsworth's lofty argument for the heroism of the private sensibility. And at such times we long for art of a more public order, a type of art rooted more firmly in the things of this world.

[17] *Anatomy of Criticism*, p. 202.

CHAPTER NINE
THE PRELUDE IN LITERARY HISTORY

1. THE PRELUDE AND THE WORDSWORTH CANON

WORDSWORTH'S own conception of the subordinate position of *The Prelude* within the scheme of the larger and uncompleted *Recluse* has badly obscured the poem's rightful place at the center of his work. In the preface he attached to *The Excursion* when it was published in 1814 he distinguishes as follows between the still unpublished *Prelude* and *The Recluse* itself, to which it is prefatory and of which *The Excursion* is the second and only complete part:

"The preparatory poem [*The Prelude*] is biographical, and conducts the history of the Author's mind to the point when he was emboldened to hope that his faculties were sufficiently matured for entering upon the arduous labour which he had proposed to himself; and the two Works [*The Prelude* and *The Recluse*] have the same kind of relation to each other, if he may so express himself, as the ante-chapel has to the body of a gothic church. Continuing this allusion, he may be permitted to add, that his minor Pieces . . . will be found . . . to have such connection with the main Work as may give them claim to be likened to the little cells, oratories, and sepulchral recesses, ordinarily included in those edifices" (PW, V, 2).

Wordsworth's statement is significant, I think, in several ways. For one thing; it voices his lofty conception of his long poem as the central structure—or nave, to use his own figure—of his work; his shorter poems, as had been true of Spenser and Milton, are relegated to the position of "minor pieces." But he reverses the proper positions of *The Prel-*

ude and of *The Recluse*: in quality and magnitude the ante-chapel has come to seem the central part of his large, uncompleted cathedral.

Yet Wordsworth's evaluation of the respective importance of the parts of his philosophical poem persisted until at least our own century. When *The Prelude* was published in 1850, directly after the poet's death, *The Excursion*, whether or not one read it, was acknowledged as his masterpiece. For instance, when Ruskin, writing to his father from Venice more than a year after the publication of *The Prelude*, referred to *The Excursion*, he commented, "I class Wordsworth as a thoroughly religious book"[1]—the name Wordsworth within this context being synonymous with *The Excursion*, as Milton with *Paradise Lost*. The reviewers and early readers of *The Prelude* only rarely discerned its superiority to *The Excursion*. Of the reviews, only two placed it above *The Excursion*, although their praise was closely qualified.[2] Several other publications proclaimed *The Prelude* among his more important works, though they all indicated reservations by listing poems to which they found it inferior. For instance, the *British Quarterly Review* placed it directly after *The Excursion*, the *Gentleman's Magazine* next to "his best lyrical ballads, his best sonnets, and his Ode to Immortality."[3] An American journal, *Graham's Magazine*, even found it inferior to the ode "On the Power of Sound."[4] It is significant, perhaps, that three of the leading journals of the time—the *Edinburgh*, the *Quarterly*, and *Blackwood's*—failed to review *The Prelude* at all, while the *Westminster* granted it only a cursory, haphazard review. The practical-minded,

---

1 *Ruskin's Letters from Venice: 1851-52*, ed. J. L. Bradley (New Haven, 1955), p. 92.

2 *Prospective Review*, VII (1851), 130; *Dublin University Magazine*, XXXVI (1850), 334.

3 *British Quarterly*, XII (1850), 579; *Gentleman's*, N.S.XXXIV (1850), 460.

4 *Graham's*, XXXVII (1850), 322.

Augustan Lord Macaulay, in what was undoubtedly the most severe condemnation of *The Prelude* by any of the eminent Victorians, found it "a poorer Excursion," complaining of "the old flimsy philosophy about the effect of scenery on the mind" and "the old crazy mystical metaphysics."[5] As late as 1896 Emile Legouis, in the introduction to his epoch-making book on Wordsworth's youth, noted, "It is to an imperfect recognition of the superior claims of *The Prelude* that we must attribute the common tendency to form a judgment of the whole of Wordsworth's moral and poetical work from the later specimens of his art, and to regard *The Excursion* as the masterpiece of the structure."[6]

When Matthew Arnold published his influential selection of Wordsworth in 1879, he deliberately opposed the efforts of such orthodox Wordsworthians as Leslie Stephen, who, like the poet himself, had given his philosophical poetry the central place in his canon. "The *Excursion* and the *Prelude*, his poems of greatest bulk, are by no means Wordsworth's best work," Arnold wrote in the famous preface. "His best work is in his shorter pieces."[7] But even in 1850 the less pious reviewers were willing to place *The Prelude* below the shorter poems, as, for example, *Tait's Magazine*, which, taking up Wordsworth's own metaphor, stated that it preferred his "little cells and oratories" to his "chapels and ante-chapels."[8]

Serious reconsideration of the central importance of *The Prelude* did not begin until the turn of the century, especially through the work of two men, A. C. Bradley, whose incisive analysis of the visionary element placed the poem in the mainstream of European idealism, and Le-

---

[5] G. O. Trevelyan, *Life and Letters of Lord Macaulay*, IV, 45.
[6] *Early Life of William Wordsworth*, p. 12.
[7] *Poems of Wordsworth* (London, 1879), p. xi.
[8] *Tait's*, XVII (1850), 521.

gouis, whose close scrutiny of the poem and its historical and biographical backgrounds revealed a portrait of Wordsworth substantially different from the one the Victorian age had known.[9] In our own time, although no responsible critic would hesitate to call *The Prelude* Wordsworth's masterpiece, our attitude toward the poem has remained somewhat ambivalent. There is no longer, of course, any competition between *The Prelude* and *The Excursion*, which, except for its great first book, has little more currency today than the eighteenth-century poem of the same name by David Mallet. Yet we are so unaccustomed to reading long meditative poems, and the traditional distinctions between a poet's major and minor poems have become so alien for us, that we tend to acclaim *The Prelude* for its "best parts" rather than the work as a whole. Josephine Miles, who has argued more persuasively than any other critic of our time in favor of Wordsworth's discursive poems, has shown how the poet's modern critics tend to rest their cases on shorter poems and passages, above all, those that exemplify "the fresh and natural particularity which he helped to foster and which has become the major poetic substance of our era."[10] Though our critical canons have changed considerably since Matthew Arnold sought to establish Wordsworth's reputation on his short poems, we still prefer a short lyric to a longer poem, or a poem which disguises its larger pretensions with oblique statements, to one which, like *The Prelude*, does not hesitate to assert its meanings with full rhetorical force. Yet, as we move restlessly away from the conceptions of poetry established early in this century by Eliot, Pound

9 Bradley's statements on *The Prelude* appear in his lectures delivered at Oxford in 1903—*Oxford Lectures on Poetry*, pp. 99-145, but I have been told that his class lectures at the University of Glasgow in the 1890's reveal substantially the same point of view toward the poem.

10 *The Major English Romantic Poets*, ed. C. D. Thorpe *et al.* (Carbondale, Ill., 1957), p. 38.

and Yeats, the time may come when we accept *The Prelude* as the center of Wordsworth's contribution to literature, with his shorter pieces—the best of the sonnets, lyrics and short meditative poems—occupying that lower, but honorable position within his work that Milton would have reserved for "Lycidas," or Dante for his *canzoni*.

2 . THE PRELUDE AND
ENGLISH LITERARY HISTORY

Wordsworth, when he resolved to be a poet, feared competition only with Chaucer, Spenser, Shakespeare, and Milton.

H. C. Robinson, On Books and their Writers

Without *The Prelude* it would be difficult to set Wordsworth next to the major figures with whom he himself chose to compete. For Matthew Arnold it was possible to include him in this hierarchy on the basis of the short poems alone, since his greatness, to the nineteenth century at least, consisted in the larger conception of life embodied in his work, and, more specifically, it consisted in the "healing power" which could radiate from a single line such as Arnold's Wordsworthian touchstone, "Of joy in widest commonalty spread." But Wordsworth's philosophy is no longer close to us, no more so, at least, than that of Goethe or any other major poet of the age, and less, indeed, than that of many still earlier writers with a more tragic perspective on life.

Yet by the time *The Prelude* appeared in 1850, even its philosophy was not enough to assure it a place among the living literature of the day. Like Diderot's *Neveu de Rameau* and Büchner's *Woyzeck*, it is one of a small group of major posthumous works which appeared so long after their creation that the impact they might have had at the time of their composition seemed precluded by the changes of taste and sensibility that inevitably follow from one generation to the next. In the half century between its composition and publication England had passed through political, technological, and social changes far vaster in scale than during any comparable period in her history. "This is a voice that speaks to us across a gulph of nearly fifty years," the *Examiner* opened its review of the poem. "But only those whose memory still carries them so far back, can feel within them any reflex of that eager excitement, with which the news of battles fought and won, or mail-coach copies of some new work of Scott, or Byron, or the *Edinburgh Review*, were looked for and received in those already old days."[11] To an age preparing to demonstrate its progress and cosmopolitanism at the Great Exhibition Wordsworth's world must have seemed quaint and provincial. Yet none of its early reviewers was willing to recommend it as a period piece—it was obviously too introspective to stand next to such vivid reconstructions as *A Tale of Two Cities* and *The French Revolution*. At the same time its early readers, however praiseworthy some of them found the poem to be, failed to recommend it for its relevance to their own world. The Christian Socialist F. D. Maurice, writing to Charles Kingsley, called *The Prelude* "the dying utterance of the half-century we have just passed through, the expression—the English expression at least—of all that self-building process in which, according to their different schemes and principles, Byron, Goethe, Wordsworth, the Evangelicals . . . were all engaged . . . in which God . . . was still the agent only in fitting them to be world-wise, men of genius, artists, saints."[12] As social criticism, Wordsworth's picture of the teeming metropolis of 1791 doubtless seemed tame to an age which had accepted "The Song

11 *Examiner*, July 27, 1850, p. 478.
12 *Life of Frederick Denison Maurice*, ed. F. Maurice (London, 1884), II, 59.

of the Shirt" and "The Cry of the Children" as images of contemporary urban squalor, while the social convictions voiced by Michel Beaupuy must have seemed unduly elementary to those responsive to the urgency and complexity of early Victorian social thought. As political reflection, *The Prelude* has communicated more successfully with our own age—disillusioned as it is about the possibilities of human progress—than with the vigorously reformist period in which it appeared. Moreover, *The Prelude* obviously failed to grapple with that peculiarly Victorian form of disillusionment brought on by the impact of evolutionary doctrines—a failure which stands out all the more sharply through the phenomenal success of a poem published only a few weeks later, *In Memoriam*. Indeed, to compare the reviews of the two poems, let alone their respective sales, is to realize how untimely *The Prelude* was when it appeared: in no review was it allowed to stand next to the greatest poems of the past, whereas Tennyson's poem was compared by various reviewers to *The Divine Comedy*, *Paradise Lost*, the sonnets of Petrarch and Shakespeare, and, significantly, to *The Excursion*.[13]

On a specifically literary level, one wonders if *The Prelude* contained too much of the quiet, reflective quality of eighteenth-century meditative verse to move the mid–nineteenth-century reader with the assertiveness to which he had become accustomed by later Romantic poetry and the early Victorian novel. On the surface, certainly, many themes of *The Prelude* remained among the central preoccupations of the mid-century. But though the Victorian reader was not deficient in his love for nature, he was more easily "moved" by a lyrical apostrophe to the cuckoo or the celandine than by lengthy reflections on the interaction of man and nature. Though he was obviously interested in

[13] See E. F. Shannon, Jr., *Tennyson and the Reviewers* (Cambridge, Mass., 1952), p. 152.

the processes of a child's growing up, he found the growth of a poet's mind far less touching than the sufferings of a Jane Eyre or David Copperfield. Though he expected his authors to put on the prophet's mantle, he found the brassy admonitions of *Sartor Resartus* and the melodious consolations of *In Memoriam* more compelling than Wordsworth's less blatant record of how he managed to overcome despair. *The Prelude* must surely have seemed cool and austere next to the other books the Victorians were reading. Moreover, the very sound of its verse must have fallen heavily on the Victorian ear, which, after the intense development the shorter lyric had undergone during the preceding half century, had come to expect more music from its poetry: even the blank verse of Tennyson's *Idylls*, as Miss Miles has suggested, was freer in motion than Wordsworth's. Perhaps more fundamental yet, if we cannot understand the Victorian failure to grasp the visionary experiences in *The Prelude*, Macaulay's statement about the "old crazy mystical metaphysics," though not wholly representative of Victorian thought, should remind us that *The Prelude* appeared long after the transcendental impulse in English romanticism had flowed into other, less speculative channels.

Had *The Prelude* appeared soon after its composition, one wonders if it might have initiated a tradition of *Bildungsgedichte* in England akin to the vogue of novels established in Germany (and later, indeed, in England) by Goethe's *Wilhelm Meister*. Moreover, one suspects that *The Prelude* might have proved even more potent than *Lyrical Ballads* in effecting the type of conversion recorded by men such as John Stuart Mill and William Hale White. Certainly Wordsworth's intimates, who knew *The Prelude* in manuscript, revealed an understanding of the poem far beyond that of its reviewers and Victorian readers. For

instance, De Quincey, who used *The Prelude* as a source
for some biographical sketches of Wordsworth in 1839,
stressed the significance of the poem as a record of inward
experience.[14] However, Coleridge, in his poem "To William Wordsworth: Composed on the Night after His Recitation of a Poem on the Growth of an Individual Mind"
(1807), gets closer to the fundamental meaning of *The
Prelude* than any critic before the turn of the century:

> Theme hard as high!
> Of smiles spontaneous, and mysterious fears
> (The first-born they of Reason and twin-birth),
> Of tides obedient to external force,
> And currents self-determined, as might seem,
> Or by some inner Power; of moments awful,
> Now in thy inner life, and now abroad,
> When power streamed from thee, and thy soul
>   received
> The light reflected, as a light bestowed. . . .

For Coleridge, unlike many of its early readers, there
was obviously no problem as to *The Prelude*'s particular
genre or theme. In 1804, before it was completed, he had
referred to it as "the biographical, or philosophico-bio-
graphical Poem to be prefixed or annexed to the Recluse."[15] Wordsworth and his family customarily spoke of
The Prelude as the "poem on his own life" or the "poem
addressed to Coleridge" (EL, 489, 517, 547, 561). De
Quincey called it a "great philosophical poem . . . absolutely unique in its class."[16] But by the time the poem
descended upon the Victorian literary world, its readers
showed discomfort with its generic and, indeed, thematic
uniqueness. If taken as a poem, why could its passion not

---

[14] See, for instance, the passage I quoted at the opening of Chapter Two.
[15] *Collected Letters* (Oxford, 1956), II, 1104.
[16] *Literary Reminiscences*, I, 319, 362.

be sustained?[17] If an autobiography, why did it not possess the richness of detail of such models as Goethe's *Dichtung und Wahrheit*?[18] If a commentary on Cambridge, London, and revolutionary France, why so many trivial incidents?[19] It seems no mere accident of literary history that *The Prelude*'s greatness was first generally recognized by the age that produced the introspective fiction—deriving as it does from the double stream of poetry and the novel—of Proust, Lawrence, and Virginia Woolf. I suggested the poem's affinities with the experimental fiction of our century in the chapters on Wordsworth's "time-consciousness." Moreover, *The Prelude* bears enough affinities with the concerns of our present age that it no longer seems necessary, as it did a generation ago, to insist on the modernity of certain of Wordsworth's themes. For instance, F. W. Bateson's interpretation of Wordsworth as "Heroic Victim" and D. G. James' emphasis upon the role of "visionary dreariness" have revealed a poet who, for all his reputed optimism, still has something to offer an anxiety-minded age.[20] Moreover, Wordsworth's record of his disillusionment in the French Revolution re-creates more powerfully than any record by an English or American poet of the 1930's and 1940's the inner turmoil which Western liberals underwent during this period. In its external themes, as well, *The Prelude* anticipates some of the central subject matter of the literature of the last century: university life, the life of the modern metropolis, the portrait of the artist growing up, the poem as its own *art poétique*.

There is still another perspective within which we may

---

[17] See, for instance, the generally laudatory review in the *Prospective Review*, pp. 94-131, from which I quote at the beginning of Chapter Four.
[18] See the review in the *British Quarterly Review*, p. 554.
[19] See the review in the *Examiner* cited above.
[20] Bateson, *Wordsworth: A Re-interpretation*, see especially pp. 197-203; James, *Skepticism and Poetry* (London, 1937), pp. 131-169.

view Wordsworth's relation to English literary history: his conception of the English poetic tradition as virtually complete. "He was not sanguine as to the future of English poetry," Aubrey De Vere recalled the aged Wordsworth saying. "He thought that there was much to be supplied in other departments of our literature, and especially he desired a really great history of England; but he was disposed to regard the roll of English poetry as made up, and as leaving place for little more except what was likely to be eccentric or imitational."[21] Although he conceived of himself as competing only with Chaucer, Spenser, Shakespeare, and Milton,[22] he must also have felt himself decidedly the last of the classical poets. It is significant, I think, that, beginning in 1800, after the inspiration which had fed *Lyrical Ballads* and the early books of *The Prelude* was running out, he undertook a close study of at least three of these writers. By drawing on the great voices of the past, Wordsworth was seeking modes of language through which he himself could speak and, in effect, find a new voice which would be his own. The major achievements that resulted from this study now seem to us so thoroughly Wordsworthian that we almost forget the process through which their language came into being. Take, for example, these famous lines from "Resolution and Independence":

> We Poets in our youth begin in gladness;
> But thereof come in the end despondency and
> madness.

The marvelously rough-hewn quality of these lines would seem to reveal to us the essential Wordsworth, or at least

[21] *Essays, Chiefly on Poetry*, II, 284.
[22] The hierarchy of four whom Wordsworth mentioned to Crabb Robinson had long been established as the central figures in the English canon. Note, for instance, the panegyric addressed to these four in Thomson's "Summer" (lines 1563-1579); Wordsworth eulogized the three Cambridge-educated poets in similar fashion in the Cambridge section of *The Prelude* (III, 276-293).

one of his most typical voices. But it is a voice which he achieved only through his study of another, far earlier poet's language. Compare the lines above with these from Wordsworth's translation of "The Cuckoo and the Nightingale," a poem attributed to Chaucer in Wordsworth's time (though now thought to be Sir John Clanvowe's):

> For thereof come all contraries to gladness;
> Thence sickness comes, and overwhelming sadness,
> Mistrust and jealousy, despite, debate,
> Dishonour, shame, envy importunate,
> Pride, anger, mischief, poverty, and madness.
>
> (PW, IV, 223)

It is a commonplace of literary history to point to Dorothy Wordsworth's journal entry of October 3, 1800, which records the meeting with the leech-gatherer, and marvel at what happened to the incident after Wordsworth recollected it in tranquillity two years later for the poem. Yet an essential part of the recollection process was his study (and translation) of Chaucer in the intervening year, for it gave him the proper voice (and also the stanza, for that matter) through which he could re-create and interpret the incident. Wordsworth's use of the past is in one sense no different from Spenser's, who also discovered a voice of his own by invoking Chaucer. But Spenser's use of Chaucer seems to me more distinctly parallel to what Wordsworth was doing when he imitated the language and rhythms of folk ballads in *Lyrical Ballads*: in each case we see an attempt to revitalize the language of poetry by discarding the accumulated conventions of the recent past and returning to earlier, fresher modes of speech. What distinguishes Wordsworth from Spenser is the fact that he was able to range so much more widely throughout the English literary tradition in search of voices. In *The Borderers*, for instance, he could speak like Shakespeare:

>   I perceive
> That fear is like a cloak which old men huddle
> About their love, as if to keep it warm.
>
>   (PW, I, 129)

The prophetic voice of his patriotic sonnets came, in turn, from Milton, who also provided the rhetoric which Wordsworth needed to sustain his long autobiographical poem. The "Stanzas Written in My Pocket-copy of Thomson's 'Castle of Indolence' " speak a triple language: Wordsworth echoing Spenser by way of Thomson. If his feeling that the roll of English poetry was "made up" ever discouraged him in his own efforts, it also gave him the opportunity to speak through more significant voices than any other major poet before him.

But if Wordsworth merely assimilated earlier voices within his own, poets of our century have sometimes suppressed their own voices altogether as a means of finding their own. The early Eliot not only assumed the voice of Laforgue in "Prufrock," and of the Jacobean dramatists in "Gerontion," but pretended to speak through the masks of dramatic characters. Ezra Pound was able to achieve his own identity as a poet only by speaking through the mouths of a wide diversity of men—Browning, Propertius, Gautier, Cavalcanti, Confucius, and thence on through all the literatures. There is something, indeed, of the ventriloquist in the modern poet and, in fact, among modern artists as a whole: witness that arch-ventriloquist among composers, Igor Stravinsky, who has gone variously to the fifteenth-century Flemish masters for his *Mass* of 1948, to Pergolesi for *Pulcinella*, to Mozart for *The Rake's Progress*. It is a condition, perhaps of our modern Alexandrianism, of our need to break through the essentially private world of the modern artist by invoking the loud and firm public voices of the past. In Wordsworth we note perhaps the beginnings of a tendency: the very mention of Alexandrianism suggests the gap that separates his world from ours.

3. THE PRELUDE AND EUROPEAN ROMANTICISM

Of the major English writers with whom he feared to compete—Chaucer, Spenser, Shakespeare, and Milton—Wordsworth has doubtless played the least imposing role in the annals of comparative literature. The continental influences upon him, except for the Neoplatonic writers whom he picked up from Coleridge's conversations, are of little consequence. Even the influence of Rousseau, which I have stressed in several places, was probably less in the nature of direct impact than an absorption, on Wordsworth's part, of notions that were already much "in the air." Even more conspicuous than the lack of outside influences upon him is the failure of his work to find an audience outside the English-speaking countries. It goes without saying that *The Prelude*, whose classical status was acknowledged in his own country only during the present century, has never captured the imagination of any foreign reading public. And although Wordsworth, through the rest of his work, determined the course of nineteenth-century English literature as much as any man, his continental influence has been minute. Of all the luminaries of European letters in his century, only Sainte-Beuve, who claimed to have read only here and there in Wordsworth, shows the impact of the English poet; and even here it was essentially the Biedermeier Wordsworth —the Wordsworth of plain living rather than high thinking, of *ethos* rather than *pathos*—who attracted the Frenchman.[23]

[23] See M. A. Smith, *L'influence des Lakistes sur les romantiques français* (Paris, 1920), pp. 27-28, 100-101. On the basis of Smith's evidence one

The reasons one might suggest for European indifference to Wordsworth are beyond the scope of this essay.
But one suspects the usual reasons—above all, that there
were other writers in other countries who embodied a
theme and sensibility similar to Wordsworth's. ("Das ist
ein Englischer Göthe!!!" the German poet Ludwig Tieck
exclaimed when Crabb Robinson showed him two of
Wordsworth's sonnets.[24]) Beyond that there are the inevitable accidents of literary history: despite the efforts of that
inveterate mediator Robinson, there was no one to make
an international myth out of Wordsworth—least of all
Wordsworth himself—as there was for such lesser poets as
Byron and Poe. But Wordsworth's insularity—symbolized
by the absurd isolation which he and Dorothy maintained
during their winter in Germany—was also a consequence
of what he stood for as man and poet. Quite unlike Goethe,
he was totally unsuited to play the man of letters, a role
forced upon him by his later eminence in his own country.
His opinions on continental writers, recorded largely during his later years, are notorious for their stubborn and
unenlightened provinciality. Lamartine, whose role in
French poetry has affinities with his own in English, was
dismissed as "a poor writer of verses not having the least
claim to be considered a statesman."[25] Rousseau, as I have
pointed out, goes virtually unmentioned, except for a
negative remark on his "paradoxical reveries" (co, 335).
Goethe's *Wilhelm Meister*, which has far more in common
with *The Prelude* than Wordsworth would have dared to

---

could postulate a probable line of descent from *Lyrical Ballads* through
Sainte-Beuve's very influential poem "Les rayons jaunes" to the city
poems of Baudelaire and Rimbaud.

[24] *Correspondence of Crabb Robinson with the Wordsworth Circle*, I,
30. It is worth noting that Robinson showed Tieck two rather indifferent
sonnets, "Praised be the Art . . ." and "Hail, Twilight."

[25] Kurt Lienemann, *Die Belesenheit von William Wordsworth* (Berlin,
1908), p. 240.

think, was left mostly unread, as "it was full of all manner of fornication . . . like the crossing of flies in the air" (CO, 266). One often suspects that within the larger realm of letters Wordsworth should have maintained with even greater rigor the solitude which he advocated so powerfully in his poems.

Yet, with the larger perspective which we possess today, we can affirm with Hazlitt, though in a more specifically literary-historical context, that "Wordsworth's genius is a pure emanation of the Spirit of the Age."[26] Friedrich Schlegel, whose criticism we now see as one of the cornerstones of Romanticism, characterized the prevailing tendencies (*Tendenzen*) of his age as the French Revolution, Fichte's transcendental philosophy, and *Wilhelm Meister*.[27] In a general but very real sense Wordsworth's major poetry —*The Prelude* and its satellite poems, "Tintern Abbey," "Home at Grasmere," the "Immortality Ode"—is centered about and, in fact, attempts to fuse the three realms of which Schlegel speaks: the political, philosophical, and literary. It is scarcely necessary to stress once more the role that the Revolution plays in Wordsworth's poetry. Indeed, despite the reservations I voiced earlier about his insight into politics, *The Prelude* deals more trenchantly with the Revolution than any major literary work of its generation. And although one cannot demonstrate the direct influence of German philosophy on *The Prelude*, one need no longer, as Bradley did a half century ago, make a point of the poem's affinities with the idealistic German philosophies of the time. In fact, the recent study of E. D. Hirsch, Jr., *Wordsworth and Schelling*, provides considerable evidence to show how closely Wordsworth's thinking parallels the thought of the idealist philosopher. *Wilhelm Meister*, despite "all manner of fornication," stands with *The Prelude*

---

26 *Complete Works*, ed. P. P. Howe (London, 1932), XI, 86.
27 *Kritische Schriften*, ed. W. Rasch (Munich, n.d.), p. 46.

(and Rousseau's *Confessions*) as the first major literary
work to concentrate on the growth and development of the
young man of sensibility.

But the mention of Friedrich Schlegel, with his interest
in irony and "arabesques" and his demand for a new
mythology, points up the limits within which one may
seek affinities between Wordsworth and his contemporaries.
Within that loose coalition of interests which we call Romanticism, Wordsworth—and above all, the Wordsworth
of *The Prelude*—represents a distinctly meditative, reflective phase, one quite removed from the sensuous, fanciful
Romanticism of Keats and the German school, or from the
ironic Romanticism so characteristic of the Germans and
only of Byron in England. "The hemisphere / Of magic
fiction, verse of mine perhaps / May never tread" (vi, 102-
104), Wordsworth wrote, distinguishing his own talent
from Spenser's, but also, in effect, defining the distance
which separates him from much we have come to call Romantic. Although we sometimes characterize his verse as
passionate, his is essentially the passion of lofty utterance,
rather than the intense lyric passion of, say, *Prometheus
Unbound*. When Matthew Arnold joined the Wordsworth
Society in 1883 he compared his entrance into the society
to joining a monastery: "The two things are not so very
different," Arnold told the Wordsworthians; "a monastery
is under the rules of poverty, chastity and obedience—well,
and he who comes under the discipline of Wordsworth
comes under the same rules."[28] In our own day John Crowe
Ransom, after commenting that "Wordsworth was willing
to throw away most of the tropology with which poetry
was commonly identified," calls *The Prelude* "the greatest
locus of the plain style."[29] Paul Van Tieghem, surveying

[28] *Transactions of the Wordsworth Society*, v (1883), 5.
[29] "William Wordsworth: Notes toward an Understanding of Poetry,"
Kenyon Review, xii (1950), 504, 508.

the whole range of writers of the period, finds that "Wordsworth représente un des aspects les plus tempérés du ro-
mantisme européen."[30] The monastic rigor of *The Prelude*
is revealed not only in Wordsworth's dispensing with the
usual poetic ornaments, but also in his insistence on doing
without a larger mythological framework; however instrumental he may have been in restoring mythology to English poetry, the influence came from later works, from the
now-neglected "Laodamia," for instance, or from his advo-
cacy (though distinctly not his practice) of mythology in
Book IV of *The Excursion*.[31] The severe classicism that controls his work has doubtless prevented his acceptance by
many modern readers who might otherwise have been attracted to the mystic element in his poetry. For instance,
those current proponents of "cosmic consciousness,"
Messrs. Shapiro and Miller and Miss Slote, for whom Whitman has become the arch-poet, trace the "cosmic" tradition
in poetry back to Blake and Wordsworth, but they dismiss
Wordsworth with these words, "[He] was a nature mystic,
but he preferred the literal to the rhapsodic tone, and his
physicality was limited to nature."[32] If richness and sensuous fullness are necessary attributes of the Romantic tradition in literature, then Wordsworth is scarcely a Romantic. Indeed, as J. C. Smith has pointed out, the senses which
Wordsworth employs in his poetry include only sight and,
to a lesser degree, sound; touch, smell, and taste are virtually missing, while he rarely attempts to create color even in
his visual images[33] (one of his distinctive achievements, as
I have suggested earlier, is his ability to evoke emptiness).
One can, in fact, speak of a principle of parsimony at work

[30] *Histoire littéraire de l'Europe et de l'Amérique* (Paris, 1946), p. 169.
[31] See the Wordsworth chapter in Douglas Bush's *Mythology and the
Romantic Tradition in English Poetry* (New York, 1957), pp. 56-70.
[32] Karl Shapiro *et al.*, *Start with the Sun* (Lincoln, Nebr., 1960), p. 6.
[33] *Wordsworth* (Edinburgh, 1946); see the chapter entitled "Organic
Sensibility," pp. 1-14.

in Wordsworth's poetry: his disdain for artifice, his refusal to plot, the doggedness with which he sticks to the literalness of things—all betray a type of imagination which needs to work within rigorous limitations to unleash its characteristic power.

If one must discriminate among the Romanticisms, Wordsworth could be called the prototype of the Romantic philosophical poet—philosophical not in the sense that he expounds a paraphrasable philosophy, but that he renders the feeling of the philosophical process, of ideas being made, prophecies in the course of being pronounced. His particular mode was unique in English Romanticism, although under his influence Byron (in *Childe Harold*) and Shelley (in "Alastor" and "Mont Blanc") sometimes approached it. His true compeers are meditative poets of the order of Hölderlin and Leopardi, perhaps also Lamartine. In each of these we discern great generalizing power, a loftiness of stance that demands eloquent language to define its proper role:

> E come il vento
> Odo stormir tra queste piante, io quello
> Infinito silenzio a questa voce
> Vo comparando: e mi sovvien l'eterno,
> E le morte stagioni, e la presente
> E viva, e il suon di lei. . . .

("L'Infinito")

> Töne mir in die Seele noch oft, dass über den Wassern
> Furchtlosrege der Geist, dem Schwimmer gleich, in der Starken
> Frischem Glüke sich üb', und die Göttersprache, das Wechseln
> Und das Werden versteh', und wenn die reissende Zeit mir

Zu gewaltig das Haupt ergreifft und die Noth und
   das Irrsaal
Unter Sterblichen mir mein sterblich Leben
   erschüttert,
Lass der Stille mich dann in deiner Tiefe gedenken.
                       ("Der Archipelagus")

Et moi, me voici seul sur ces confins du monde!
Loin d'ici, sous mes pieds, la foudre vole et gronde;
Les nuages battus par les ailes des vents,
Entrechoquant comme eux leur tourbillons
   mouvants . . .
                       ("La Solitude")

   And now recovering, to my Soul I say
   I recognise thy glory; in such strength
   Of usurpation, in such visitings
   Of awful promise, when the light of sense
   Goes out in flashes that have shewn to us
   The invisible world, doth Greatness make abode,
   There harbours whether we be young or old.
   Our destiny, our nature, and our home
   Is with infinitude, and only there;
   With hope it is, hope that can never die,
   Effort, and expectation, and desire,
   And something evermore about to be.
                    (*Prelude*, VI, 531-542)

   In each, as well, we note that quality which Keats described in Wordsworth when he spoke of the "egotistical
sublime." However much these poets may differ in the
ideas one could cull out of them—Hölderlin and Leopardi
would emerge as pessimists, Wordsworth and Lamartine
as optimists—they represent a type of poetic sensibility
distinguishable from that of their contemporaries (it is
significant, I think, that Hölderlin and Leopardi canno

comfortably be classified as Romantics according to the usual definitions of Romanticism in their respective literatures). I shall not attempt to describe Wordsworth's affinities with Lamartine (a poet of lesser stature than the other three), though it is worth noting that an early reviewer of *The Prelude* attempted to disparage Wordsworth by claiming the superiority of the French poet in this type of verse —"The Englishman contemplates; the Frenchman soars— Wordsworth looks reverently upon things divine; Lamartine is lost therein . . . Wordsworth celebrates Duty; Lamartine pants after God"[34]—which was only to stress once more that austere aspect of *The Prelude* which made the poem so hard for the lyric-minded Victorians to read. The parallel with Leopardi was developed in considerable detail a generation ago in a British Academy lecture by Geoffrey L. Bickersteth, who, besides their affinities in their treatment of nature and politics, stressed the attempt of each poet to achieve sublime effect in a similarly contemplative mode.[35]

Sir Herbert Read drew a brief parallel between the poetic theory of Wordsworth and Hölderlin in an essay on the former poet,[36] but I do not otherwise recall seeing the two poets linked, except in a remark made by T. S. Eliot in his late and, for once, appreciative essay on Goethe: "At his best, [Wordsworth's] flight was much higher than that of Byron, and as high as that of Goethe. . . . Yet he will never mean to Europeans of other nationality, what he means to his own compatriots. . . . Similarly . . . it seems to me possible to maintain that Hölderlin was at moments more inspired than Goethe: yet he also, can never be to

---

[34] *Prospective Review*, p. 105.
[35] *Leopardi and Wordsworth* (London, 1927). For a comparative study of the poetic treatment of solitude in Leopardi and Lamartine, see Ulrich Leo, "Zwei Einsamkeiten," *Archivum Romanicum*, XVI (1932), 521-539.
[36] *The True Voice of Feeling: Studies in English Romantic Poetry* (New York, 1953), pp. 52-54.

the same degree a European figure. Into the possible account of the differences between the two kinds of poet, I do not propose to enter. . . ."[37] An adequate account of these differences would go well beyond the scope of my present study, much as it would of Eliot's study of Goethe; but it seems to me worth suggesting that Wordsworth and Hölderlin were both the kind of philosophical poet I attempted to describe above. Obviously narrower in range than Goethe, lacking his virtuosity, richness, and witty playfulness, they strove for an uncompromisingly lofty type of effect which Goethe, except for some isolated moments in his *Sturm-und-Drang* period, was willing to dispense with.

Born within a few weeks of one another, Wordsworth and Hölderlin both grew up in an intimacy with nature which they attempted valiantly to restore as the self-consciousness of adulthood set in. Indeed, both experienced only a short period of poetic power: if Wordsworth's great period—to use Bateson's dates—can be circumscribed 1797-1806,[38] Hölderlin's encompasses an even shorter, though also contemporaneous span, roughly 1798-1803. Each, in turn, after his moment of significant utterance, was destined to a long decline—Wordsworth to a virtual half-century of unimaginative stability, Hölderlin to an almost equally long period (he died in 1843) of insanity, which he spent in a lonely tower room. Moreover, just as *The Prelude*—in which Wordsworth comes closest to Hölderlin's mode—did not gain its just place in the literary canon until the present century, so Hölderlin, who has since come to occupy a place in German poetry only next to Goethe's, remained almost totally unrecognized throughout his own century. I do not claim to make two uniquely great poets seem like one. Their differences are

---

[37] *On Poetry and Poets* (London, 1957), p. 212.
[38] *Wordsworth: A Re-interpretation*, p. 8n.

conspicuous enough. In ideas Wordsworth comes much closer to Hölderlin's schoolmate Schelling than to Hölderlin himself. Wordsworth, moreover, spoke in a greater variety of voices, while Hölderlin's tone, despite an amazing stylistic development during his short career, remained essentially elegiac. Although it is marked by something of the same austerity which we noted in Wordsworth, Hölderlin's poetry was able to assimilate, quite unselfconsciously, a large range of mythological and Christian reference that Wordsworth's was forced to do without. Hölderlin is perhaps at his most Wordsworthian in lines such as these:

> Da ich ein Knabe war,
> Rettet' ein Gott mich oft
> Vom Geschrei und der Ruthe der Menschen
>
> . . .
>
> Mich erzog der Wohllaut
> Des säuselnden Hains,
> Und lieben lernt' ich
> Unter den Blumen.
>
> Im Arme der Götter wuchs ich gross—
> ("Da ich ein Knabe war . . ."; probably 1798)

lines in which, like Wordsworth in "Tintern Abbey," the "Ode" and *The Prelude*, he attempts to restore something of his former intimacy with nature through the poetic evocation of his past bliss. But the parallel I have tried to develop is of a more general order: it is perhaps better suggested by those awesome (though less specifically "Wordsworthian") lines from "Der Archipelagus" which I quoted earlier. Throughout this study I have stressed Wordsworth the contemplative, sublime poet; in the past we have had enough portraits of Wordsworth the Lake poet, or Wordsworth as the poet of humble men and small and homely things. But the Wordsworth of philosophical loftiness is the Wordsworth who once filled Coleridge and

Keats with awe, and it is also the Wordsworth, I suspect, whose greatness we shall most be willing to grant in the future. If he is not thereby the type of "European figure" Mr. Eliot discerned in Goethe, he at least belongs to that small band of austere solitaries inspired by the same philosophic muse in his time.

APPENDIX ONE

1805 OR 1850?

LIKE *Hamlet, The Prelude* exists in two versions, neither of them altogether satisfactory. The textual problem is not, as with *Hamlet*, a matter of getting back to the author's original intentions, but of distinguishing between two different sets of intentions—those of the poet at the time he was writing the poem and those of the aged poet reflecting and improving upon a manuscript long since laid aside. The relative merits of the two versions have provoked considerable discussion since De Selincourt first published the 1805 text in 1926; and the justness with which he appraised Wordsworth's changes, both stylistic and ideological, has not, I think, been surpassed by any later commentators. For De Selincourt the ideal text would be a composite of the two:

"The ideal text of *The Prelude*, which the lover of Wordsworth may construct for himself from the material here presented to him, would follow no single manuscript. It would retain from the earliest version such familiar details as have any autobiographical significance. Of purely stylistic changes from that text, it would accept those only which Wordsworth might have made (and some he would certainly have made), had he prepared the poem for the press in his greatest period, changes designed to remove crudities of expression, and to develop or clarify his original meaning: but it would reject those later excrescences of a manner less pure, at times even meretricious, which are out of key with the spirit in which the poem was first conceived and executed. Most firmly would it reject all modifications of his original thought and attitude to his theme" (*Prel.*, p. lxiii).

But publishers are obviously forced to commit themselves to one version or the other, and although the 1805 version has been available for a whole generation, it is still the later version that appears in editions designed for the classroom and the general reader. Indeed, although many have deplored the revisions that Wordsworth made to adjust to his changing re-

ligious and political commitments, the consensus among those
of Wordsworth's commentators who have taken up the issue is
that, stylistically, at least, the 1850 version is by far the superior
performance.[1] I am not here concerned with the ideological
changes to which Wordsworth subjected his manuscript: as has
often enough been said, it is extraordinary that Wordsworth
did not go further than he did in erasing his radical and pantheistic past from the poem, though I for one am irritated by
the revision of lines such as these:

> Prophets of Nature, we to them will speak
> A lasting inspiration, sanctified
> By reason and by truth,   (XIII, 442-444)

so that the last three words are changed to "blest by faith"
(XIV, 446 [1850]). I am far more concerned with the stylistic
changes which, by and large, strike me as ruinous to much of
the effect of the early version. The usual argument for the
stylistic superiority of the 1850 *Prelude* is that Wordsworth was
able to improve the poem by condensing, sharpening, by making slack and prosaic lines more vivid and poetic. And, in fact,
if we compare individual lines from the two versions out of
context, the revision usually seems the superior one. Consider
changes such as the following:

> And almost make our Infancy itself
> A visible scene,   (I, 662-663)

to

> And almost make remotest infancy
> A visible scene   (I, 634-635 [1850])

or even the example above, in which the phrase "sanctified /
By reason and by truth," became "sanctified / By reason, blest
by faith." In each case, the revision seems an "improvement":

[1] I refer, for instance, to the remarks in F. R. Leavis' essay in *Revaluation*, pp. 155-158; R. D. Havens' frequent attacks in his notes to *The
Prelude* (*The Mind of a Poet*, II) on the monosyllabic and "pedestrian"
lines in the early version; and Mary E. Burton's full-length study of the
revisions to the poem, *The One Wordsworth* (Chapel Hill, N.C., 1942),
which attempts to justify the superiority of the later version at every point.
The only relevant defenses of the 1805 text I have been able to find are
those of Donald Davie (in *Articulate Energy*, pp. 112-116) and William
Empson, from whom I quote below.

we would normally bestow such critical compliments as "tightness" or "economy" upon it. But tightness and economy are
perhaps not such absolute values in poetry as we should like
to think; the 1805 *Prelude*, at any rate, is likely to confound
them. Compare the following lines from the early version:

> Spring returns,
> I saw the Spring return, when I was dead
> To deeper hope, yet had I joy for her,
> And welcomed her benevolence, rejoiced
> In common with the Children of her Love,
> Plants, insects, beasts in field, and birds in bower,
> (XI, 23-28)

with these from 1850:

> Spring returns,—
> I saw the Spring return, and could rejoice,
> In common with the children of her love,
> Piping on boughs, or sporting on fresh fields,
> Or boldly seeking pleasure nearer heaven
> On wings that navigate cerulean skies.
> (XII, 32-37 [1850])

The later version is by all odds better "writing," if by this
term we distinguish its greater economy, concreteness, vividness, strictness of syntax. But the poetry also sustains great loss.
We no longer follow the waywardings of the thinking mind—
"I saw the Spring return, when I was dead / To deeper hope,
yet had I joy for her"—while the images of the natural world,
for all their "concreteness" in the later version, have the heavy
feel of a set piece ("wings that navigate cerulean skies"), which
I, for one, find less in keeping with the context than the simple
catalog of "plants, insects, beasts in field, and birds in bower."
The 1850 *Prelude* always retains the quality of "competent,"
"finished" verse, while the early version has a delicacy and
spontaneity that the later Wordsworth was often bent on vio-
lating. But the essential difference cannot be demonstrated by
sampling short passages; rather, it is a difference in total effect,
one which I have come to feel only after repeated readings of
each version as a whole. Foremost, perhaps, among the impressions one gains of the two versions is that the later Wordsworth

had forgotten much that the younger poet was trying to do in *The Prelude*. For one thing, in the process of tidying up stray phrases here and there, he had forgotten that much of the success of the poem—especially of the mystical passages and those of inner turmoil—depends upon the conversational tone, the off-handedness, the struggle toward definition which he was trying to portray. Moreover, one suspects he had also forgotten the manner in which he had built up the various spots of time. In an earlier chapter I attempted to demonstrate the design of these passages, which start out in a casual, matter-of-fact tone and gradually build toward bolder poetic assertions. Wordsworth's revisions often work to undercut the casualness which is so important a part of the total effect of these passages. Take, for instance, the beginning of the ascent of Mt. Snowdon; the early version reads as follows:

> In one of these excursions, travelling then
> Through Wales on foot, and with a youthful Friend,
> I left Bethkelet's huts at couching-time,
> And westward took my way to see the sun
> Rise from the top of Snowdon.   (XIII, 1-5)

Prosaic though they are, these rambling lines provide the factual base from which Wordsworth moves to his loftier vision. In the later version he attempts to poeticize these lines:

> In one of those excursions (may they ne'er
> Fade from remembrance!) through the Northern tracts
> Of Cambria ranging with a youthful friend,
> I left Bethgelert's huts at couching-time. . . .
>   (XIV, 1-4 [1850])

"Travelling then / Through Wales on foot" is romanticized to "Through the Northern tracts / Of Cambria ranging," and the grand-style exclamation "May they ne'er / Fade from remembrance" is injected to make sure the reader properly recognizes the urgency of the occasion. As in nearly all the other major spots of time the build-up is blurred in order to ensure a more evenly "poetic" texture. But I suppose the most precise statement of what happened between the two versions is that of William Empson, who dismisses the ideological revisions as insignificant, but concentrates on the effect of Wordsworth's stylistic "improvements":

". . . This improvement, which was mainly a process of packing the lines more fully, meant invoking Milton and his sense of the unrelaxing Will; whereas the whole point and delicacy of the first version was to represent a wavering and untrammelled natural growth. The improvement was, therefore, about the most destructive thing he could have done, far worse than changing the supposed opinions."[2]

But spontaneity also can make for banality, and after repeated readings of the 1805 text one wishes Wordsworth had pruned his "untrammelled natural growth" here and there at the time he first wrote. I have sometimes hoped that some editor with a special sensitivity to Wordsworth's language would put together a popular, composite edition of *The Prelude*, an edition based principally on the 1805 text, yet one which shears off its most bathetic lines, omits such longer passages as "Vaudracour and Julia" and "The Matron's Tale," and adds the passage on the Chartreuse (written soon after he finished the 1805 text), plus some individual lines—like the one on Newton, "Voyaging through strange seas of Thought, alone"—which do not violate the "natural growth" of which Empson speaks (the Wordsworth of the 1830's, if he was nothing else, was still the master of the single line). But the serious reader is left where he was when De Selincourt published his monumental edition: he will continue moving across the page from one version to the other, or read through each version alternately—an appropriate enough procedure for the first major imaginative work to deal centrally with the nature of the creative process.

[2] *The Structure of Complex Words*, p. 294.

APPENDIX TWO

1798-99 OR 1804-5?— A NOTE ON
WORDSWORTH AND MILTON

THE composition of *The Prelude* encompasses two distinctly
separate phases of Wordsworth's development, at the beginning and the end, respectively, of his great period. If we separate the poem into its two chronological parts, it is clear the
critical consensus would overwhelmingly favor the sections
which Wordsworth wrote in 1798-99—all of the first two books
except the introduction to Book I, plus such great passages in
the later books as "There was a Boy" and the visit to the
murderer's gibbet near Penrith. For *The Prelude* of 1798-99
shows the characteristically visionary Wordsworth: here one
finds most of the great spots of time, and it is here that his language of personal vision—what I have called his "rhetoric of
interaction"— is most powerfully exemplified.

In Chapter Four I argued the danger of reading *The Prelude*
for its visionary passages alone, as some critics have done; in
value as well as meaning, I contended, a long poem such as *The
Prelude* amounts to something more than the sum of its best
parts. Yet we must not demand too even a tone from the poem
as a whole. *The Prelude* of 1798-99, to be sure, speaks in largely
a single voice—the voice of enraptured memory, for which
"Tintern Abbey" sets the keynote. But *The Prelude* of 1804-5
speaks in many voices. At times, as in the ascent of Snowdon,
it recaptures the voice of the earlier *Prelude*. But there is also
the voice of inner turmoil which dominates the books on the
French Revolution and its aftermath. At times—and here the
modern reader feels least at home—it assumes the voice of
didactic satire:

> And here was Labour, his own Bond-slave, Hope
> That never set the pains against the prize,
> Idleness, halting with his weary clog,
> And poor misguided Shame, and witless Fear,
> And simple Pleasure, foraging for Death,

Honour misplaced, and Dignity astray,

(III, 630-635)

and on one particularly impressive occasion, in the passage about the Quixote-like Arab, it launches into dream allegory.

Apart from the fact of this variety of voices and attitudes, perhaps the most notable feature of the language of the 1804-5 *Prelude*, as compared to that of the earlier parts, is the pervasive presence of Milton—both the Milton whom Wordsworth studied directly and the Milton whom he approached through his eighteenth-century imitators. There are Miltonic elements, of course, in the 1798-99 *Prelude*, as there are in all non-dramatic blank verse before the twentieth century. But Wordsworth's verse does not become noticeably Miltonic until after the period—beginning with his residence in Grasmere in 1800 —that he undertook an intensive study of the earlier poet. It is significant, for instance, that the list of direct Miltonic echoes in *The Prelude* which appears in R. D. Havens' monumental study of Milton's influence on English verse is virtually limited to the parts of the poem written in 1804-5[1]. There can be no doubt, I think, that the Miltonic element in *The Prelude*— and it is something in the very grain of the poem, in the syntax, the tone, the meaning—has made the poem relatively roughgoing for the modern reader, who, after the successful revolt of Eliot and Pound against the "damage" that Milton did to English verse, is rarely prepared to respond favorably to any sort of Miltonizing, good or bad. But the Miltonic influence on the 1804-5 *Prelude* takes a variety of forms, and I shall be concerned here with suggesting some distinctions between these forms. When Empson, in the passage quoted in Appendix One, refers to Wordsworth's "invoking Milton and his sense of the unrelaxing Will," he is speaking of the revisions to which Wordsworth subjected the poem during the 1830's. But Empson's statement is applicable also to what Wordsworth wrote in 1804-5. For one thing, the unrelaxing Miltonic Will helped give Wordsworth himself the will—in the form both of rhetoric and epic ambitions—to create a long and fully worked out poetic structure from what would otherwise have remained a group of inspired, but unconnected fragments of blank verse.

[1] *The Influence of Milton on English Poetry* (Cambridge, Mass., 1922), pp. 609-611.

Though Empson does not take the matter much further, he indicates at least one favorable aspect of Milton's influence:

". . . I think there was also a good influence of Milton . . . which came from a very different side of that author's feeling about the world; it is remarkable surely that the first paragraph of *The Prelude*, describing how Wordsworth is now free to wander where he chooses and write as much as he likes, makes two distinct quotations from the throwing out from Paradise of Adam and Eve ('The earth is all before me' [i.14], 'Whither shall I turn' [i.26]). Indeed the repeated claims that it was somehow a good thing to have lost his first inspiration are a rather close parallel to Milton's baffling but very strong feelings about Paradise."[2]

As I remarked in Chapter Six, Wordsworth deliberately uses such echoes as these to establish an entirely different context. Contrast, for instance, the somber, sublime surroundings of these lines at the close of *Paradise Lost* with the freshness of vision at the opening of *The Prelude*—it is the sort of passage Arnold had in mind when he wrote of Wordsworth, "He laid us as we lay at birth / On the cool flowery lap of earth."

But the essential Miltonic influence on *The Prelude* is of a different order (for that matter, it is still uncertain whether the echoes which Empson cites were injected as early as 1795 or in the later stages of the poem's composition). In several places one finds the deliberately humorous Miltonizing (or mock-Miltonizing) which Cowper exploited so well, for instance, in Wordsworth's portrait of the fashionable London preacher (vii, 546-565) or in the playful line describing his entrance into Cambridge, "And at the *Hoop* we landed, famous Inn" (iii, 15) a line which Arnold, incidentally—in the only touchstone he ever drew from *The Prelude*—misread while trying to illustrate the negative effect of Milton's influence on English poetry in general ("What leagues of lumbering movement! what desperate endeavors . . . to render a platitude endurable by making it pompous!")[3]

Most frequently Miltonic language serves Wordsworth as a ready means of achieving a poetic and formal tone to counterbalance the matter-of-factness which Coleridge found so distressing in his verse. At its best it takes the form of a single

2 *The Structure of Complex Words*, p. 294.
3 *Mixed Essays, Irish Essays and Others* (New York, 1883), p. 200.

Miltonic phrase in an otherwise conversational sentence, as, for instance, in the following lines:

> Sometimes, mistaking vainly, as I fear,
> Proud spring-tide swellings for a regular sea,
> I settle on some British theme, some old
> Romantic tale, by Milton left unsung.

(I, 177-180)

Up to the final phrase, with its inverted Miltonic syntax, Wordsworth speaks fully in his own voice—casual, in fact ("as I fear," "some old / Romantic tale"), with hints of his language of personal vision ("proud spring-tide swellings"). The concluding phrase, which itself echoes Milton's statement rejecting an heroic British theme ("the better fortitude / Of Patience and Heroic Martyrdom / Unsung"—P.L., IX, 31-33), serves to lift the tone to a more formal level, to interrupt his meanderings of thought with a new and sterner perspective on his search for a proper theme. In such instances the interplay between Wordsworthian and Miltonic voices gives life to his language, but once the balance is destroyed, as often in the later Wordsworth, the Miltonic takes over and deadens the whole. At its worst it appears in a line such as the one addressed to Coleridge convalescing in Sicily—"Thine be those motions strong and sanative" (X, 978). But this is a rare instance in *The Prelude*; it is essentially a lapse of tone, of the sort that Wordsworth was capable of even during his best years: one could, in fact, divide his lapses into two distinct categories —those in the direction of matter-of-factness ("My drift hath scarcely, / I fear, been obvious"—V, 290-291) and those, like the one above, which take a "poetic," that is, Miltonic, direction. Indeed, there is often only a thin line between such lapses and total control; Wordsworth patched up, though he did not omit, the above examples when he prepared the 1850 version, but many such corrections, as I indicated earlier, have themselves destroyed the touchy balance between formality and matter-of-factness which he had achieved in his early version.

There is a particular type of Miltonic passage in *The Prelude* which, though it reads as the sort of set piece which may bore or irritate the modern reader, has a functional enough role within the scheme of the poem. An example is the description of the gardens of Gehol, whose role in the poem I discussed in Chapter Four. The Miltonic formality of this description is occasioned by the fact that Wordsworth cites these gardens as an artificial paradise, like Milton his "faire field / Of Enna," to contrast with a more genuine image of paradise; and afterwards, when Wordsworth comes to speak of his real paradise, the language gradually takes on a more conversational tone. For Wordsworth, being formal means being more or less Miltonic, and at numerous points it suits his purposes, within the design of the poem, to don Milton's formal singing robes; the modern reader, demanding a certain tension in poetry at all points, refuses to make such concessions in favor of the larger design.

The history of Wordsworth's use of blank verse is also the history, in a sense, of the gradual Miltonization of his language. Least in number before 1800, the Miltonic elements are still kept largely within bounds in *The Prelude* of 1804-5. But the crucial difference in the way they affected the quality of his poetry is not so much between 1798-99 and 1804-5, but between the latter period and the composition of *The Excursion* during the following decade. Virtually the only parts of *The Excursion* that can still be read as living literature are those, like *The Ruined Cottage* and some parts of Book IV, which were composed during, or before, the period of *The Prelude*; the rest of *The Excursion* is written in a pseudo-Miltonic language through which the poet can no longer speak with his own voice nor give free play to the thinking mind:

> With such foundations laid, avaunt the fear
> Of numbers crowded on their native soil,
> To the prevention of all healthful growth
> Through mutual injury! Rather in the law
> Of increase and the mandate from above
> Rejoice!   (IX, 363-368)

At its worst, as here, a falsely poetic manner is employed to disguise a theme that calls for plain-speaking matter-of-factness. What is good in the post-*Prelude* Wordsworth is not to be found in his blank verse, but in sonnets, stanzaic poems, octosyllabics, and, above all, in individual lines. And it goes without saying once more that the indiscriminate Miltonizing of his later days was largely responsible for what is bad in the revisions to which he subjected *The Prelude*.

APPENDIX THREE

SOME TRADITIONAL TOPICS AND FIGURES
IN *THE PRELUDE*

THE impact of Ernst Robert Curtius' *European Literature and the Latin Middle Ages* during the last decade has made us aware—perhaps even too startlingly so—of the conventional aspect of innumerable images and themes which persisted even after the cult of originality, which still dominates our literary theory, set in during the eighteenth century. It takes no great effort to pick out a sizable number of *topoi* and traditional metaphors in Wordsworth; when, for instance, he writes of Beaupuy, "Let the Name / Stand near the worthiest of Antiquity" (IX, 425-426), and when, in the same passage, he praises his friend for combining philosophic depth and military talent, we recognize at least two features of traditional panegyric—praise of a contemporary both as worthy of comparison with ancient heroes and as combining the often irreconcilable virtues of *sapientia* and *fortitudo*.[1] Nor should it be surprising that *The Prelude* shows so many evidences of traditional rhetoric, when we consider Wordsworth's intimate knowledge of the Roman prose writers[2] as well as the close study he devoted to the major English poets, above all, Chaucer, Spenser, and Milton, during the composition of the poem. But what seems most striking in his use of traditional figures and motifs is the fact that we can observe once again how Wordsworth looks both before and after in his allegiances: if the classical poet in Wordsworth chose some particular figure, the modern poet in him saw fit to shape it to his characteristically modern ends.

1. THE POEM AS JOURNEY

It is significant that of the four epic similes in *The Prelude* (IV, 247-268; VIII, 711-751; IX, 1-9; X, 402-414), two utilize the ancient figure of the poem as a journey over water. Just as Dante opens the *Purgatorio* with the lines:

[1] Cf. Curtius, *European Literature and the Latin Middle Ages*, tr. W. R. Trask (New York, 1953), pp. 165-166, 178-179.
[2] See Jane Worthington's *Wordsworth's Reading in Roman Prose.*

Per correr miglior acqua alza le vele
  Omai la navicella del mio ingegno,
  Che lascia dietro a sè mar sì crudele . . .

so Wordsworth begins the second half of *The Prelude*:

As oftentimes a River, it might seem,
Yielding in part to old remembrances,
Part sway'd by fear to tread an onward road
That leads direct to the devouring sea
Turns, and will measure back his course, far back,
Towards the very regions which he cross'd
In his first outset; so have we long time
Made motions retrograde, in like pursuit
Detain'd.   (IX, 1-9)

But it is also significant that Wordsworth chooses not the sea,
but a smaller body of water, as in an earlier simile he had
chosen a lake:

As one who hangs down-bending from the side
Of a slow-moving Boat, upon the breast
Of a still water, solacing himself
With such discoveries as his eye can make,
Beneath him, in the bottom of the deeps . . .
—Such pleasant office have we long pursued
Incumbent o'er the surface of past time
With like success.   (IV, 247-264)

As Curtius reminds us in his discussion of nautical metaphors,
"The epic poet voyages over the open sea in a great ship, the
lyric poet on a river in a small boat."[3] The very modesty with
which Wordsworth chooses his bodies of water, combined with
the Miltonic elaborateness of his similes, indicates in still another way how *The Prelude* hovers between the poet's epic
conception and its less traditionally epic subject matter. Moreover, Wordsworth's tendency, evident in these similes, to ex-
cuse himself for delaying the progress of his story, serves to
remind us of the uniqueness of so much private, often seemingly miscellaneous matter (note the image of the hidden world
beneath the water's surface in the simile of the "slow-moving
Boat") in a long poem.

[3] *European Literature and the Latin Middle Ages*, p. 128.

Yet, however much they may reflect upon Wordsworth's relation to an older rhetorical tradition, the stream and the journey are both fundamental to the central conceptions underlying the poem. In the last book, while summing up, he not only alludes to the stream once more, but he associates it directly with the imagination:

> This faculty hath been the moving soul
> Of our long labour: we have traced the stream
> From darkness, and the very place of birth
> In its blind cavern, whence is faintly heard
> The sound of waters; follow'd it to light
> And open day, accompanied its course
> Among the ways of Nature, afterwards
> Lost sight of it . . .   (XIII, 171-178)

Thus the stream symbol is inextricably tied to the whole complex of water imagery that runs through the poem. In some passages it functions as one of the "images of interaction" which I described in Chapter Three:

>   The brook and road
> Were fellow-travellers in this gloomy Pass,
> And with them did we journey several hours
> At a slow step. The immeasurable height
> Of woods decaying, never to be decay'd,
> The stationary blasts of water-falls . . .
>   (VI, 553-558)

In these lines from the description of the Simplon Pass, as the stream progresses from brook to water-fall, thence to a "raving stream," and finally to a "lordly River, broad and deep," the image is used primarily to suggest and explore, to comprehend something essentially bigger than itself. Yet in other passages the stream is used in a rhetorically more traditional way, as a figure that defines and limits, but attempts nothing more, as in the description of Anne Tyson:

> Her talk, her business pleas'd me, and no less
> Her clear though shallow stream of piety,
> That ran on Sabbath days a fresher course.
>   (IV, 215-217)

2. THE POET'S MODESTY

In the first chapter I tried to interpret such a line as "Alas,
I feel / That I am trifling" as an example of Wordsworth's
uneasiness about the propriety and importance of his subject
matter. But one might look at this statement in still another
way, as Wordsworth's perhaps unconscious echo of the convention of affected modesty. The convention, as Curtius has
observed,[4] usually takes two forms—the writer questions his
ability to handle his chosen theme, or he shows concern about
boring the reader. Wordsworth, however, never picks up the
convention directly: his concern is not with his own powers, but
rather with the inadequacy or complexity ("My drift hath
scarcely, / I fear, been obvious") of his subject. Even when he
comes closest to the convention, as in these lines,

> This is, in truth, heroic argument,
> And genuine prowess; which I wish'd to touch
> With hand however weak; but in the main
> It lies far hidden from the reach of words,
> (III, 182-185)

it is the resources of the language itself, not his own resources,
which he sees fit to blame. If the poet's modesty cannot express
itself as affectation or convention in the realm of the egotistical
sublime, it *can* take the form of sincere confession, as in the
passage where he tells of his failure to carry out his proposed
epic subjects:

> This is my lot; for either still I find
> Some imperfection in the chosen theme,
> Or see of absolute accomplishment
> Much wanting, so much wanting, in myself,
> That I recoil and droop, and seek repose
> In listlessness from vain perplexity,
> Unprofitably travelling towards the grave,
> Like a false Steward who hath much received
> And renders nothing back.   (I, 263-271)

3. NOURISHMENT

It is doubtless out of Christian tradition, from the mystics
and Jakob Boehme in particular, and probably through Cole-

[4] *Ibid.*, pp. 83-85.

ridge's intercession,[5] that Wordsworth developed his figure of nourishment to symbolize processes of interaction. In its traditional form the figure is used to indicate the transfer of divine knowledge to man, for instance in the Biblical example, "As newborn babes desire the sincere milk of the word, that ye may grow thereby: if so be ye have tasted that the Lord is gracious" (1 Peter 2:2-3); or, to take one of Curtius' medieval examples, the writings of Augustine are referred to by Gregory the Great as wheat flour, his own writings as bran.[6] Wordsworth's book of knowledge, significantly, is neither the revealed nor written word, but nature itself:

> I held unconscious intercourse
> With the eternal Beauty, drinking in
> A pure organic pleasure from the lines
> Of curling mist, or from the level plain
> Of waters colour'd by the steady clouds,
>
> (I, 589-593)

or, more explicitly, though less characteristic of the Wordsworthian rhetoric of interaction,

> O Nature! Thou hast fed
> My lofty speculations; and in thee,
> For this uneasy heart of ours I find
> A never-failing principle of joy,
> And purest passion.   (II, 462-466)

The figure occurs about a dozen times in the course of *The Prelude* and, like its Biblical prototype, gives sensuous embodiment to the relation between man and his source of spiritual inspiration. In its most audacious form—and here Wordsworth comes closest to Boehme's use of the figure—it occurs in the last book of the poem, where Mt. Snowdon is called

> The perfect image of a mighty Mind,
> Of one that feeds upon infinity . . . .
>
> (XIII, 69-70)

Here the interaction is no longer between man and nature (or the spirit immanent in nature), but between an object of nature visible to man and a higher realm from which it—and, in effect, man—draws its sustenance.

[5] For a full discussion of the Boehme influence, see Stallknecht, *Strange Seas of Thought*, pp. 42-72, 101-125.

[6] *European Literature and the Latin Middle Ages*, p. 135.

INDEX

Individual poems are listed under author's name. Passages in *The Prelude* are cited in order of their occurrence in the poem.

INDEX

INDEX

INDEX

Wordsworth, Bishop Christopher, 97

Wordsworth, Dorothy, x, 163, 285; as "character" in *The Prelude*, 7-8, 20-21, 36-37, 39, 78, 157-58, 212, 214; *Journals*, 160-62, 176, 282

Wordsworth, John (1741-83), 134, 135-36, 212

Wordsworth, William, "Apology for the French Revolution," 268; "Autobiographical Memoranda," 134-37; *The Borderers*, 138, 226, 261, 282-83; "Character of the Happy Warrior," 34; *The Convention of Cintra*, 138, 265-68; "The Cuckoo and the Nightingale," 282; "Dear native regions . . . ," 136; *Descriptive Sketches*, 8, 65-66, 67, 132, 236, 254; *Ecclesiastical Sonnets*, 175; "Essay upon Epitaphs," 17-19, 26-27, 223-24; *An Evening Walk*, 8, 132, 236, 238; *The Excursion*, ix, 44, 50, 59, 112, 122, 124, 144, 166, 207, 210, 227, 228, 229, 256, 257, 259-60, 267, 271, 272, 273, 274, 277, 288, 304, *see also The Ruined Cottage*; "Fragment of a 'Gothic' Tale," 175; "The French Revolution," *see The Prelude*; *Guide to the Lakes*, 79n, 82n, 94; *Guilt and Sorrow*, 8, 225-26; "Hail, Twilight," 285n; "Home at Grasmere," ix, 28-29, 163-66, 188n, 224-25, 286; "The Idiot Boy," 193; "Imitation of Juvenal," 238; "Immortality Ode," 32, 34, 165, 201, 272, 286, 293; "Influence of Natural Objects," *see The Prelude*; "Laodamia," 288; letter to the Bishop of Llandaff, *see* "Apology for the French Revolution"; letter to Charles James Fox, 206-7, 251; "Look at the fate of summer flowers . . . ," 188n; Lucy poems, x, 78, 187-88, 211, 214, 216; *Lyrical Ballads*, ix, 30, 60, 119, 166, 201, 207, 209, 211, 215n, 221, 272, 278, 281, 282,

284-85n; "Memory," 175; "Michael," 29, 30, 149, 217-18, 246, 247; "The Old Cumberland Beggar," 216-17; "On the Power of Sound," 272; "Praised be the Art . . . ," 285n; preface to *The Excursion*, 271, *see also* "Home at Grasmere"; preface to *Lyrical Ballads*, 4, 27, 201, 206-7; preface to edition of 1815, 9, 13, 43-44

The Prelude: preamble, 70-71, 95, 162; difficulties in choosing theme, 27-28, 64, 109-11, 118, 197, 265, 302-3, 308; summer bathing in Derwent, 159, 160; plunder of birds' nests, 88, 159-60, 222; theft of boat, 5-6, 23, 47, 71-72, 84, 87, 88, 90-91, 102, 146, 209; "Influence of Natural Objects" (skating scene) and succeeding passage, 7, 72, 87, 111, 167, 201, 214, 218; description of card games, 122; description and defense of plans for *The Prelude*, 11-12, 143, 181, 296; excursions to islands on Lake Windermere, 23, 45, 79-80, 81-82, 147-48; "Bless'd the infant Babe," 61-62; descriptions of childhood visionary power, 46, 57-58, 77-78, 178n, 309; Cambridge, 14, 46, 87, 102, 107, 136, 167, 168, 169, 170, 178, 180, 182, 186, 192, 233, 280, 281n, 300-301, 302; tribute to Newton, 212, 299; definition of poem's "heroic argument," 12, 308; tribute to, and description of Anne Tyson, 15-18, 105-6, 307; description of summer vacation, 72-73, 77, 192, 306; scene of dedication to poetry, 6-7, 11, 144-47, 174; meeting with discharged soldier, 84-85, 157, 181, 188, 208-9, 211, 214, 216, 218, 219, 221; dream of Arab carrying shell and stone, 82n, 157, 211, 216, 301; tribute to poet's mother, 157-58; criticism of children's education, 119, 168; "There was a Boy," xii, 41-